ANTHROPOLOGICAL PAPERS OF
THE UNIVERSITY OF ARIZONA
NUMBER 26

EXCAVATIONS AT PUNTA DE AGUA

in the Santa Cruz River Basin,
Southeastern Arizona

J. CAMERON GREENLEAF

THE UNIVERSITY OF ARIZONA PRESS
TUCSON, ARIZONA 1975

About the Author...

J. CAMERON GREENLEAF's fruitful association with Tucson Basin archaeology follows a varied career during which he served as a U.S. Navy Lt. Commander in World War II, then worked for 12 years as a mining engineer and marketing specialist. In 1957 he moved to Tucson from New York state and enrolled in the graduate program in the Anthropology Department of the University of Arizona. Since then he has participated in a number of excavations for the Arizona State Museum including work with the Arizona Archaeological and Historical Society at the Whiptail site northeast of Tucson, at Johnny Ward's Ranch in Santa Cruz County, and at the mission site of San Gabriel Guevavi on the Santa Cruz River. He has also worked at the Fortified Hill site near Gila Bend with the late William W. Wasley, then state archaeologist, and at the Mission San Xavier del Bac with Bernard Fontana, state ethnologist. In the winter of 1965-66 he concluded the excavations at Punta de Agua, the results of which are reported here.

Contributions to Highway Salvage
Archaeology in Arizona No. 40

THE UNIVERSITY OF ARIZONA PRESS

Copyright ©1975
The Arizona Board of Regents
All Rights Reserved
Manufactured in the U.S.A.

I. S. B. N. 0-8165-0497-0
L. C. No. 74-83334

CONTENTS

LIST OF ILLUSTRATIONS	6
LIST OF TABLES	7
ACKNOWLEDGMENTS	9
THE SETTING	11
1. ENVIRONMENTAL AND ARCHAEOLOGICAL BACKGROUND	15

    Local Environment   15
    Tucson Basin Archaeology   16
        History of Research
        Summary of Prehistoric Cultures
        Cultural Continuity and Ethnographic Parallels

2. THE PUNTA DE AGUA SITES   20
    Site Descriptions   20
        Arizona BB:13:50
            Unit 1
            Unit 2
            Stratigraphic Tests in Borrow Pits
        Arizona BB:13:49
        Arizona BB:13:43
            Unit 1
            Unit 2
        Arizona BB:13:41
            Unit 1
            Unit 2
            Unit 3
        Arizona BB:13:16
    Architecture   35
        House Plans
            Squared
            Oval
            Rectangular
            Subrectangular
        Construction Details
            Squared Plan
            Oval Plan
            Rectangular Plan
            Subrectangular Plan
            Discussion
        Late Rincon–Tanque Verde Transition
        Special Architectural Features
            The Curb Rim Plan
            Entryway Adobe Cones
        Identification of Architectural Wood
    Summary   44

3. THE CERAMICS   45
    Introduction   45
        Punta de Agua: Colonial Period
            Cañada del Oro Phase
                Cañada del Oro Red-on-brown
            Rillito Phase
                Rillito Red-on-brown
        Punta de Agua: Sedentary Period
            Rincon Phase
                Rincon Red-on-brown
            Tanque Verde Phase
                Early Tanque Verde Red-on-brown
                Tanque Verde Red-on-brown
                Topawa Red-on-brown (Tucson Variety)
    Plainware   54
        Snaketown Phase
        Cañada del Oro Phase
        Rillito Phase
        Rincon Phase
        Tanque Verde Phase
    Redware   59
        Intrusive Redware
        Local Redware
            Rincon Red
    Late Rincon Ceramics   60
        Rincon Red-on-brown
            Bowls with Interior Decoration
            Bowls with Exterior Decoration
            Bowls with Interior and Exterior Decoration
            Jars
            Pitchers
    Summary   66
    Rincon Polychrome   67
        Introduction
        General Description
        Forms
        Designs
            Principal Design on Exterior of Bowls
            Principal Design on Exterior of Jars
            Principal Design on Interior of Bowls
            Secondary Design on Interior of Bowls
            Elements
        Discussion
    Intrusive Ceramics   73
        Introduction
        Gila Polychrome
        Gila Basin Types
        Papaguería Types
        Mimbres District
        San Pedro Valley (Dragoon Series)
        Trincheras District
        Tonto-Roosevelt District
        El Paso District

4. CERAMIC ARTIFACTS   78
    Modeled Spindle Whorls   78
    Human Figurines and Effigies   79
        Arizona BB:13:50
        Arizona BB:13:16
        Arizona BB:13:41 and BB:13:43
    Animal Figurines and Effigies   81
    Perforated Discs   82
    Other Classes of Worked Sherds   82
        Discs
        Jar Cover: Unfired

5. STONE ARTIFACTS   85
    Projectile Points and Drills   85
        Arizona BB:13:50
        Arizona BB:13:16
        Arizona BB:13:41
        Arizona BB:13:43
    Turquoise   86
        Arizona BB:13:50
        Arizona BB:13:16
    Carved Stone Ornaments   86
        Arizona BB:13:50
        Arizona BB:13:16
    Palettes   86
        Arizona BB:13:50
            Rincon Phase
        Arizona BB:13:16

5. STONE ARTIFACTS (continued)

    Rillito Phase
    Rincon Phase
      Arizona BB:13:41
      Rincon Phase
  Stone Bowls   88
    Arizona BB:13:50
      House 5: Fill
      House 12: Floor
      House 25: Floor
    Arizona BB:13:16
      Cremation 4: Cache
      Cremation 7: Cache
    Arizona BB:13:41
      House 13: Floor
    Arizona BB:13:43
      House 2: Floor
  Axes and Mauls   90
    Arizona BB:13:50
      House 3: Fill
      House 22
    Arizona BB:13:16
      Test 89
  Arrowshaft Tools   90
    Arizona BB:13:16
      Trench 9
      House 6: Floor
  Miscellaneous Stone Artifacts   91
    Arizona BB:13:16
      Test 10
    Arizona BB:13:49
      Mound 1
  Metates   91
  Manos   92
  Mortars   92
    Arizona BB:13:50

      Houses 15 and 16
      House 19A
  Pestles   93
  Anvils   94
  Handstones   94
  Choppers   95
  Hammerstones   95
  Pottery Polishers   95
  Knives and Saws   95
  A Complete Stone Tool "Kit"   96
    Arizona BB:13:41
      House 15
  Minerals
    Arizona BB:13:50
    Arizona BB:13:16
    Arizona BB:13:41
    Arizona BB:13:43
    Comment

6. OTHER TECHNOLOGY   98
  Bone Artifacts   98
  Shell Artifacts   98

7. MORTUARY PRACTICES   101
  Cremations   101
    Arizona BB:13:16
    Arizona BB:13:50
    Discussion
  Inhumations   104
  Death Practices   105

8. FOOD RESOURCES   106
  Faunal Remains   106
  Vegetal Remains   106

9. CONCLUSIONS   108
  APPENDIX A: Architectural Data   111
  APPENDIX B: Rincon Polychrome Summary   113
  APPENDIX C: Cremation and Inhumation Data   115
  REFERENCES   117
  INDEX   121

ILLUSTRATIONS

A.	Sites of the Sedentary and Classic periods in southern Arizona	10
B.	Prehistoric phase correlations in southern Arizona	12
C.	Aerial photograph of the Punta de Agua excavation	14
1.1.	Archaeological sites in the Tucson Basin	17
2.1.	Punta de Agua and other excavated sites	20
2.2.	Site map of Arizona BB:13:50, Units 1 and 2	21
2.3.	Arizona BB:13:50, Unit 1, superimposition of House 19B over 19A	22
2.4.	Arizona BB:13:50, Unit 1, superimposition of House 2 cutting entry of House 1	22
2.5.	Arizona BB:13:50, Unit 2, principal house cluster showing superimposition	23
2.6.	Arizona BB:13:50, Unit 2, second house cluster showing superimposition	24
2.7.	Site map of Arizona BB:13:43, Units 1 and 2	26
2.8.	Arizona BB:13:43, Unit 1, House 4 — Oval plan	27
2.9.	Arizona BB:13:43, Unit 1, House 10	27
2.10.	Arizona BB:13:43, Unit 1, House 1	27
2.11.	Arizona BB:13:43, Unit 1, House 5	28
2.12.	Arizona BB:13:43, Unit 1, House 2	28
2.13.	Arizona BB:13:43, Unit 2, House 7	28
2.14.	Arizona BB:13:43, Unit 2, House 6	29
2.15.	Site map of Arizona BB:13:41, Units 1, 2, and 3	29
2.16.	Arizona BB:13:41, Unit 1, House 1	30
2.17.	Arizona BB:13:41, Unit 1, House 5	30
2.18.	Arizona BB:13:41, Unit 1, House 4	30
2.19.	Arizona BB:13:41, Unit 2, House 7	31
2.20.	Arizona BB:13:41, Unit 2, House 6	31
2.21.	Arizona BB:13:41, Unit 3, House 12	31
2.22.	Arizona BB:13:41, Unit 3, House 13	32
2.23.	Site map of Arizona BB:13:16	33
2.24.	Arizona BB:13:16, superimposition of House 6 over House 7	34
2.25.	*Photograph:* Arizona BB:13:16, House 8	34
2.26.	Arizona BB:13:16, House 3	34
2.27.	Arizona BB:13:16, House 4 — Rectangular plan	34
2.28.	Arizona BB:13:16, House 5	35
2.29.	Squared plan — Arizona BB:13:50, Unit 2, House 16	36
2.30.	*Photograph:* Squared plan — Arizona BB:13:50, Unit 2, House 16	36
2.31.	*Photograph:* Oval plan — Arizona BB:13:43, Unit 1, House 4	37
2.32.	*Photograph:* Arizona BB:13:50, House 18 (with House 22 in foreground)	38
2.33.	Arizona BB:13:50, Unit 1, House 25. Subrectangular plan: Earlier type with short, straight-sided entry	38
2.34.	Arizona BB:13:50, Unit 2, House 11. Subrectangular plan: Earlier type with short, straight-sided entry	38

2.35. *Photograph:* Arizona BB:13:50, Unit 2, House 21 (with House 13A in background). Subrectangular plan: Earlier type with short, straight-sided entry ... 38
2.36. Arizona BB:13:50, Unit 1, House 6. Subrectangular plan: Later type with large, bulbous entry ... 39
2.37. *Photograph:* Arizona BB:13:50, Unit 2, House 23. Subrectangular plan: Later type with large, bulbous entry ... 39
2.38. Arizona BB:13:50, Unit 2, House 14. Subrectangular plan: Later type with long, straight-sided entry ... 39
2.39. *Photograph:* Arizona BB:13:50, Unit 2, House 14. Subrectangular plan: Later type with long, straight-sided entry ... 39
2.40. *Photograph:* Arizona BB:13:41, Unit 2, House 3. Subrectangular plan: Later type with long, straight-sided entry ... 39
2.41. Arizona BB:13:50, Unit 1, House 3. Late Rincon-Tanque Verde transition ... 40
2.42. *Photograph:* Arizona BB:13:50, Unit 1, House 3. Late Rincon-Tanque Verde transition ... 40
2.43. *Photograph:* Arizona BB:13:16, House 5. Curb rim during excavation ... 41
2.44. Arizona BB:13:16, House 5. Detail of curb rim ... 41
2.45. Arizona BB:13:16, House 6. Detail of adobe cones and entry ... 42
2.46. Arizona BB:13:50, House 6. Detail of adobe cones and entry ... 42
2.47. *Photograph:* Adobe cone showing interior fluting from entry of House 6, Arizona BB:13:50 ... 43
3.1. *Photograph:* Cañada del Oro and Rillito vessels ... 46
3.2. *Photograph:* Ceramic vessels from a cremation near Arizona BB:13:43 ... 47
3.3. Coyote design on Rillito Red-on-brown sherd ... 48
3.4. *Photograph:* Rincon Red-on-brown bowls ... 49
3.5. *Photograph:* Rincon Red-on-brown jars ... 50
3.6. *Photograph:* Rincon Red-on-brown mortuary vessels ... 51
3.7. *Photograph:* Early Tanque Verde Red-on-brown vessels and Tanque Verde plainware jars ... 52
3.8. Early Tanque Verde Red-on-brown: Plans of two bowls ... 53
3.9. Early Tanque Verde Red-on-brown sherds ... 53
3.10. Topawa Red-on-brown sherds: Interior design ... 55
3.11. Topawa Red-on-brown sherds: Exterior design ... 55
3.12. *Photograph:* Four plainware bowls and two plainware jars ... 57
3.13. *Photograph:* Two Rincon phase plainware bowls and two plainware jars ... 58
3.14. Late Rincon Red-on-brown: Interior decoration on two hemispherical bowls ... 61
3.15. Late Rincon Red-on-brown: Interior decoration on hemispherical bowl sherds ... 62
3.16. Late Rincon Red-on-brown: Plan view of interior decoration on large, outcurved bowl ... 63
3.17. Late Rincon Red-on-brown: Exterior decoration on small, incurved bowl sherds ... 63
3.18. Late Rincon Red-on-brown: Exterior decoration on recurved bowl sherds with flared rims ... 64
3.19. Late Rincon Red-on-brown: Recurved jar sherds with flared rims (globular and shouldered varieties) ... 65
3.20. Late Rincon Red-on-brown: Recurved jars with low, flared rims (one restored, two sherds) ... 66
3.21. Rincon Polychrome: Sherds ... 68
3.22. *Photograph:* Rincon Polychrome: Two bowls and one jar ... 69
3.23. Rincon Polychrome: Hemispherical bowl and low, shouldered bowl ... 69
3.24. *Photograph:* Rincon Polychrome: Sherds ... 70
3.25. Rincon Polychrome: Plan view of design ... 71
3.26. *Photograph:* Intrusive ceramics ... 76
4.1. *Photograph:* Spindle whorls ... 78
4.2. *Photograph:* Human figurines and effigies ... 79
4.3. Enlargement of head with headdress and facial features (front and side views), and fragmentary *adorno* ... 80
4.4. *Photograph:* Animal effigies ... 81
4.5. *Photograph:* Ceramic artifacts ... 83
5.1. *Photograph:* Projectile points ... 85
5.2. *Photograph:* Bird effigy pendant ... 86
5.3. *Photograph:* Palettes ... 87
5.4. *Photograph:* Stone bowls and miscellaneous objects ... 89
5.5. *Photograph:* Axes and mauls ... 90
5.6. *Photograph:* Metate-mano pairs ... 91
5.7. *Photograph:* Manos ... 92
5.8. *Photograph:* Mortar with two grinding stones ... 93
5.9. *Photograph:* Large pestles ... 93
5.10. *Photograph:* Small pestles ... 93
5.11. *Photograph:* Handstones, hammerstones, chopper ... 94
5.12. *Photograph:* Polishing tools ... 95
5.13. *Photographs:* Knives and saws ... 96
5.14. *Photograph:* Stone tool kit from Arizona BB:13:41, House 15 ... 97
6.1. *Photograph:* Shell bracelets ... 98
6.2. *Photograph:* Various shell ornaments ... 99
7.1. Cremation area at Arizona BB:13:16 ... 101
7.2. *Photograph:* Examples of cremations from the Rillito and Tanque Verde phases ... 103

TABLES

2.1. Tentative archaeomagnetic dates — Arizona BB:13:50 ... 21
2.2. Ceramics from stratigraphic tests in borrow pits — Arizona BB:13:50 ... 26
2.3. Distribution of adobe cones ... 42
3.1. Intrusive ceramics listed by provenience ... 73
8.1. Faunal remains from Punta de Agua ... 106
8.2. Vegetal remains from Punta de Agua ... 107

ACKNOWLEDGMENTS

This final report on two seasons' work on the San Xavier Indian Reservation, 12 miles south of Tucson, Arizona, was made possible by the great cooperation of many institutions and individuals.

First, thanks are due Robert C. Stifler of the Arizona Highway Department for negotiating the contracts for I-19-1(47) and I-19-1(50) with the Arizona State Museum. The highway salvage archaeology was conducted under the supervision of R. Gwinn Vivian, then Assistant Archaeologist at the Museum. Homer Jenkins, Superintendent of the Papago Agency at Sells, Arizona, provided necessary clearance for excavation.

The first season (June 21 to September 11, 1965) was led by James Sciscenti. The second season (December 1, 1965 to March 2, 1966) was directed by the author of this report.

Linus Hohendorf O.F.M., at Mission San Xavier del Bac, helped immeasurably by recruiting a work force on the San Xavier Indian Reservation and providing equipment storage space.

Significant new information was supplied by the following scholars: Vorsila L. Bohrer, Hugh C. Cutler, and Jonathan D. Sauer who have published the analysis of carbonized plant remains discovered at the sites in question. Robert L. DuBois submitted a series of tentative archaeomagnetic dates that corroborated other internal evidence concerning the length of certain phases in the Tucson Basin.

William J. Robinson identified charred tree-ring material which gave insight into local cultural changes. Walter H. Birkby reported on the cremated remains from the various sites with his usual care and thoroughness. Additional identifications were provided by Walter B. Miller (shell); R. T. O'Haire (minerals) and J. J. Saunders (faunal bone). Charles C. DiPeso, Director of the Amerind Foundation, generously loaned rare vessels for study and comparison.

The excellent drawings and maps accompanying this report were prepared with infinite care by E. W. Jernigan. Additional house plans and corrections were cheerfully completed by Charles Sternberg. All the photographs, except those in the field, are the result of the skill of Helga Teiwes-French.

In the field a loyal corps of students and friends made the two seasons' work possible. During the first phase William Barrera was the assistant archaeologist. Bruce Harrill and E. T. Hemmings helped when they were called. The writer was aided, during the second season, by assistants Paul Shewan and David Acton. Invaluable voluntary digging and mapping came from the zeal of Richard Polhemus, Jonathan Gell, Valerie Jackson, and Geoffrey Clark. Throughout the whole operation, in the laboratory and the field, the hand of Sharon Urban kept the ship running. Most of the laboratory work was carried out, with patience and good humor, under the guidance of Candace Lane and Michele Brady.

My special thanks go to Julian D. Hayden for arranging the presence of backhoe operator extraordinary, Richard Throp, who, with his golden touch, warmed up a cold winter.

This report would not be here without the indefatigable cooperation of Mildred Ogg who typed the first draft, and Suzy O'Neill and Melinda Curry who typed the final draft. The final form of the work was guided by an inspired editor, Gayle Hartmann.

Countless conversations with Emil W. Haury, Julian D. Hayden, William J. Robinson, and Bernard L. Fontana are hereby acknowledged.

With his rare perseverance, Raymond H. Thompson encouraged the writer to see this through. His was the guiding hand to which I am indebted.

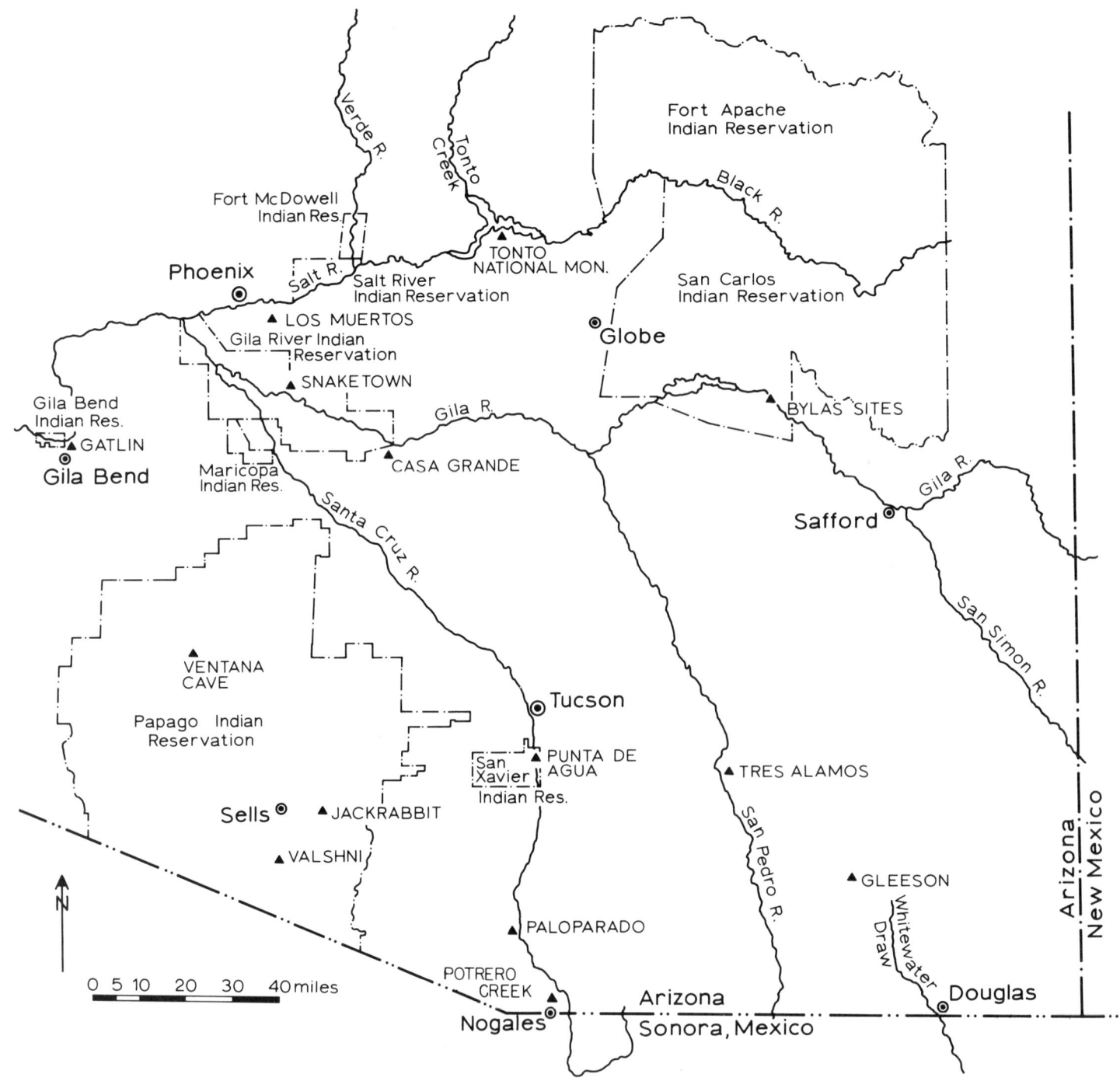

Fig. A. Sites of the Sedentary and Classic periods in southern Arizona.

THE SETTING

Of ten sites investigated in this salvage operation all except two were situated on the San Xavier Indian Reservation, Pima County, Arizona (Fig. A). The center of the occupied prehistoric zone is nearly two and one-half miles south of the present Mission of San Xavier del Bac which, in turn, is centrally located between the two most prominent landmarks in the area—Black Mountain to the west, and Sahuarita Butte (Martinez Hill) to the east. Modern Tucson lies about ten miles north, downstream on the Santa Cruz River.

Most of the surveyed sites were found on ridges between arroyos or on the upper terrace of the earlier west channel of the Santa Cruz River. The important areas in the right-of-way were marked by low trash mounds or sherds and debris eroding from higher levels. After close scrutiny four prehistoric sites were not tested and are, therefore, not included in this report. These were Arizona BB:13:42, BB:13:44, BB:13:45, and BB:13:48 and were all comprised of washed-down surface material. A fifth site, the large, historic Punta de Agua ranch will be reported separately in another highway salvage report.

The name given the excavations, Punta de Agua, was originally established in 1851 from its mention in a Mexican land grant to José María Martínez, who drew water from the aquifer by means of the "Acequia de la Punta de Agua" (Olberg and Schanck 1913:10). In 1855, Fritz and Julius Contzen built the Punta de Agua ranch just north of Arizona BB:13:16. The ranch passed to Juan Elias in 1868. The place name has variously been recorded as Punta del Agua and Punta Agua on early maps. The property was acquired by the United States government as part of the San Xavier Indian Reservation in 1874.

Surface material at the prehistoric sites consisted mainly of sherds which represented pottery from types described by Kelly (n.d.) from the Hodges site just north of Tucson. The Hodges site is a large, late Pioneer through early Classic community and is the type site for the ceramic phase structure in the Tucson Basin (Fig. B). The phase sequence was chosen, in 1938, to reflect a parallel development to that at Snaketown, the home of the Hohokam proper. The two earliest phases of the local sequence possess names and ceramics indistinguishable from those at Snaketown. The earliest architecture thus far discovered within the Tucson Basin, is at the Hodges site and has been assigned to the Snaketown phase or about A.D. 500 (Officer 1961:I:30).

The surface material recovered at Punta de Agua included pottery from the Cañada del Oro to Tanque Verde phases, although the local Rincon phase ceramics dominated the collection. In similar situations these ceramic types are correlated with small villages of relatively permanent agriculturalists. Such villages were utlimately unearthed, but unexpected divergence from the Gila River Hohokam was far greater than anticipated.

During the first season no mechanical equipment was available. The difficulty of locating buried architectural features led to an exploratory rubidium magnetometer survey by Elizabeth K. Ralph of the Applied Science Center of Archaeology, University of Pennsylvania. Because of the nature of prehistoric adobe walls and floors, however, no magnetic anomalies could be located.

At Arizona BB:13:50, when the second season started, a skilled backhoe operator proceeded to cut long test trenches between trash mounds through

TIME PERIOD (A.D.)		PAPAGUERÍA	TUCSON	GILA BASIN	SAN SIMON	PALOPARADO
1450	Classic	Sells	Tucson	Civano	(?)	Ootam Reassertion
1300			Tanque Verde			
1225				Soho		
1200	Sedentary	Topawa	Late Rincon (Cortaro)	Santan		Hohokam Intrusion
1150						
1100			Early Rincon	Sacaton	Encinas	
900		Vamori				
800	Colonial		Rillito	Santa Cruz	Cerros	Santa Cruz
700						
500			Cañada del Oro	Gila Butte		
	Pioneer	(?)	Snaketown	Snaketown	Galiuro	Formative Ootam
A.D. 1			Sweetwater	Sweetwater	Pinaleño	
				Estrella	Dos Cabezas	
300 B.C. (?)				Vahki	Peñasco	
	Pre-Pottery	Amargosa II	San Pedro	San Pedro	San Pedro	(?)
		Amargosa I	Chiricahua		Chiricahua	
		San Dieguito I & II	Sulphur Spring		Sulphur Spring	

Fig. B. Prehistoric phase correlations in southern Arizona.

promising village sites. Due to the deep overburden and vast area, the result was most rewarding, as a final aerial photograph shows (Fig. C).

Additional salvage work during the second season was made possible by a planned new highway interchange. Under contract I-19-1(50) negotiated with the Arizona Highway Department and Bureau of Public Roads, further excavation proceeded at Arizona BB:13:16 and BB:13:41. The huge site, Arizona BB:13:50, was unearthed at the borrow pit which provided fill for the interchange.

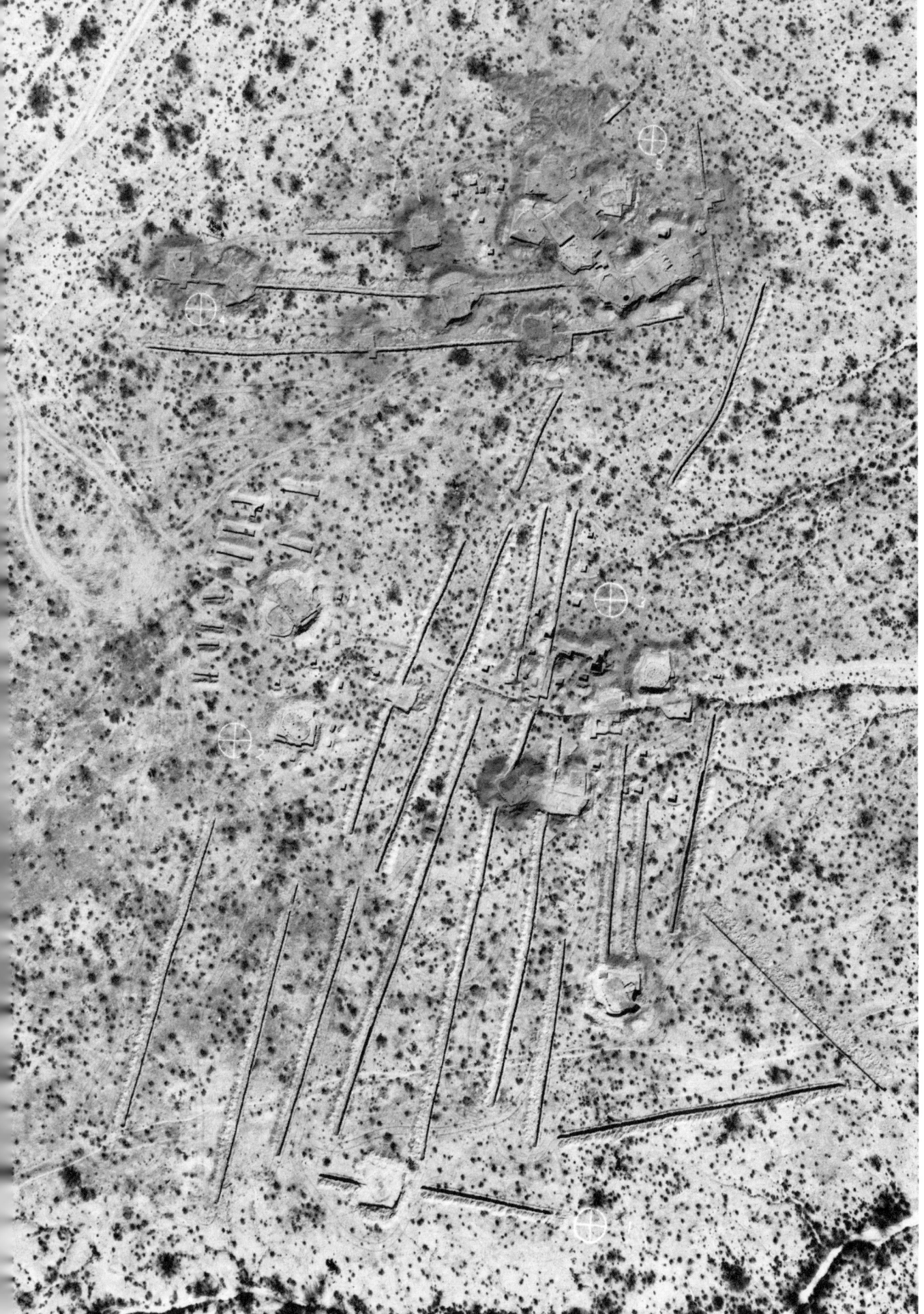

Fig. C. Aerial photograph of Punta de Agua excavation. North is to the top.

1. ENVIRONMENTAL AND ARCHAEOLOGICAL BACKGROUND

LOCAL ENVIRONMENT

Interstate 19 enters the San Xavier Indian Reservation on the east side of the Santa Cruz River, then crosses to the west bank at the narrows opposite Sahuarita Butte (Martinez Hill). From this point south, the right-of-way cuts a series of low ridges which are intersected by northeast-trending arroyos. It is on these ridges that the largest settlements were constructed. Below the ridges beyond the upper terrace is the west and older channel of the Santa Cruz River. Recent maps indicate that the main channel has moved about one mile to the east primarily due to continued erosion in the stream bed. The elevations found within the salvage area range from 2490 to 2725 feet above mean sea level.

The reservation lies within the Sonoran Desert, which shows wide variation in its great extent—from Needles, California on the north to include most of the Mexican states of Sonora and Baja California on the south (Shreve 1943). This desert region is the lowest and the hottest of the North American deserts. Its elevation ranges between sea level and about 3800 feet. The area is considered part of the Lower Sonoran life zone (Lowe 1964) and is dominated by two major plant communities, the paloverde-sahuaro *(Cercidium-Cereus)* on the better drained, higher slopes and the creosotebush-bursage *(Larrea-Franseria)* at lower elevations. The section embraced by southern Arizona is commonly designated, physiographically, the basin and range province (Dice 1943). The notable characteristic of the topography is the series of north-south trending mountain ranges separated by broad dissected valleys.

Specifically, the plain of the Tucson Basin is contained on the east by the Catalina and Rincon mountains which attain heights over 9000 feet, on the west by the lower, discontinuous Tucson and Sierrita mountains, and on the south by the Santa Rita Mountains.

The geology of the San Xavier Indian Reservation has been thoroughly summarized by Heindl (1959:156). Most of the reservation is underlain by alluvial deposits of the following types:

(1) Older alluvium of probably late Tertiary and Quaternary age, which includes the deposits that underlie the broad slopes, or bajadas, of the Santa Cruz and Avra Valley basins; (2) talus deposits which mantle the steep flanks of Black Mountain and other high hills; (3) floodplain deposits of the Santa Cruz River; (4) adobe-flat deposits, all of Quaternary age; and (5) recent stream channel deposits.

In the area of this study the older alluvium has an average thickness of about 200 feet and rests on an uneven surface. The surface now is cut by northeast-trending valleys separating ridges upon which the sites were constructed.

The most common and accessible rock outcrops at San Xavier lie in the vicinity of Black Mountain. They include a local variety of rhyolite, andesite porphyry, flows of basalt and andesite, and an indigenous conglomerate structure (Heindl 1959:154-155). It is safe to say that most of the heavier tools and metates were fashioned from these materials.

The mean yearly precipitation in the area is about 11 inches and is bi-seasonal. Nearly one-half of the total falls in the two hottest summer months (July and August) when the native grass and shrubs experience their main growth. The secondary rainy season occurs mainly in December and January with an average of less than two inches (Sellers 1960.) From early June through mid-September, the temperature may reach 110° Fahrenheit during the day. The average length of the frost-free growing season in modern times is 250 days (Smith 1956). Small variations in the amount of rainfall and changes in the onset of summer rains could have had serious effect on the yield of prehistoric fields whether or not irrigation was used.

Both the Santa Cruz and the San Pedro rivers flow north (an unusual occurrence) and their courses intersect the rapidly changing gradients of seasonal rainfall. These gradients apparently have a close correlation with the natural vegetation change and, possibly, with the recent phenomenon of arroyo cutting (Hastings and Turner 1965:12-15). Perhaps erratic rainfall had serious short-term effects on the farmers of the twelfth and thirteenth centuries as well.

The noticeable choice of high ridges for settlement early in the Classic period might be correlated with the necessity to farm the more confined tributary valleys (with the aid of check dams). Balancing this proposal, there are investigators who feel that increasing population of the local valleys forced the Indians to develop new, supplementary, farming zones.

The vegetation along the Santa Cruz is strictly Lower Sonoran and, in addition to many varieties of grasses and shrubs with food value, is characterized by paloverde, mesquite, acacia, creosotebush, saltbush, numerous types of cholla, and prickly pear. The sahuaro cactus may be found on the slopes of adjacent

Black Mountain and Martinez Hill. The gourds *Cucurbita foetidissima* and *C. digitata* are found throughout the district. A review of the historic changes in groundcover locally may be found in a study of Lower Sonoran relic vegetation on Black Mountain (Ferguson 1950).

A remarkable feature in the floodplain of the Santa Cruz River, opposite the excavated sites, is the dense mesquite forest. A study of the fauna in this thick stand (Arnold 1940) recorded these native species: coyote, bobcat, raccoon, grey fox, cottontail, and jackrabbit. Besides many rodents, the area contains Gambel's quail, roadrunner, and the common birds of prey. Desert mule deer inhabit all the neighboring mountains. Big horn sheep were prevalent in the taller ranges in early historic times, but now only a remnant breeding population exists on the western ridges of the Catalina Mountains.

TUCSON BASIN ARCHAEOLOGY
History of Research

Previous archaeology in the Tucson Basin has been confined to the largest and most accessible sites along the principal water courses (Fig. 1.1). The first complete report, from what became the Tanque Verde type site (Arizona BB:14:1) was by Haury (1928). The site was again considered by Haury (1932:54-56) in relation to the findings at Roosevelt 9:6. The distinctive Tanque Verde pottery found in the Tucson Basin was first described by Fraps (1935). A supplementary report on Tanque Verde Red-on-brown was published by Danson (1957).

A survey of ceramics in the Papaguería by W. and H. S. Gladwin (1929) followed. The next year saw extensive excavation at the Classic period ruin near Martinez Hill (Gabel 1931). The work of three seasons (1930-33) at the University Ruin by Cummings was reported by Kelly (1936).

In the same year testing at the Hodges Ruin (Arizona AA:12:18) was undertaken by Carl Miller. Archaeological excavations were continued there by Isabel Kelly for two more seasons under the auspices of Gila Pueblo. Her original summary forms the keystone for the chronology in the Tucson area (Kelly n.d. and Officer 1961).

During the late 1930s Emil W. Haury and students returned to the University Indian Ruin and, in addition, tested the Freeman site (Arizona BB:14:3). Julian D. Hayden (1957) published his 1940 work at the University Indian Ruin and reviewed its connection with Classic period sites on the Gila and Salt rivers.

Only sporadic digging and survey reports filled the years between 1940 and the highway salvage work described here. Wright and Gerald (1950) described a small excavation at the Zanardelli site south of San Xavier. An analysis of the stone walls, trails, and house foundations on Black Mountain, just to the west of the highway salvage area, was presented by Fontana and others (1959). This was followed by a wide-ranging study of historic Papago ceramics and possible prehistoric antecedents by Fontana and others (1962).

A second look at the villages near the Tanque Verde type site was published by Zahniser (1966). In addition, work has been conducted at the Whiptail site, another Tanque Verde community (Arizona BB:10:3) on Agua Caliente Wash east of Tucson, under the direction of Paul Grebinger for the Arizona Archaeological and Historical Society.

No work in southern Arizona can proceed without acknowledging its debt to the pioneering report of the Snaketown sequence on the Gila River (Gladwin and others 1937) which is the basis for all area correlations up to the Classic period.

The detailed summary from Ventana Cave (Haury 1950) presents the longest cultural sequence in southern Arizona. In conjunction with the work at Jackrabbit Ruin (Scantling 1939, 1940) and at Valshni Village (Withers 1941, 1944) the reconstruction of events in the Papaguería have direct bearing on the development at Punta de Agua.

More removed, but still applicable to cultural changes in the Tucson Basin, are the descriptions of Sobaipuri Indians on the San Pedro River (DiPeso 1953) and the intrusive Western Pueblo village, the Reeve Ruin, on the same drainage (DiPeso 1958). The archaeological sequence at Tres Alamos, on the San Pedro River, covers much of the same period as that encountered at San Xavier (Tuthill 1947).

The major southern outpost of the Hohokam on the Santa Cruz River at Paloparado has also been published by DiPeso (1956). Up to the Classic period the events here were synchronous with the phases represented at San Xavier. Numerous examples of analogous material and similar architectural traits are cited in this report.

The latest archaeological work in the vicinity of the salvage area is continuing at the modern San Xavier Mission itself. Robinson (1963) summarized the early findings within and on the west side of the present structure which aided in establishing the historic building sequences. However, any continuity of aesthetic or material traits between historic Sobaipuri or Papago culture and the late prehistoric phases could not be established.

A most significant excavation near Bylas on the San Carlos Indian Reservation delineated a new phase on that portion of the Gila River. The Bylas phase (A.D. 1100-1200) incorporated a specialized ceramic inven-

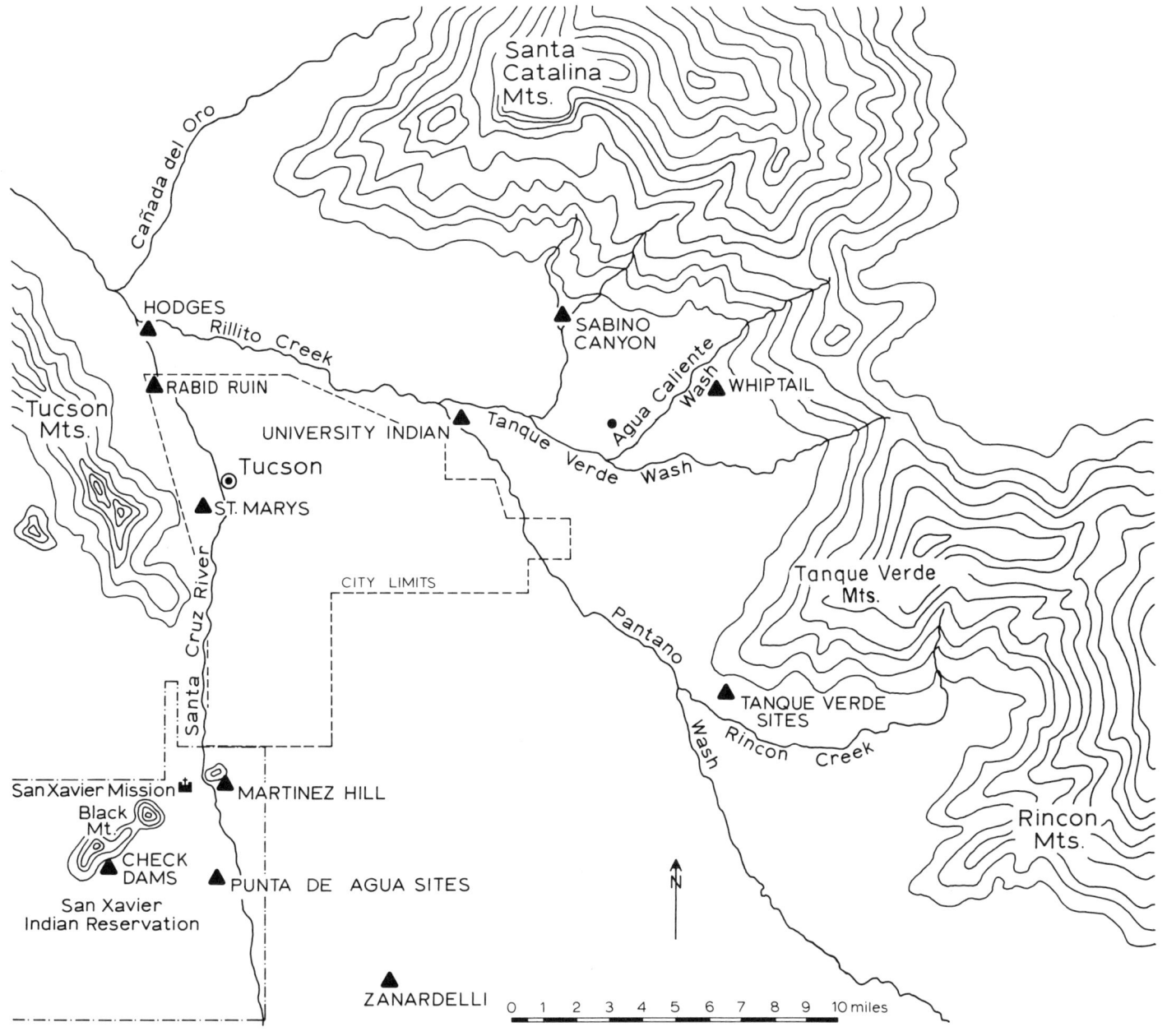

Fig. 1.1. Archaeological sites in the Tucson Basin.

tory and settlement pattern (Johnson and Wasley 1966) which was repeated at sites on the San Pedro River and, notably, at the Whiptail site twelve miles east of Tucson. It is probable that the intrusive pottery and other material culture traits from the Bylas district first entered the Tucson Basin as a full assemblage at Whiptail and at the University Indian Ruin.

Completing the recent work near Tucson was the important salvage operation at the Rabid Ruin (Arizona AA:12:46). This was a Tanque Verde phase site located on the west bank of the Santa Cruz River and marked by exclusive use of primary cremations (Hammack n.d.).

Summary of Prehistoric Cultures

A long-standing gap exists in the Tucson Basin record regarding peoples and settlements in the Pioneer period of the Hohokam sequence. Surface surveys have produced a smattering of pottery resembling that of the Vahki through Snaketown styles of the Gila Basin Hohokam. However, some of the identifications are equivocal as the early pottery types of the Gila River and San Simon sequences are practically indistinguishable, and there are generally no other remains.

So far as evidence of actual settlement in the Tucson Basin is concerned, only at the Hodges site has an early house been excavated. It is attributable to the Snaketown phase of the Pioneer period (Officer 1961:I:30).

Other collections from along the Santa Cruz River have produced pottery resembling that assigned to the earlier Sweetwater phase. At Paloparado (DiPeso 1956:259-264, Fig. 40, and 346-356) for example, some Snaketown and Sweetwater ceramics were found, but these were not associated with any architecture of a comparable phase. Two extensive surveys along the upper and middle Santa Cruz by Danson (1940) and Frick (1954) respectively identified no settlements prior to the Colonial period.

A similar phenomenon has recently been reported at the Potrero Creek site (Ariz. EE:9:53) near Nogales (Grebinger 1971:28-71). There a scattering of sherds from the Sweetwater and Snaketown phases of the Gila sequence were present, but the first physical evidence of a settlement dates from the Santa Cruz phase (Rillito in the Tucson Basin).

The same conditions seem to exist in the San Pedro Valley east of Tucson. Surface collections have produced some of the early red-on-brown types, but at sites excavated, the settlements date to the Colonial period (DiPeso 1953:254-255).

In the Empire Valley, which comprises the upper drainage of Pantano and Rillito creeks, Eddy (1958:65-81) uncovered a probable pit house containing ceramics he assigned, in a tentative fashion, to the Estrella phase. Previously Swanson (1951:30-32) recorded a Peñasco phase structure and Dos Cabezas phase ceramics in the Empire Valley. This area had been, therefore, considered an extension of the Mogollon-San Simon Red-on-brown culture district.

In order to fill the Pioneer period gap along the Santa Cruz River authors of chronological charts have often gratuitously transposed phases either from the Gila Hohokam or San Simon phase structures. However, there is little evidence to substantiate these Tucson Basin phases.

At the present state of our knowledge, therefore, we are left with a twilight zone between the well-documented Amargosa I-II and San Pedro stages of the earlier hunting and foraging groups and the beginning of the Colonial period—a period of over 500 years. Haury (1950:530-543) has shown long continuity at Ventana Cave emphasizing the earlier periods. Rogers (1958) outlined the San Dieguito and Amargosa development in the Tucson Basin and then Rogers (1966) correlated all the latter horizons in the far west.

In southeast Arizona the Cochise culture (Sayles and Antevs 1944) accounted for preceramic horizons upon which most of the regional prehistory was built. Hayden (1970) proposed a bold version of this area's continuity which links the Amargosa and Cochise stages as ecological variants of the same horizon.

We are left, locally, with a rather unsatisfactory understanding of cultural events. There is no question that the Hohokam spread out and colonized neighboring river valleys around A.D. 500, but who did the colonists meet in the Tucson Basin? Perhaps the few Pioneer period sites were happily situated in foothill locations and are as yet undiscovered by investigators. Throughout the basin, including Punta de Agua, the ceramic inventory always maintained the brownware and red-on-brown traditions of the Mogollon, perhaps reflecting the Sonoran brownware background as well.

Hohokam irrigation practices soon compelled the scattered local dwellers to concentrate in villages along the river terraces. The increase of the Hohokam population in the Tucson Basin was not absolutely synchronous with that in the Gila heartland. Environmental and ecological differences surely played an important factor in the divergence. In summary, the Tucson development was not built upon a pure Gila Hohokam base.

Cultural Continuity and Ethnographic Parallels

On the face of it, the prehistoric house clusters excavated seem to fit ethnographic data remarkably well. For this reason we will now review selected ethnographic details concerning the historic Indian populations.

Many investigators have tried, without much success, to find analogous traits which would link up the Pima, Papago, or Sobaipuri Indians with the former inhabitants of the twelfth century. It is a difficult task primarily due to lack of datable post-Hohokam pottery and poor ethnographic material available from the Spanish contact period. To say that a viable continuity of social or religious organization lasted for over 500 years would be pure sophistry.

There is evidence for extraordinary cultural upheavals at Punta de Agua and throughout the Gila Basin, during the three centuries after the establishment of our villages. The first manifestations of Western Pueblo (Haury 1945:204-213) advancement were already appearing by A.D. 1200 at late Rincon phase houses at Arizona BB:13:50. For example, a distinctly new regional polychrome incorporating elements from the White Mountain Redware series (Carlson 1970) was developed.

After the abandonment of the Great Houses near the end of the fifteenth century, the Western Pueblo culture and organization withered. Such a political collapse probably was accompanied by the actual dispersal of some of the social units. We speculate that they left those they had so dominated to eke out their existence as their forefathers had done hundreds of years before. The Pima creation myth (Russell 1908:206-230) and a summary of Papago myths (DiPeso 1958:158-160) embody legendary events (perhaps reliable) about their ancestors' rebellion. The survivors had assimilated many pueblo traits as well as genes. These people were first identified as Sobaipuri at San Xavier del Bac and as Pima along the Gila River (Bolton 1936:247-249).

A review of the social organization of the Pima (Russell 1908), the Sobaipuri (DiPeso 1953) and, for good measure, the Papago (Spicer 1941), reveals that all three groups reckoned descent in the male line and practiced patrilocal residence. A single house might, therefore, have a nuclear family and, at the same time, parts of older and younger generations that formed the extended family. As the sons married and built nearby, closely situated clusters sprang up providing architectural evidence of a full-blown extended family.

After the collapse of the political and economic organization of the Classic period, the local population reverted to the simple wattle and daub structures of earlier times. The villages along the Santa Cruz River were probably organized in much the same way as historic rancherías, that is, loose groups of houses that probably represented the residence of one or more closely related families.

The historic Papago are noted for their establishment of summer and winter villages, but prehistorically the sites under study here show no evidence of seasonal occupation. They might have been partially deserted for the sahuaro fruit gathering and hunting activities, but as the area near Punta de Agua was a well-watered agricultural zone, the inference is that the communities were inhabited on a year-round basis.

More recently, the Papago and Pima made use of a community house that was circular in plan and slightly larger than the normal wattle and daub structure. This was the Rain or Cloud House and, when not in use, it was the regular dwelling of the Keeper of the Smoke. Intravillage secular and ceremonial meetings took place in these structures (Spicer 1941:23). A peculiar fact is that no readily identifiable prehistoric ceremonial house has been identified from the Colonial and Sedentary periods. However, in Chapter 2 we have tentatively advanced the suggestion that a newly discovered housetype with more formal and careful construction in each contemporaneous group might have had some ceremonial significance for a kin group.

Especially during the Rincon phase we find ballcourts near the larger settlements. These probably served an integrative function on a higher, perhaps intercommunity level. It has recently been suggested that these courts did not serve the same purpose as the ballcourts further to the south in Mexico. Ferdon (1967:8-12) proposed that the Papago *Vikita* ceremony could have had its origin in a ceremony held in what archaeologists have termed ballcourts. In this view, the main purpose of the *Vikita* was flood prevention, instead of rain-making.

My impression is that these prehistoric villages were more formally cohesive than ethnographic examples and that there could have been stronger political forces operating than observed historically. Thus, the Hohokam ballcourt "could represent the fundamental socio-religious organization needed to construct and maintain the large irrigation systems" on a cooperative intervillage basis (Ferdon 1967:12). Consistent with this, the two ballcourts near Martinez Hill were within the integrated zone where historic irrigation was practiced at the time of the Spanish contact (Kelly 1963:100-101).

2. THE PUNTA DE AGUA SITES

SITE DESCRIPTIONS

This chapter includes a synopsis of the architectural discoveries at four of the excavated sites: Arizona BB:13:50, Arizona BB:13:43, Arizona BB:13:41, and Arizona BB:13:16. One additional site, Arizona BB:13:49, which was a trash mound area, is also reviewed (Fig. 2.1).

Certain terms are introduced in this discussion regarding the dispersal of houses at the principal sites. Each site is separated into "units." A unit is nothing more than an arbitrary grouping of houses in one part of a site, spatially separated from the rest. Such a determination aided in describing the houses and, often, led to perceiving possible cultural development. A corollary term, "cluster," is employed to describe two or more houses within a unit that might have been functionally related, or similar in style, or perhaps are residual evidence of an extended family grouping.

New to the archaeological literature of southern Arizona is the term "adobe cone." The description and function of this architectural embellishment is found in the discussion below.

Throughout the discussion reference is made to the methods used in developing the relative placement of the houses within the phases of the Tucson Basin chronology. The controls are outlined below which enabled the seriation of architecture to be internally consistent.

The majority of the structures are from the Rincon phase (A.D. 900-1215). The relative placement of structures within this phase rests upon the following criteria:

1. House plans analogous to those at other Hohokam sites.
2. House superimposition. One major and four minor series of stratified house floors became the key to the local series.
3. Ceramics directly associated with each house. When the refinements to the Rincon phase decorated pottery were worked out, the seriation of houses in accordance with early or late pottery designs was feasible.
4. Relative dating by intrusive pottery, some of which had been previously dated by dendrochronology.
5. House or hearth remodeling. Most instances of enlargement or relocation of hearths were looked upon as an indication of more lengthy occupation. Major changes usually signaled a phase transition.

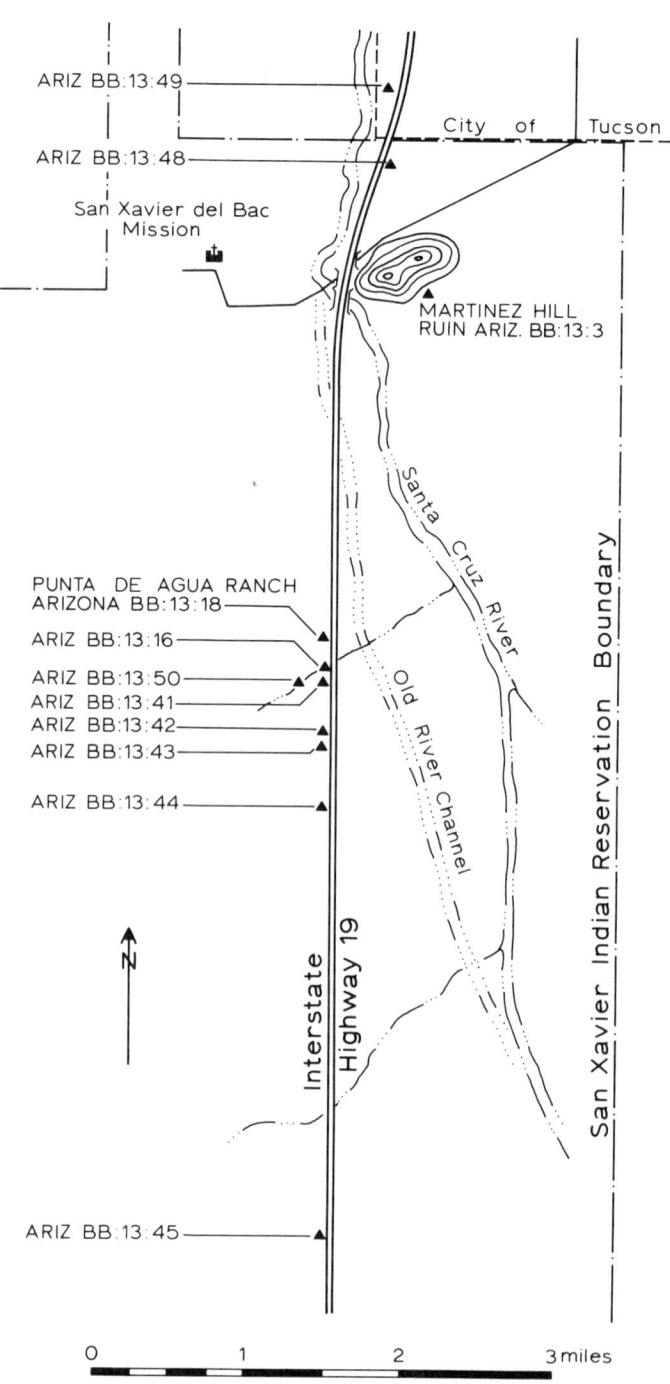

Fig. 2.1. Punta de Agua and other excavated sites.

TABLE 2.1
**Tentative Archaeomagnetic Dates
Arizona BB:13:50**

Provenience	DuBois Number	Date Range (A.D.)	Remarks
Hearth, House 14 Unit 2	101	1205 ± 25	Late Rincon
Hearth, House 23 Unit 2	102	1160 ± 20	Late Rincon
Hearth, House 2 Unit 1	103	1210 ± 21	Late Rincon
Hearth, House 18 Unit 2	104	1240 ± 65	Tanque Verde
Hearth, House 22 Unit 2	105	1215 ± 20	Late Rincon
Hearth, House 10 Unit 2	106	1155 ± 20	Late Rincon

6. Increase of relative abundance of redware. The unwritten rule has been that as the Classic period was approached an increase of redware manufacturing also occurred.
7. A final check was provided by preliminary archaeomagnetic dates from six houses at Arizona BB:13:50. These were all from late structures and corroborated the placement of the late Rincon phase houses.

The results of the proposed architectural seriation based on the above criteria were checked against the preliminary dates from six hearths at Arizona BB:13:50 as shown in Table 2.1 (DuBois 1968).

It was reassuring to find that the dates tended to affirm the existence of clearly defined late Rincon activity up to about A.D. 1215; another pair of dates fell near A.D. 1160. From these, it is proposed that the late Rincon phase covers the period from A.D. 1150 to about A.D. 1215. The complement of architecture and other material traits in the Tucson Basin shows that the time period was not just a local transition, but was a distinct regional development.

Arizona BB:13:50

Exploratory trenching was conducted on this large site with a backhoe. As the backhoe was only available for a few days, the overburden was removed mechanically to within 30-40 cm of the floor when trash or a house floor was exposed. Twelve structures were discovered in this manner.

The architectural groups at Arizona BB:13:50 were separated into two units which will be discussed separately. The division into Units 1 and 2 seems to be a natural one that existed in prehistoric times (Fig. 2.2).

Unit 1 produced 11 houses, a trash mound, 3 trash pits, and 1 ramada or covered storage and work area. A recent wash had obliterated the major portions of Houses 4 and 8. Only a single cremation was discovered in Unit 1.

Unit 2, the greater proportion of which was on

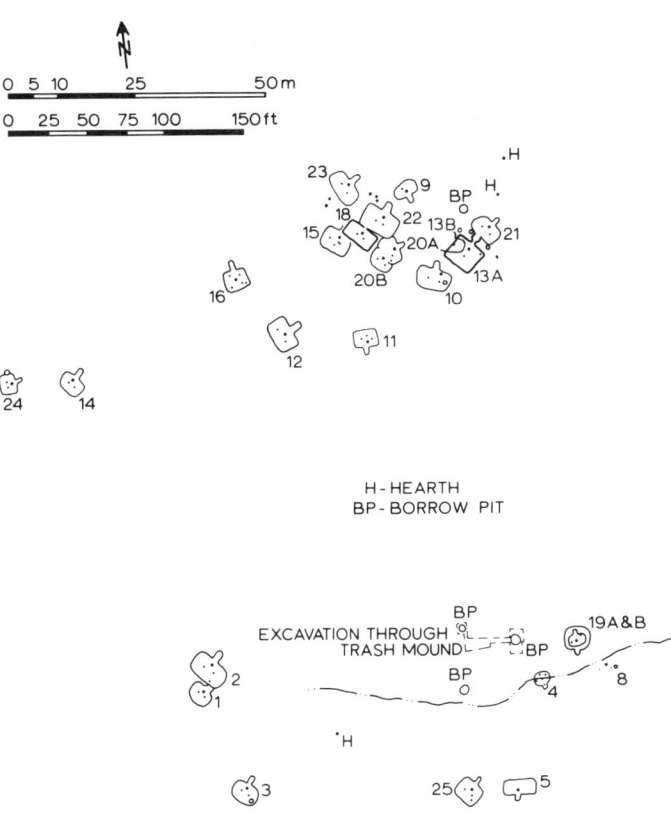
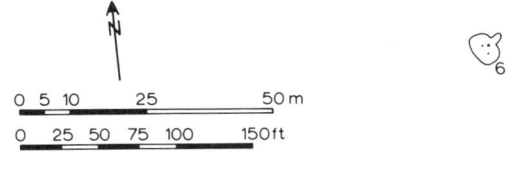

Fig. 2.2. Site map of Arizona BB:13:50, Units 1 and 2.

higher ground than Unit 1, included 15 houses, 1 large trash pit, and a variety of adobe-lined cooking pits and outside hearths. The principal burial zones were not located. Only two cremations, both of the Tanque Verde phase, were discovered.

Two other houses were located in Unit 2, but insufficient time precluded their excavation. House 17 was deep in the trench between Houses 11 and 15. No artifacts were recovered, but the amount of overlying trash indicated that it was a relatively early house. Under the north part of House 13 another hearth and floor were exposed only 6 cm down. The floor sherds made a late Rincon assignment probable.

UNIT 1

Continuous occupation in Unit 1 from the Rillito, through all stages of the Rincon and up to the Tanque Verde transition, was confirmed. The 11 houses of the unit were strung out in a discontinuous pattern with the Rillito settlement represented by Houses 19A and 4. Each plan was based on the squared, four-post arrangement with a short, rounded, entrance passage. Both structures were overlain by a trash mound.

A newer and smaller oval house was built entirely within the walls of House 19A. The floor of this early Rincon structure, House 19B, consisted of 5 cm of caliche plaster over the earlier floor. Its entry faced north in opposition to House 19A, the earlier house (Fig. 2.3). [For details of superimposition see Appendix A.]

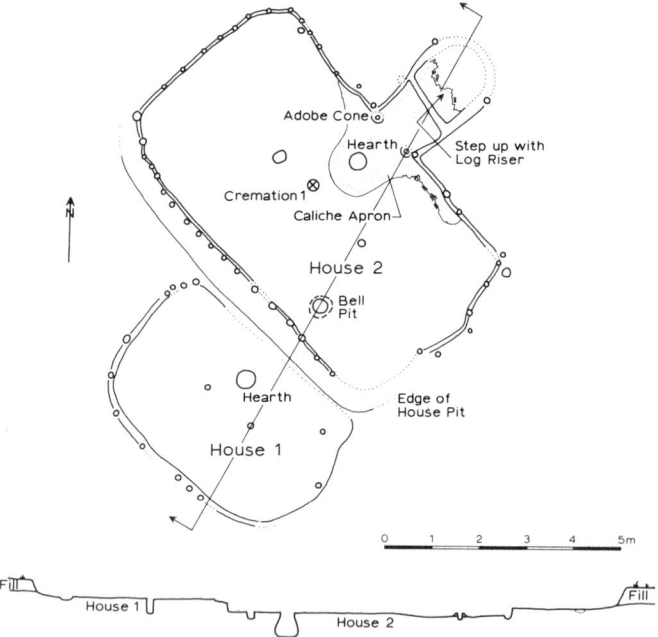

Fig. 2.4. Arizona BB:13:50, Unit 1, superimposition of House 2 cutting entry of House 1.

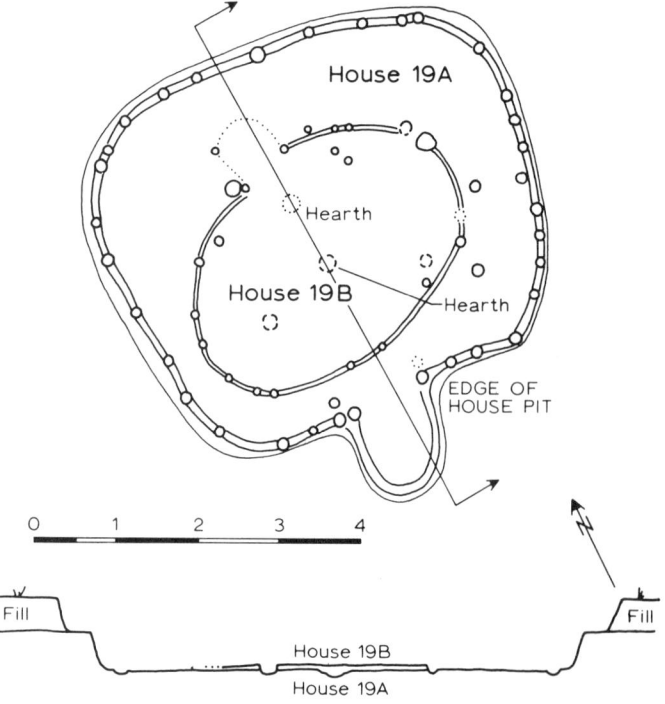

Fig. 2.3. Arizona BB:13:50, Unit 1, superimposition of House 19B over 19A.

The community started to expand in mid-Rincon times. The variety of house plans was most likely a reflection of experimentation during the time of rapid population growth. Only in the last half of the Rincon phase did the house plans assume two characteristic shapes.

House 5, the narrowest discovered at Punta de Agua, was rectangular and possessed a short, rounded entry. Even though the shape recalls Colonial period types, restorable vessels from the floor and nearby storage area are distinctly mid-Rincon in style.

House 25 suggests a persistence of the squared plan in that half of a four-post pattern was found on one side. However, the placement of other features and a thicker caliche apron about the hearth area reflected the late Rincon elements.

House 1, the typical mid-Rincon subrectangular shape, had its entry obliterated by the construction of the huge, late Rincon structure, House 2 (Fig. 2.4).

Isolated about 100 m to the south, House 7 was the last of the mid-Rincon units. It represented the smaller variety of the subrectangular plan with a large straight entrance.

The final stage of architecture in the Rincon phase revealed two well-built, typical, late subrectangular houses with bulbous entries. House 2, the largest found at Punta de Agua, in addition to the well-prepared caliche floor and hearth apron of fine plaster, contained a pair of separate adobe cones without fluting impressions. House 6, though smaller, had well-preserved fluted adobe cones near the entrance. Each had a stepped entry vestibule with a transverse groove that held a wooden riser.

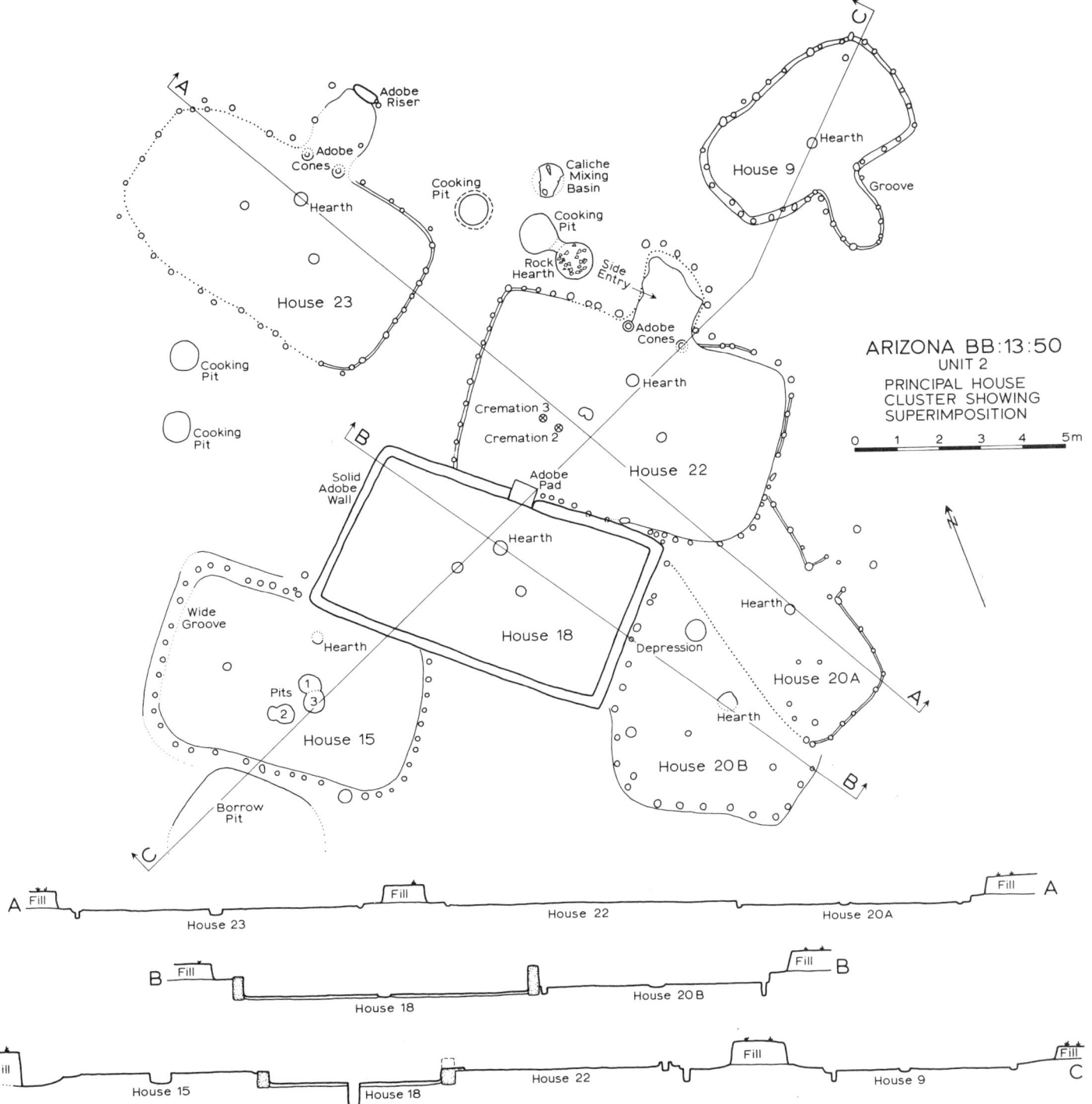

Fig. 2.5. Arizona BB:13:50, Unit 2, principal house cluster showing superimposition.

Unit 1 was notable for a peculiar structure, House 3. The well-conceived ovoid plan and abundance of late ceramics, including Rincon Polychrome, Tanque Verde Red-on-brown, and Mimbres Black-on-white led to its classification as a transitional type. The single cremation in Unit 1 (over House 2) must represent an individual from House 3. The cremation urn was an example of early Tanque Verde Red-on-brown.

UNIT 2

The 15 houses in Unit 2 provided the longest continuous sequence at Punta de Agua. The occupation reached from the end of the Rillito phase through the first part of the Tanque Verde phase.

The key to the architectural seriation at all sites at Punta de Agua was the exposure at Unit 2 of a group of five houses in the principal house cluster involving three consecutive cases of superimposition (Fig. 2.5). At the bottom of the series lay a typical squared Rillito structure, House 20B. Later, a mid-Rincon building, House 20A, was constructed over part of 20B. Then, House 22, an ideal late Rincon type, was built, partly overlaying House 20A. Finally, the solid adobe-walled Tanque Verde unit, House 18, was constructed through the south side of House 22. In fact, the Tanque Verde struc-

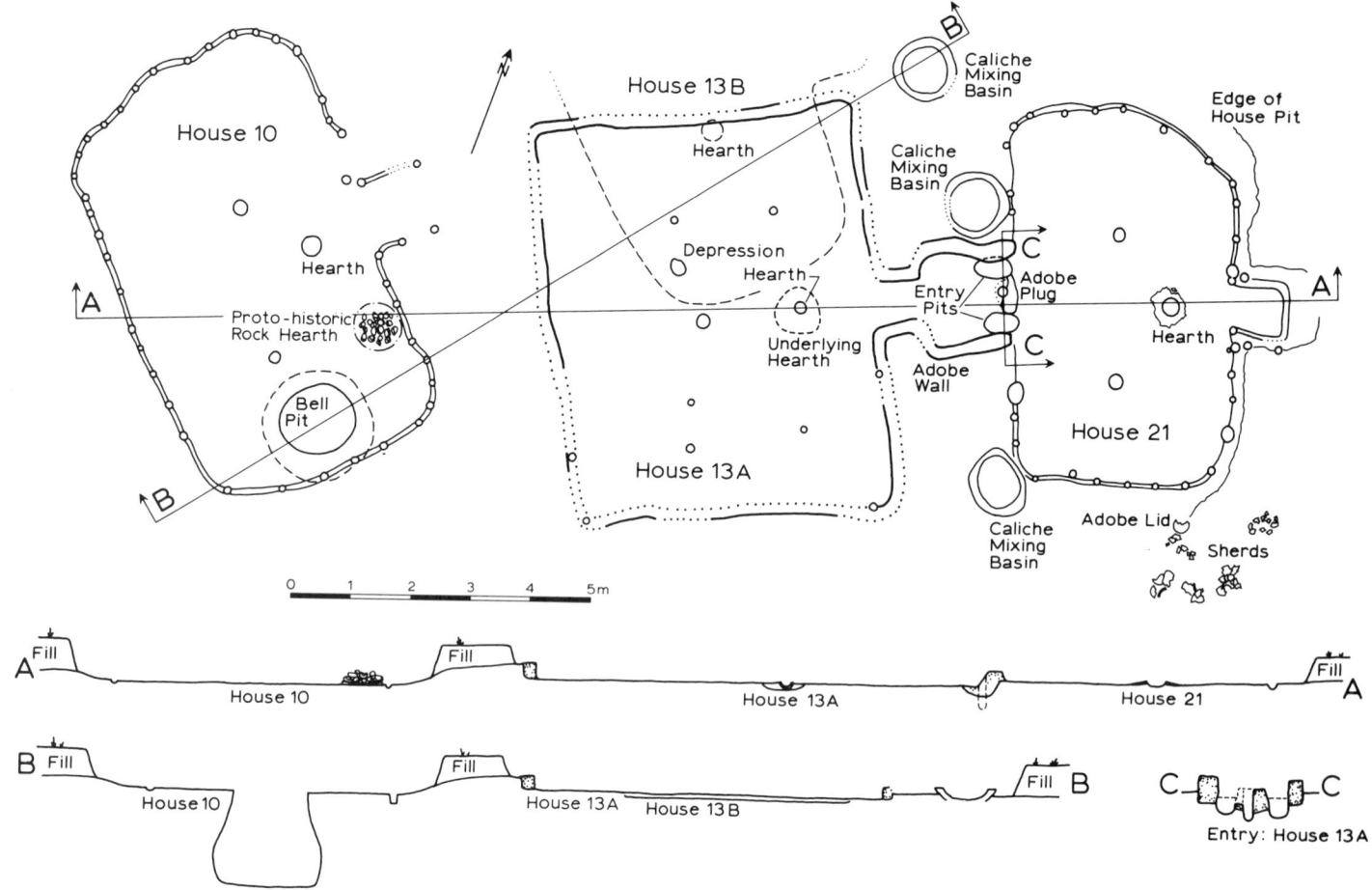

Fig. 2.6. Arizona BB:13:50, Unit 2, second house cluster showing superimposition.

ture cut through the entry of another adjacent mid-Rincon building, House 15, in the process. Houses 18 and 22 of this group have been assigned tentative archaeomagnetic dates by DuBois (1968).

Another series of superimposed structures was also discovered in Unit 2 (Fig. 2.6). A few meters to the southeast, three more houses were involved, of which only two were fully excavated. In this association, House 21, a mid-Rincon structure, was overlaid by the entry of House 13A. The entry was constructed of post-reinforced walls and was a component of the early Tanque Verde phase (see House 13 at Arizona BB:13:41).

Under the north portion of the floor of House 13A another hearth and wall section were exposed only 6 cm down. The time limit imposed by the salvage work precluded full excavation. The sub-floor unit, House 13B, did have enough pottery in its floor association to enable a late Rincon phase assignment to be made.

It is important to note that House 10, a late Rincon structure for which an archaeomagnetic date was obtained, lay just west of House 13A. A study of the plans of these two superimposed series revealed that most of the later dwellings were carefully aligned so as not to overlay the earlier structures. Some, in fact, were built so as to place the walls into direct contact with the earlier houses.

From the part of the settlement exposed, the following outline for the phase development of Unit 2 can be constructed. The Rillito phase settlement consisted of three houses, 20B, 11, and 16 in close association near the center of Unit 2. As noted, House 20B lay at the bottom of the series of superimposed structures. It and House 11 and 16 were each built according to the common squared pattern. However, House 11, being smaller, did not have four equally spaced roof supports. A notable variation in wall construction was exposed at House 16. The location of wall postholes suggested that the wall screen posts were paired within the groove. House 20B closely paralleled the configuration of House 19A of Unit 1 at Arizona BB:13:50.

The transition to the Rincon phase was abrupt. Only

House 9, a small subrectangular structure with bulbous entry, could be related to this period. Fortunately, a group of partly restorable vessels of early Rincon type were located on the floor. The bulbous entry was the earliest noted at Punta de Agua.

The marked increase of mid-Rincon structures (Houses 12, 15, 20A, and 21) gave the impression of an increase in population or, at least, of a planned concentration at Arizona BB:13:50. All houses conformed to the short entry, subrectangular type and were clustered together.

House 12 was the storeroom for this mid-Rincon group. Up to a dozen storage ollas, both plain and decorated, remained on the floor when the house was destroyed by fire. In the process, large quantities of stored corn, beans, seeds, and cholla buds became carbonized. A complete report on these plant remains has been published by Bohrer, Cutler, and Sauer (1969). Some jars held minerals and large accumulations of specular hematite. Carved stone bowls and a slate palette were in place on the floor. Most likely, they were used for grinding and mixing paints that were derived from other minerals in the collection. The storeroom inventory also included three decorated storage ollas of Rillito Red-on-brown.

Five late Rincon structures (House 10, 13A, 22, and 23) also followed the cluster pattern while two, Houses 14 and 24, were isolated to the west. The latter two had long straight entries which did not absolutely conform to the diagnostic bulbous type.

Six houses were completely excavated in Unit 2. They were assigned late Rincon dates on the basis of internal data and have now received tentative archaeomagnetic dates (Table 2.1). The data reveal that the later settlement owes its existence to two surges of construction at the end of the Rincon phase. The first activity occurred just after A.D. 1150, while the second began about A.D. 1200.

The Classic period in Unit 2 at Arizona BB:13:50 has been tentatively dated by one archaeomagnetic date from House 18 at about A.D. 1240 (Table 2.1). The architecture and ceramics confirm the date. However, House 13A represents the first transitional architecture of the early Tanque Verde phase. In this house, late Rincon and early Tanque Verde ceramics lay side by side. Its excavation revealed a large rectangular structure with post-reinforced adobe walls. Notably, the walls continued around a vestibule that was built as a more formal version of a bulbous entry. The walls in the vestibule were thicker and better preserved than the room walls. Three caliche mixing basins were aligned in front of the house, two of which overlay the west wall of House 21.

Furthermore, the hearth had been remodeled. The original basin had been filled with ash residue, then a smaller plug was placed within the first hearth. There are indications that House 13 at Arizona BB:13:41 was also extensively remodeled. Both houses reflect transitions from late Rincon phase architecture to Tanque Verde phase architecture. The final plan of House 13A at Arizona BB:13:50 bears close resemblance to House 4 at Arizona BB:14:24 (Zahniser 1966:131), and to House 31 at the Hodges site (Kelly n.d.:II:54).

The latest building in Unit 2 was House 18. It was a typical Classic period structure which showed no traces of the transitional experiments. As shown in Figure 2.5, this structure cut the south side of House 22, as well as the entry of House 15 and the juncture of Houses 20A and 20B. The plan was rectangular with a direct entry. A deep pit served as the support for the base of the solid adobe walls. Access was provided by means of an adobe pad laid over the burned debris of House 22. Directly opposite the entry, two Tanque Verde cremation urns were discovered; they presumably contained the remains of some of the last inhabitants of House 18.

Later in the Classic period, the population apparently concentrated at the large community of seven compounds near Martinez Hill about three miles north of Punta de Agua. Small dispersed communities were apparently abandoned.

STRATIGRAPHIC TESTS IN BORROW PITS

At Arizona BB:13:50 four large borrow pits were discovered. Each had ultimately been converted to a trash pit. Stratigraphic tests (using arbitrary 25 cm levels) were conducted in the two deepest pits. The first, Borrow Pit 2, was situated about 3 m north of House 21 in Unit 2; the second, Borrow Pit 4, lay 10 m west of the center of Houses 19A and 19B in Unit 1.

The complete dominance of Rincon phase pottery at all levels was unexpected. However, it reinforced the data gained from the architecture and from changes in the settlement pattern which pointed to rapid development at this site in the Rincon phase. Of the 27 houses discovered at Arizona BB:13:50, 22 were started during the same phase. The ceramic types from each level in the two pits are identified in Table 2.2.

Borrow Pit 3 was found at the west end of a test trench that connected with Pit 4. The heavy accumulation of trash in the area, which overlay Houses 19A and 19B, gave every indication of being the eroded remnant of a trash mound. No level separation was maintained in Borrow Pit 3, but the sherds found are listed in Table 2.2.

Both Pits 2 and 4 contained irregular layers of silt and sand, each layer denoting a period when the pit was open to the elements for a considerable time before the final filling.

TABLE 2.2
Ceramics from Stratigraphic Tests in Borrow Pits Arizona BB:13:50

Borrow Pit	Level	Rincon Red-on-brown	Rillito Red-on-brown	Sacaton Red-on-buff
PIT 2	1	14	1	–
	2	38	3	–
	3	45	1	1
	4	28	1	–
	5	13	1	–
	Total	138	7	1
PIT 4	1	69	–	1
	2	59	1	1
	3	52	3	–
	4	31	–	–
	5	66	2	–
	6	54	4	2
	7	31	1	3
	Total	362	11	7
PIT 3	Total	287	17	1

The rectilinear, late variety of Rincon Red-on-brown pottery was notably absent from each pit. This indicates that, by the time the late Rincon architecture was developed, the pits were filled. Most late Rincon pottery was discovered in fill over the mid-Rincon phase structures.

Arizona BB:13:49

This site was situated on the east side of the Santa Cruz River about one mile north of Sahuarita Butte (Martinez Hill) just off the San Xavier Indian Reservation. No architecture was disclosed by intensive trenching. However, from two low trash mounds, much late Rincon phase material was recovered. The site represented the disposal area of a settlement that probably was related to the late Classic period village known as the Martinez Hill Ruin where seven walled compounds suggested a more formal social and political organization as well as a large resident population.

From the ceramic analysis, the site dated to the late Rincon and early Tanque Verde phases. Thus, it has been assigned to an A.D. 1150-1215 time period. Much of the late Rincon Red-on-brown varieties were discovered here.

Arizona BB:13:43

This village lay on a relatively flat terrace on the west side of the Santa Cruz River. Recent erosion of the riverbank had exposed a burial zone which was evidently part of a larger Rillito phase village lying further east off the right-of-way. One interesting cremation was salvaged. A Tanque Verde phase settlement to the east was indicated by outlines of contiguous adobe structures.

The ten houses which were excavated were all of Rincon age and were discovered after systematic trenching. They were grouped into two discrete units. Unit 1, to the north, was composed of six houses, and Unit 2 contained four smaller houses from the earliest part of the Rincon phase (Fig. 2.7).

Within the limits of this zone, only a minimum of subsidiary evidence was noted. Three ramadas or unroofed brush shelters and one rock-filled cooking pit were located. No burial area or trash mounds were found in the right-of-way. The full extent of Arizona BB:13:43 stretched over a distance of about 145 m oriented along an approximate north-south axis.

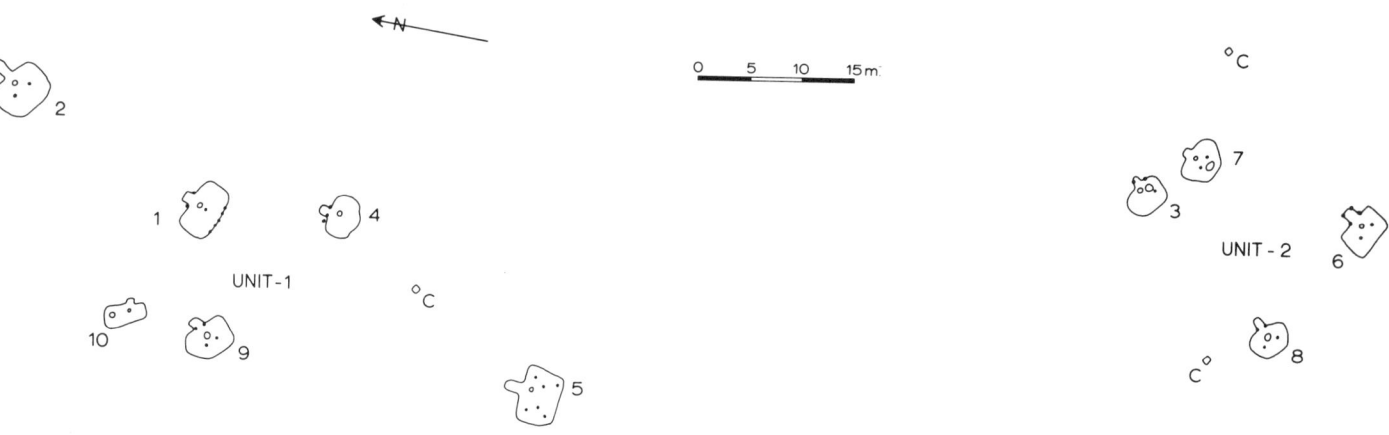

Fig. 2.7. Site map of Arizona BB:13:43, Units 1 and 2.

UNIT 1

The earliest settlement included Houses 4 (Fig. 2.8) and 10 (Fig. 2.9) and was occupied at the beginning of the Rincon phase. Each house was a small oval structure incorporating deep storage pits in the floor. The pit in House 10 was bell-shaped. It is important to emphasize here that there is no local prototype for these oval houses with bell-shaped storage pits. The plan does not occur in the Colonial Hohokam sequence. The Pioneer period structures in the San Simon Valley (Sayles 1945:19-22) which included oval houses were occupied at an earlier time. Therefore, throughout this report, the oval plan is considered as evidence of a widely scattered indigenous population which joined newly established permanent villages along the Santa Cruz River.

Houses 1 (Fig. 2.10), 5, and 9 are larger structures from the middle of the Rincon phase. House 1 bore evidence of reconstruction and enlargement. Its hearth was relocated and a new floor laid down which covered a pit at the rear containing early Rincon Red-on-brown jars.

House 9 was a modest mid-Rincon structure; a sherd of Rincon Polychrome was on the floor. This newly described pottery type is discussed in Chapter 3.

House 5 (Fig. 2.11) of the mid-Rincon phase, was constructed according to a transitional plan in that it had four equally spaced posts of the typically squared Rillito type, as well as two major centerline supports.

House 2 (Fig. 2.12) at the far northwest, was a typical Rincon example with a bulbous entry.

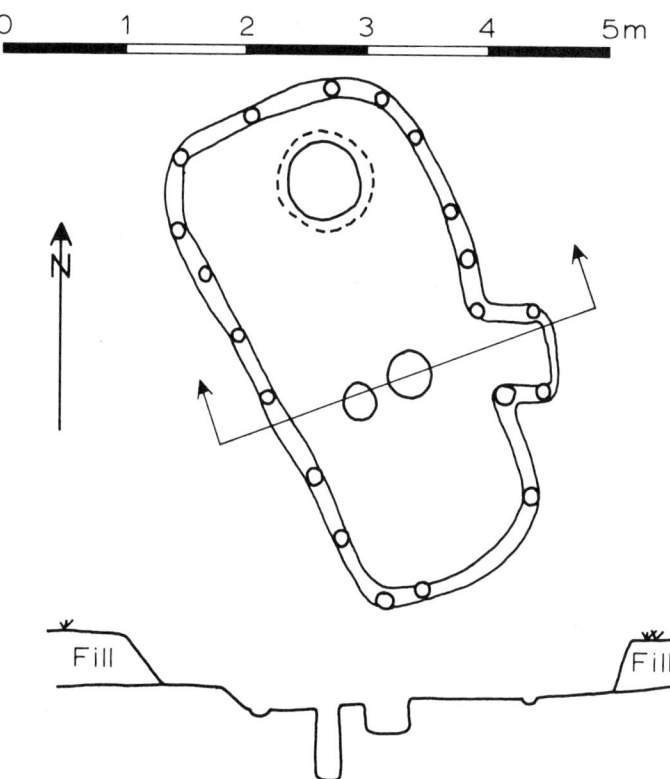

Fig. 2.9. Arizona BB:13:43, Unit 1, House 10.

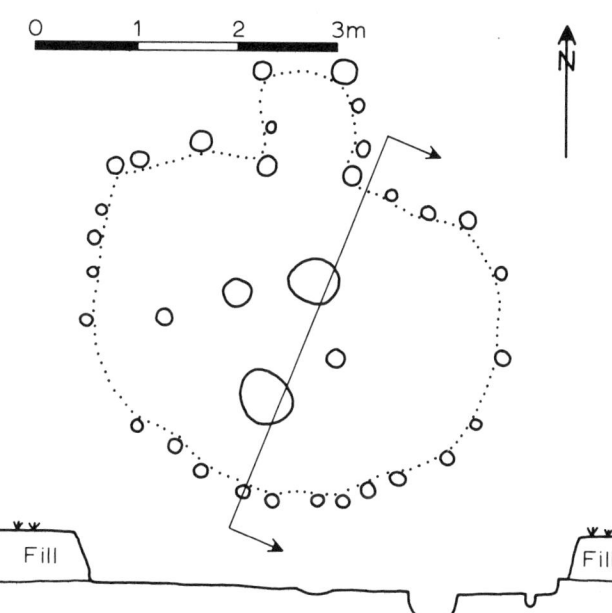

Fig. 2.8. Arizona BB:13:43, Unit 1, House 4 — Oval plan.

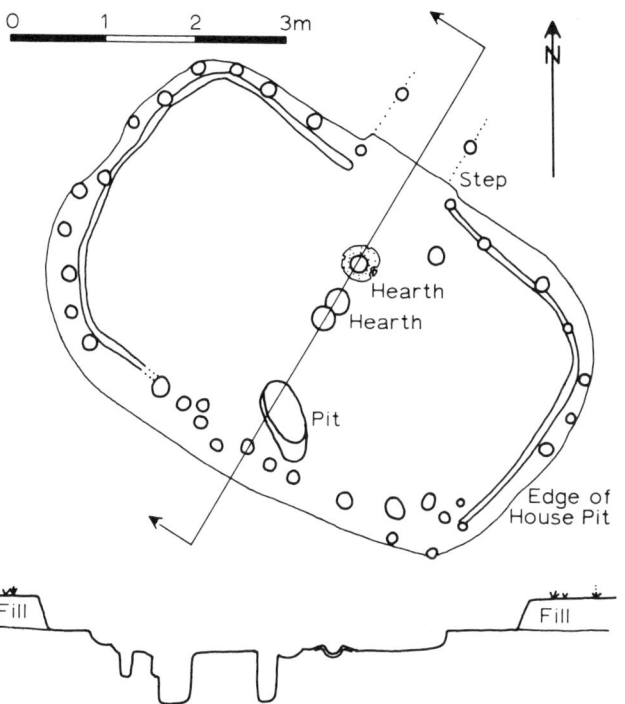

Fig. 2.10. Arizona BB:13:43, Unit 1, House 1.

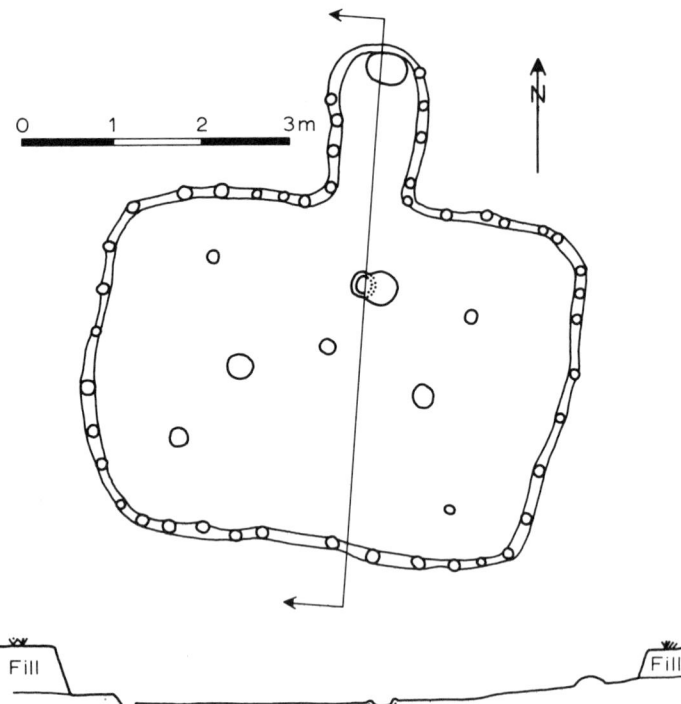

Fig. 2.11. Arizona BB:13:43, Unit 1, House 5.

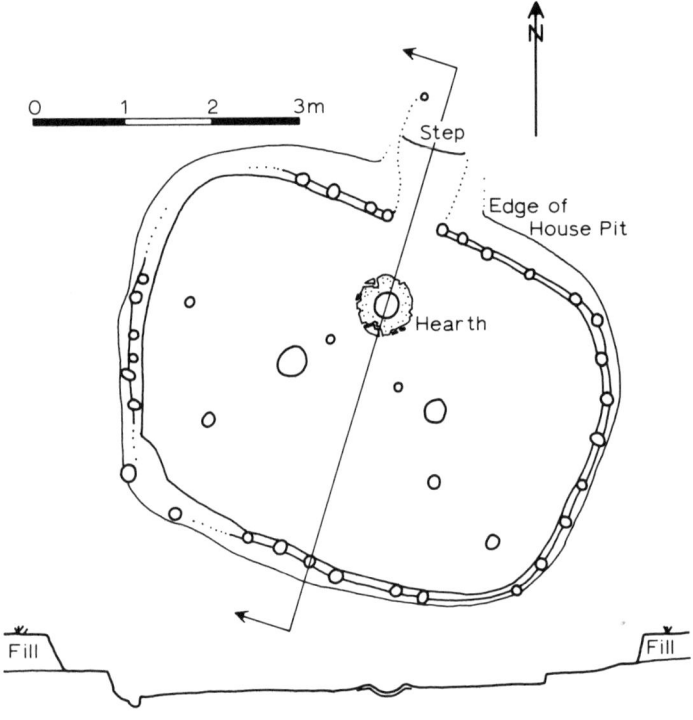

Fig. 2.12. Arizona BB:13:43, Unit 1, House 2.

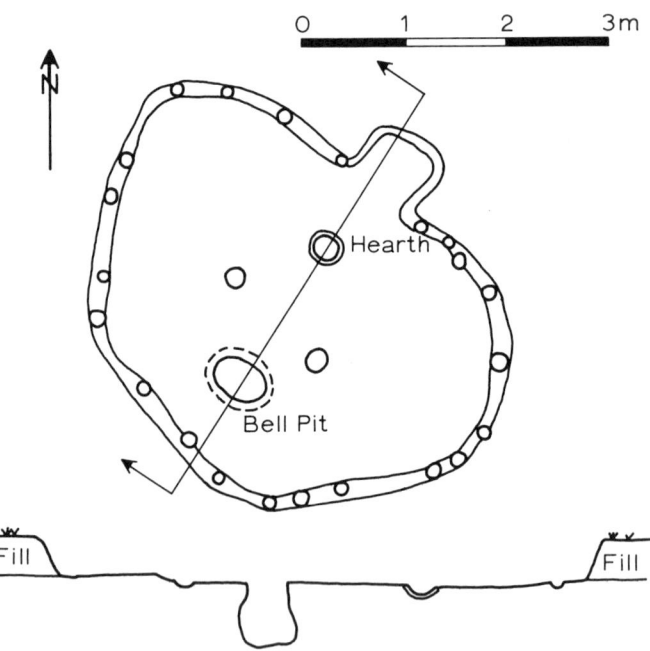

Fig. 2.13. Arizona BB:13:43, Unit 2, House 7.

UNIT 2

Unit 2 was first occupied in the early Rincon phase. It is represented by two closely associated small oval dwellings, Houses 3 and 7 (Fig. 2.13). The former had a large storage cist in the floor, while the latter had a bell-shaped pit. Both these features are hallmarks of the early Rincon phase at Punta de Agua. House 8 was poorly preserved, but contained a large sample of early Rincon plain and decorated vessels. House 6, a rectangular structure, was assigned to the mid-Rincon phase (Fig. 2.14).

From the data recovered at Units 1 and 2, it was clear that Arizona BB:13:43 was developed in the beginning of the Rincon phase. No Colonial period dwellings were located.

Arizona BB:13:41

On the west side of the Santa Cruz River, about one-third mile north of Arizona BB:13:43, a larger site containing 15 Rincon phase houses was discovered. Arizona BB:13:41 was situated between two major arroyos which cut the old terrace. The higher ground was composed of deep alluvium and much of the site had been destroyed by erosion.

That part of the site within the right-of-way extended for a distance of 130 m. The alignment of the buildings in a northeast-southwest line corresponded with the trend of the ridge and the direction of the drainage pattern. The old channel of the Santa Cruz lies about

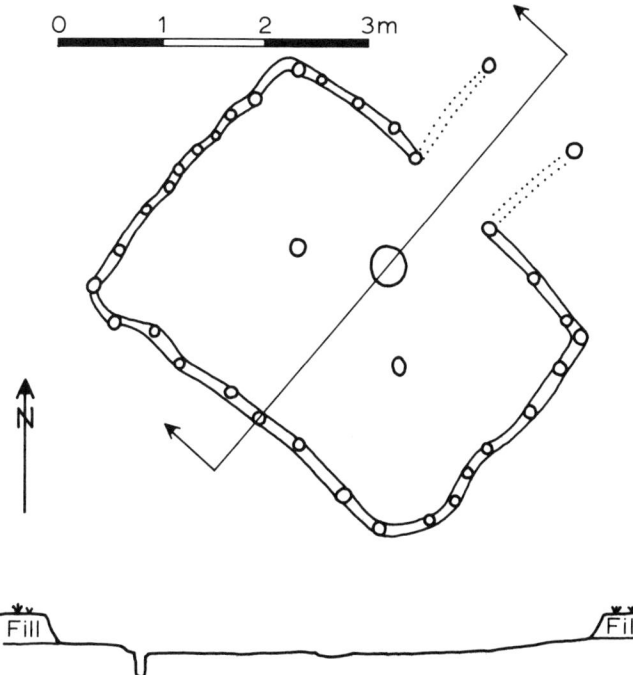

Fig. 2.14. Arizona BB:13:43, Unit 2, House 6.

PUNTA DE AGUA SITES 29

one-quarter mile to the east. Arizona BB:13:16 was on a higher ridge about 200 m to the north.

Systematic exploratory trenching revealed, in addition to the fifteen dwellings, six small cooking pits with fire-cracked rock and one carefully shaped adobe-lined pit. No burial zone or trash mounds were encountered.

For convenience, the settlement will be reported as three units (Fig. 2.15). The first two, lying about 25 m apart, form discrete groups of houses. Unit 3 includes the five dispersed houses on the south end.

UNIT 1

Using the criteria for relative dating, the four houses in Unit 1 sort themselves into two related pairs. Houses 1 (Fig. 2.16) and 5 (Fig. 2.17) were built according to the characteristic mid-Rincon plan employing a short entry.

The community was enlarged by the building of Houses 2 and 4 of typical, bulbous entry, late Rincon vintage. House 4 included the remains of a pair of separate adobe cones with reed fluting impressions. An

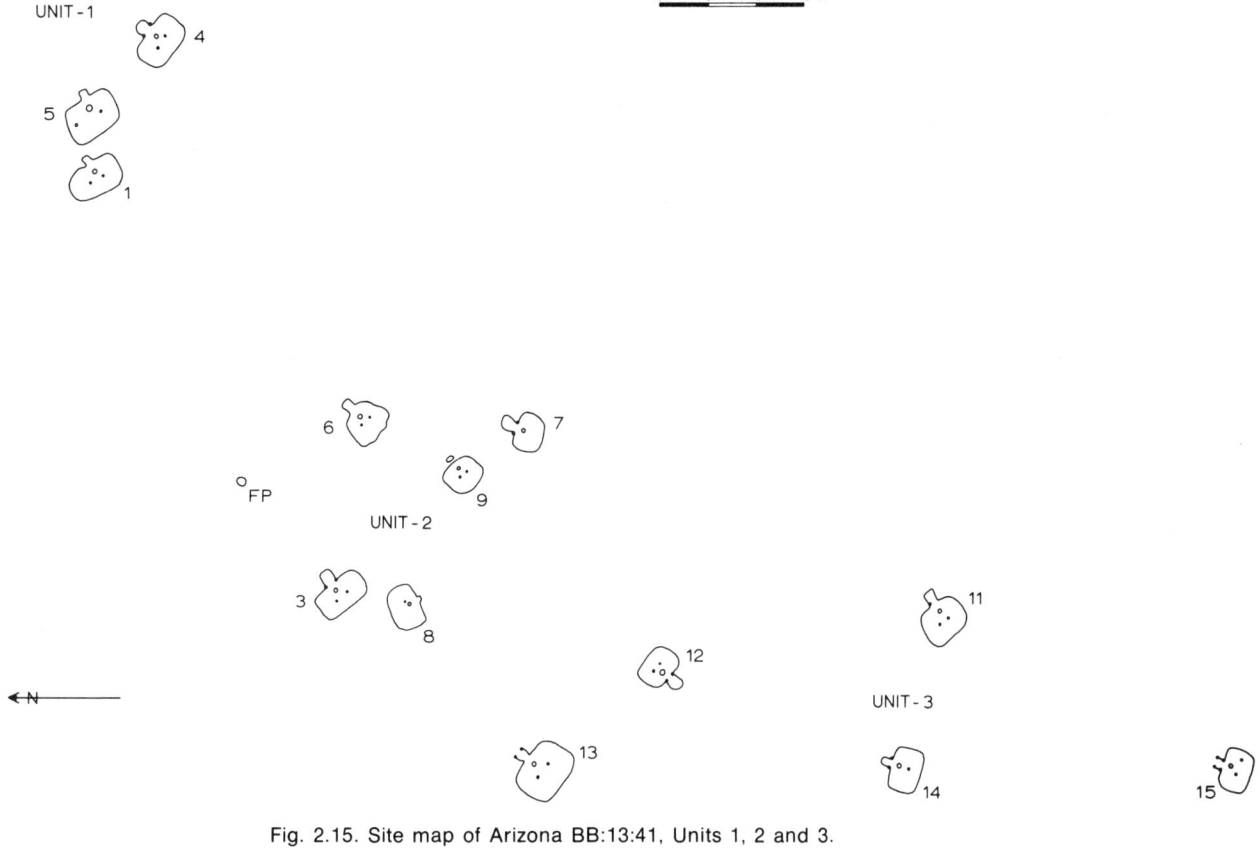

Fig. 2.15. Site map of Arizona BB:13:41, Units 1, 2 and 3.

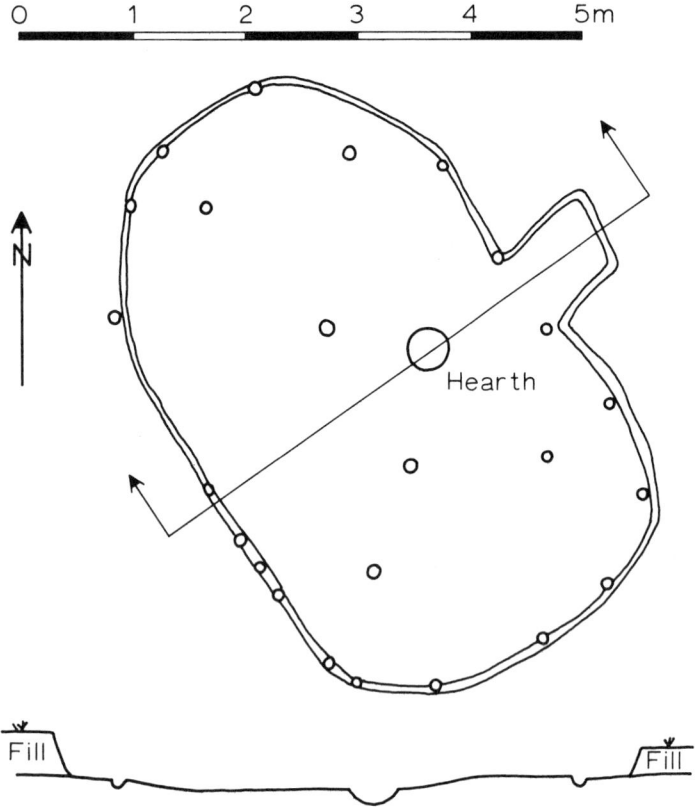

Fig. 2.16. Arizona BB:13:41, Unit 1, House 1.

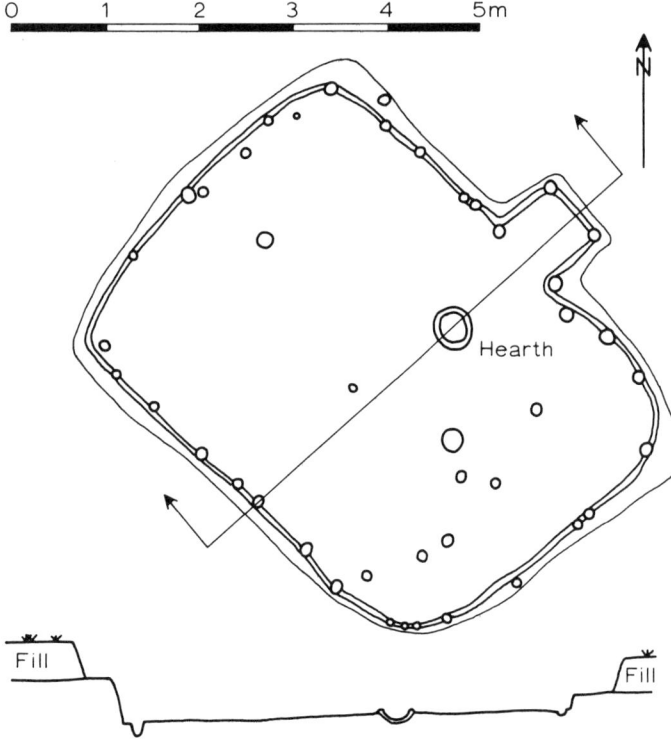

Fig. 2.17. Arizona BB:13:41, Unit 1, House 5.

Fig. 2.18. Arizona BB:13:41, Unit 1, House 4.

interesting post pattern in the southeast corner of House 4 suggested the possibility of a raised platform (Fig. 2.18).

UNIT 2

The six structures in Unit 2 reflected the same development as those in Unit 1, Houses 8 and 9 being best equated with mid-Rincon time. The latter probably continued in use to the last part of the phase, as late pottery was well represented. A ramada or work area was associated with these houses.

House 9 was unusual for it alone at San Xavier possessed a specialized entrance that seems to have provided direct access to the house from a depressed step beyond the wall line. The step was roughly oval and was apparently remodeled, the later and larger depression cutting the front edge of a smaller basin.

Three late Rincon Houses, 3, 6, and 7, were closely spaced around the nucleus. Each was a variation of the bulbous entry type. House 7 (Fig. 2.19) was a small version with a stepped entry; however, it had a pair of separate adobe cones, unfluted, near the corners of the entry.

House 6 was built according to an odd yet symmetrical plan. The rear wall was irregular (Fig. 2.20) with two pairs of large postholes just inside the wall groove for major support. The centerline postholes were surrounded by smoothed adobe collars. Parallel rows of posts extended between the hearth and entry, probably providing support for a screen or deflector.

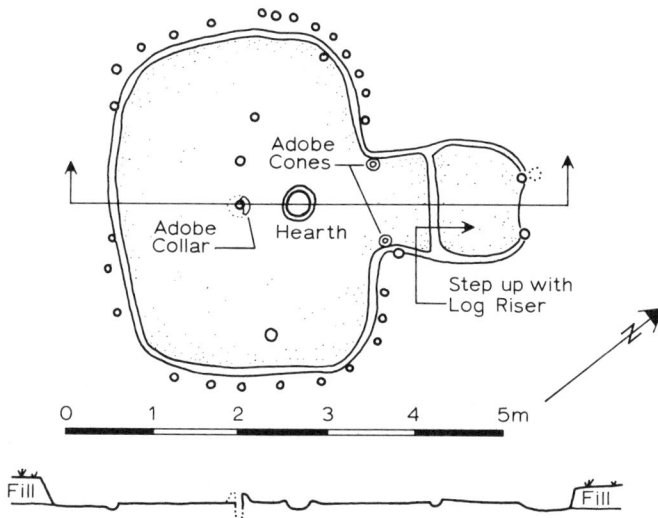

Fig. 2.19. Arizona BB:13:41, Unit 2, House 7.

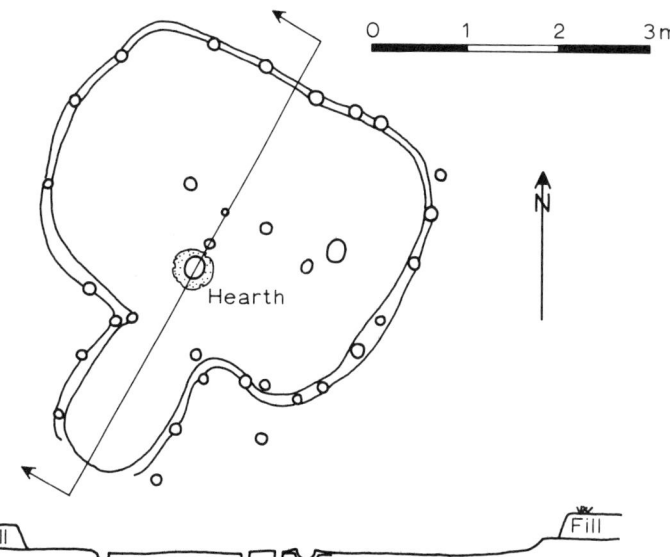

Fig. 2.21. Arizona BB:13:41, Unit 3, House 12.

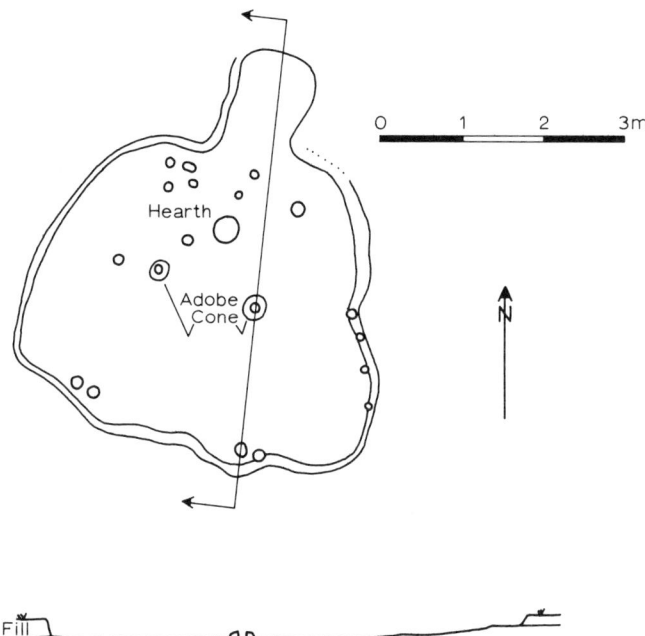

Fig. 2.20. Arizona BB:13:41, Unit 2, House 6.

UNIT 3

Unit 3 consisted of five dispersed houses. Houses 11 and 12 (Fig. 2.21) were excellent examples of the typical late Rincon subrectangular type with bulbous entries. They were isolated from Houses 13, 14, and 15.

Houses 13, 14, and 15 were arranged in a north-south alignment in which a developmental sequence was represented. Each showed architectural features that either indicated remodeling and reuse or a significant structural design that warranted close scrutiny.

House 15 was originally built in mid-Rincon times, but was slightly enlarged near the end of the phase. A later hearth was partly superimposed over the first. Due to severe weather during excavation, the shape of the vestibule was lost to the elements, but, fortunately, a selection of late Rincon Red-on-brown and a complete stone tool kit remained in place.

House 14 was a mid-Rincon structure and was the only one of its age to contain unfluted, adobe cones at entry corners. The single central roof support was within an adobe cone. The entry was short and straight.

House 13 (Fig. 2.22) was created in the last half of the Rincon phase and was thoroughly remodeled and enlarged into a post-reinforced adobe structure with thick adobe walls enclosing a bulbous entry. This unit contained Tanque Verde Red-on-brown pottery and, thus, ceramically and architecturally bridged the gap to the early Tanque Verde phase. House 13 had originally been built in a shallow pit, the rear half of which was used later as the lower support for the new thick adobe walls. The north wall of the house (the entry side) had been moved out to enlarge the floor area. The old hearth, central roof supports, and entry corner posts were plastered over. Two caliche mixing bowls were situated on the old surface just outside the west side of the entry and abutted the wall.

The final plan of House 13 is analogous to the Tanque Verde phase structures House 31 at the Hodges site (Kelly n.d.:IV:54) and House 4 at Arizona BB:14:24 (Zahniser 1966:131). One conclusion can be drawn from this similarity in plan. At widely separated points in the Tucson Basin, similar transitional houses were contem-

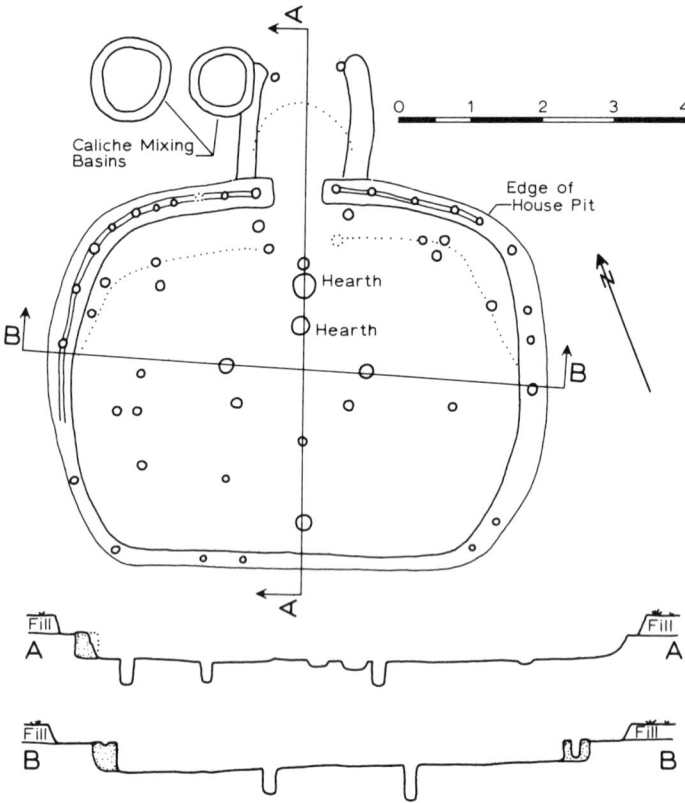

Fig. 2.22. Arizona BB:13:41, Unit 3, House 13.

porary, thus showing a cultural response to the same economic or social pressures.

In summary, Houses 13, 14 and 15 at Arizona BB:13:41 offered good corroboration for the architectural seriation presented above which was originally generated by the major superimposed series at Unit 2, Arizona BB:13:50. This is distinct from the settlement at Arizona BB:13:43, which started with early Rincon architecture and had only a light occupation in late Rincon time. Arizona BB:13:41 showed the largest late Rincon settlement and no early structures.

Arizona BB:13:16

The location of this site, like the preceding two, is at the end and on the slope of a higher, eroded ridge less than one-quarter mile from the old channel of the Santa Cruz River. A few houses of roughly the same age were noted to the southwest along the ridge, but outside the right-of-way. They formed an extension of the largest site, Arizona BB:13:50.

Arizona BB:13:16 was one part of the earliest settlement along this bank of the river and nearest to the Punta de Agua (Fig. 2.23. House 9 too far south to be shown). The site was about 15 m south of the historic ranch. The greatest number of sherds of the Colonial period types, Rillito Red-on-brown and Cañada del Oro Red-on-brown, at any of these villages, were concentrated on the surface down the slope. A cremation zone was also at the base of the slope. Some Snaketown Red-on-brown sherds, but no manifestations of earlier architecture were located.

The section of the river due east gave the impression of having been prehistorically, as it was during the nineteenth century, an area where surface water was available from seeps, lagoons, and springs. The location was presumably chosen for its proximity to easily channeled irrigation water as well as arable land found near the mouths of two arroyos and on the floodplain itself.

In the 1965 fieldwork, the lower portion of Arizona BB:13:16 was thoroughly tested. The heavy concentration of trash gave the impression that the east face of the ridge was covered by material washed down from the top. Two natural levels were established according to a change in color and consistency of the redeposited alluvium. It was hoped that these zones might indicate different occupation periods. However, after laboratory analysis, no significant changes in the percentage of pottery types were determined. The Rillito and Rincon material was thoroughly mixed by erosion.

At the end of the second season Arizona BB:13:16 included 10 houses, 15 cremations, 2 inhumations, 12 cooking pits, 2 borrow pits, and 1 ramada or outside work area.

The Rillito phase houses were predictable in style, but those of the Rincon phase did not follow the pattern established at the other sites. In fact, the architecture here revealed a greater variety of specialized plans than was identified at all the other sites. A late Rincon phase occupation was also represented. Some Tanque Verde phase pottery overlay the general trash zone. The houses from the Tanque Verde phase probably lay about 100 m further southwest along the ridge in the direction of Arizona BB:13:50.

At the south end of the site, House 9 was isolated from the others and lay equidistant between the main settlement at Arizona BB:13:16 and the west extension of Arizona BB:13:41.

The architecture at Arizona BB:13:16 included four Rillito houses. Houses 1 and 7 were small oval structures that had been subject to much erosion and deterioration. These two structures presented the first evidence at Punta de Agua of the modest wattle and daub oval house which in final analysis seems to be an indigenous expression. There are no immediate antecedents for this type except in the Pioneer period in the San Simon Valley.

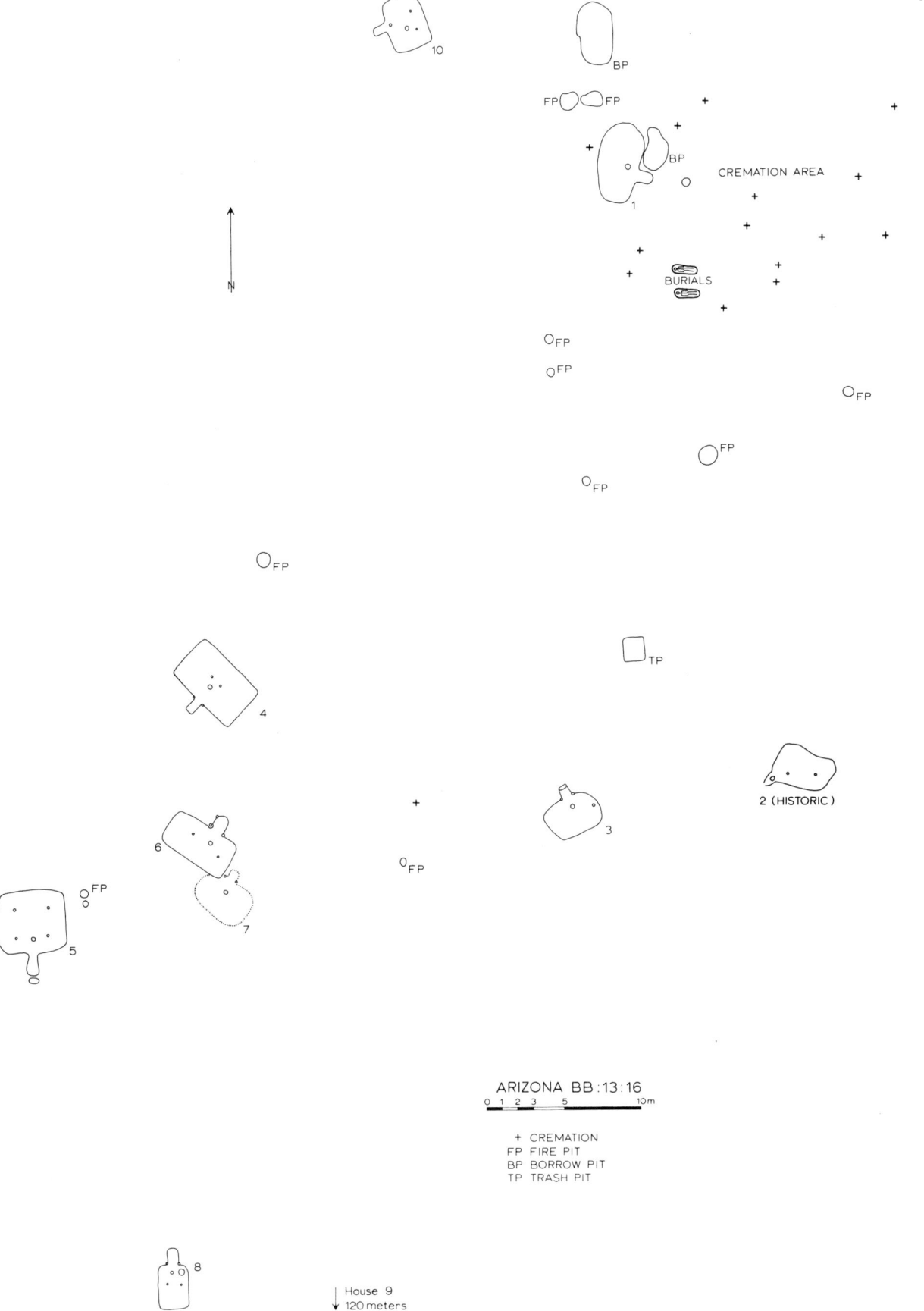

Fig. 2.23. Site map of Arizona BB:13:16.

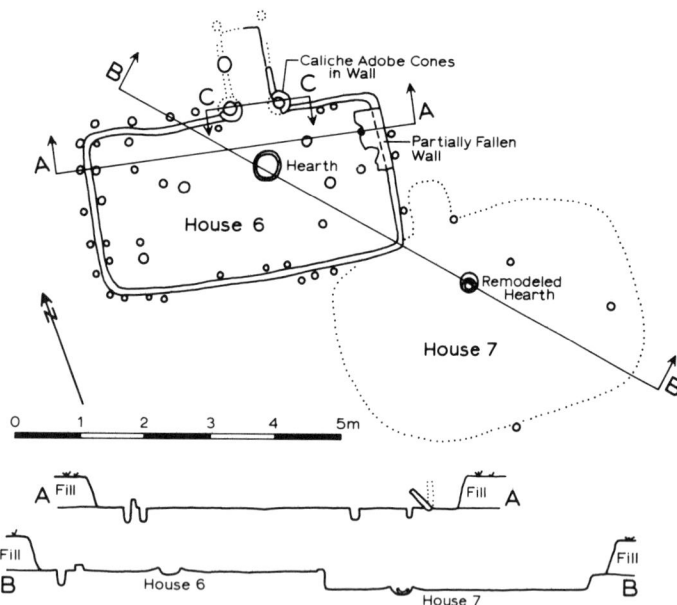

Fig. 2.24. Arizona BB:13:16, superimposition of House 6 over House 7.

House 7 was partly under the corner of House 6, a late Rincon rectangular dwelling (Fig. 2.24). House 7 contained a remodeled hearth that consisted of a later adobe plug set within the earlier basin.

House 8 (Fig. 2.25), a small Rillito unit with an unusual entry on the short side, resembled House 47, a contemporary structure at the Hodges site (Kelly n.d.:IV:61). It was almost rectangular with one central roof support and it contained a straight-sided storage pit.

The most typical Rillito structure, House 10, was quadrilateral with a long parallel-sided entry and four equally spaced roof supports.

The first part of the Rincon phase is represented by House 3, the smallest unit at Punta de Agua. The roof posts were located within the floor area, even though a complete wall groove was present (Fig. 2.26).

The plan of House 4 was rectangular with a long level entry possessing reinforced adobe walls up to 6 cm thick (Fig. 2.27). The late ceramics indicate this building was created in the transitional time prior to the

Fig. 2.25. Arizona BB:13:16, House 8.

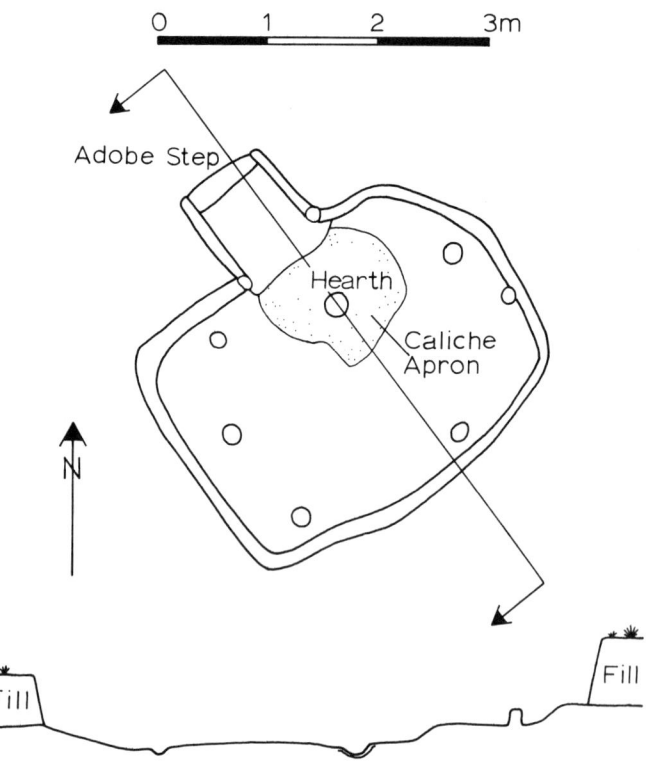

Fig. 2.26. Arizona BB:13:16, House 3.

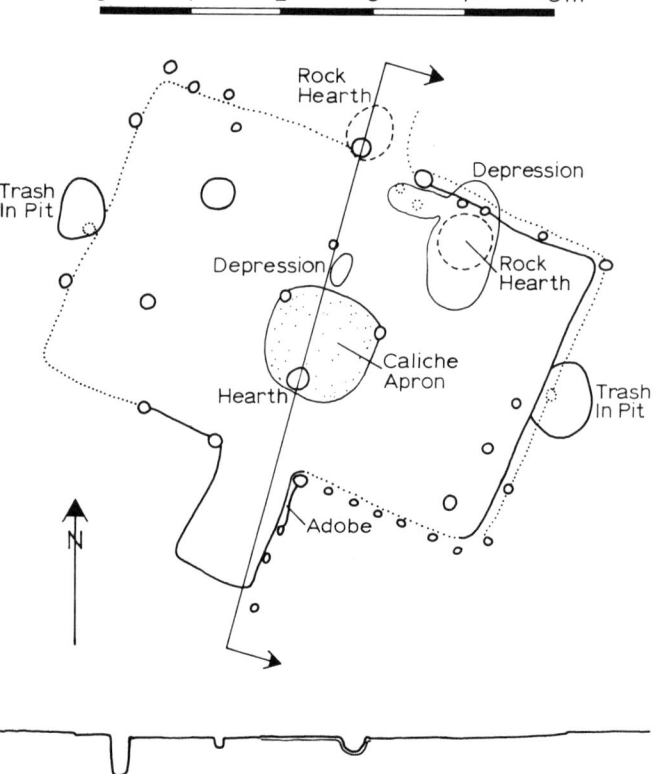

Fig. 2.27. Arizona BB:13:16, House 4 — Rectangular plan.

Tanque Verde phase. Its construction was similar to nearby House 6.

Houses 5 and 6 belonged to the late Rincon settlement. Mixed sherds, covering the range from Rillito to late Rincon, were found in the fill and on the floors. This mixture of pottery types, and the fact that each of these houses exhibited highly evolved architectural refinements, made temporal evaluation a problem.

House 5 was the only structure of its kind at Punta de Agua. It was of the squared variety and was completely outlined by a well-shaped curb. Furthermore, the curb rim was thicker next to the corner entry posts so that partial integral adobe cones were created. The corner between the rim and post bore the marks of fluting impressions (Fig. 2.28). The entry was long and level with a large adobe sill outside the curb. Four equally spaced posts were the main roof support. One of a pair of thick secondary posts was set on each side of the entry within the floor area proper.

At the Hodges site, curb rim houses also resisted accurate temporal placement, but were generally believed to be of Rillito age. House 68 at Hodges (Officer 1961:28-29) was of the same plan as House 5. At the Snaketown site, the curb rim house was a variation of the typical late Sacaton type (Gladwin and others 1937, Plate VIIb). From the ceramic analysis of a borrow pit and two cooking pits, adjacent to House 5, and from its good state of preservation, the inference is that it belonged to the late Rincon phase.

House 6, a small rectangular unit with offset entry, had sections of the entry and east wall still standing to a height of 40 cm. The wall, about 10 cm thick, was reinforced by both interior and exterior posts. As in House 5, this unit preserved the anomalous fluting impressions within the integral cones around the entry corner posts.

House 9, isolated to the south, was a surprising late example of the small oval unit common in early Rincon time. The associated pottery, and the variety of transitional ceramic types from a work area (Test 89) next to the house, indicate that the unit was in existence in late Rincon time.

Completing the inventory at Arizona BB:13:16 was House 2, a historic Papago structure which probably was associated with the Punta de Agua Ranch. The floor had been cut through prehistoric trash into sterile earth. The outlines were not well defined. Two interior posts and two perimeter postholes were exposed. The most diagnostic feature was the base of a recessed fireplace in the southwest corner reminiscent of the Mexican beehive style. The flue or chimney ran up the outside of the structure and was built of crude adobe bricks. Set partway within the floor area was an ash-filled oval basin. A Mexican five centavo coin, dated 1880 and minted in Hermosillo, Sonora, was recovered from the floor. All the historic Papago pottery discovered lay in adjacent trenches and in a square trash pit 6 m to the north. A similar exterior chimney was photographed at a chief's house at Fresnal on the Papago Indian Reservation on the W. J. McGee expedition through the Papaguería in 1894-1895.

ARCHITECTURE

From the four sites that produced houses at Punta de Agua, 61 living units were excavated. A few other houses were located in test trenches, but were not excavated.

None of the excavated structures can be properly called pit houses. The usual procedure before building was to clear the loose sand and silt down to a more compact level that was suitable for a floor surface. The depth required to reach such a surface varied from a few centimeters to a maximum of 50 cm.

The plans and methods of construction generally followed what was previously known about dwelling structures from Hohokam or Mogollon sites in southern Arizona. Certain variations and interesting transitional plans will be mentioned below when discussing the specific types and their temporal placement.

Nine houses were assigned to the Rillito phase, 47 to the Rincon phase, and 4 to the Tanque Verde phase. In addition, one historic adobe house was excavated. It was an outlier of the historic Punta de Agua Ranch (Arizona BB:13:18) that was part of the salvage operation. Since 47 of the 61 units were assigned to the Rincon phase, an attempt was made to propose an architectural sequence for that phase.

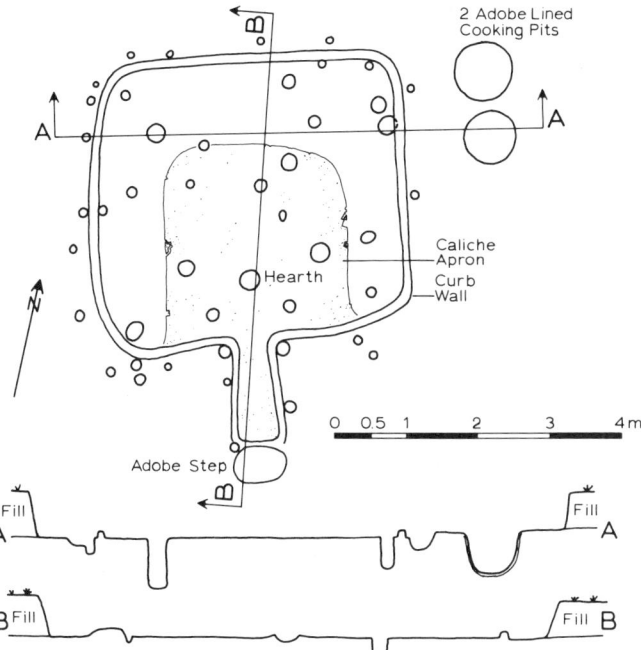

Fig. 2.28. Arizona BB:13:16, House 5.

House Plans

With few exceptions, the majority of the 61 houses were of four easily recognizable plans. Certain variations in the largest category, subrectangular, have sequential significance that relate to the delineation of the late Rincon phase.

SQUARED

This form tended to be quadrilateral with a four-post roof support pattern and was basically an indicator of the Rillito phase. In a modified form it survived until mid-Rincon times.

OVAL

Oval houses commonly contained sub-floor, bell-shaped pits, although some later examples were larger and irregular. This house style was an indicator of early Rincon settlement. Its presence seems to be strictly a regional expression.

RECTANGULAR

A truly rectangular solid-walled house was known only in the Tanque Verde phase. Precursors of this shape were found in mid-Rincon and late Rincon times especially at Arizona BB:13:16.

SUBRECTANGULAR

This plan was confined to the Rincon phase with only two exceptions. The variations listed below were markers for changes within the phase. Two centerline roof supports were normal. Other investigators term this shape rectangular with rounded corners.

A. A subrectangular plan with a short, parallel-sided entry. The surviving examples date from the middle part of the Rincon phase. In numerous structures the entry was destroyed by construction at the end of the phase.
B. A subrectangular plan with bulbous entry, either level or stepped. This common form was the hallmark of late Rincon architecture. Both large and small versions were contemporary.

Construction Details
SQUARED PLAN

This plan was similar to and patterned after the prototype reported from the Pioneer period in the Gila Basin (Gladwin and others 1937:71-78). A similar plan, although usually set in a deeper pit, persisted at San Simon Village from the Dos Cabezas through the early Cerros phases (Sayles 1945:23-26).

This house type was squared, almost quadrilateral, with rounded corners and was built in a shallow, but well-defined pit (Figs. 2.29 and 2.30). Two types of entries were excavated—the first was a long parallel-sided passage, the second was shorter and rounded (Fig. 2.3).

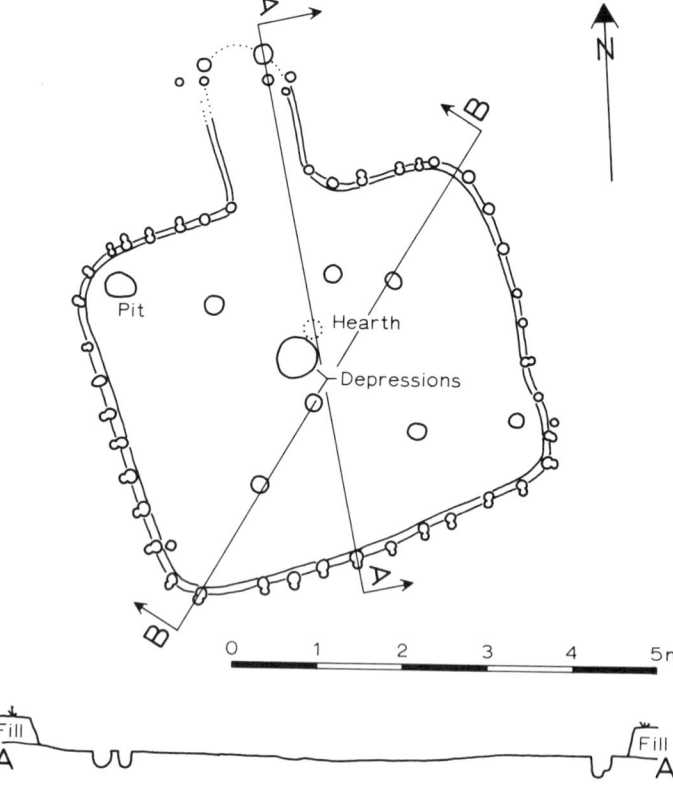
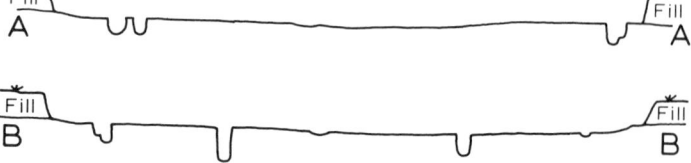

Fig. 2.29. Squared plan — Arizona BB:13:50, Unit 2, House 16.

Fig. 2.30. Squared plan — Arizona BB:13:50, Unit 2, House 16.

Basic construction features were four, equally-spaced, major roof supports, relatively wide grooves for wall posts, and an adobe-lined, shallow hearth directly in line with the doorway.

One unit had double wall posts at each position. Bell-shaped storage pits sometimes were present in the Rillito phase.

OVAL PLAN

This distinctive plan was found in both the Rillito and Rincon phases, but the houses with better temporal data show that it was more characteristic, and more numerous, in the early Rincon stage.

It is not easy to find satisfactory prototypes in the literature for this type. The plan was a dominant feature of the Peñasco and early Dos Cabezas phases in the San Simon area (Sayles 1945:19-23) and during Mogollon stages 1 and 2 (Wheat 1955:40-46). However, too much time elapsed between these horizons and the late Colonial at Punta de Agua to expect direct relationships. The oval plan was not isolated, as a type, at Snaketown.

Several factors indicate that this plan may be an expression of local preference. First, DiPeso (1958:11, 146) described three small oval units at the Bidegain site on the San Pedro River. This site was a small ranchería ceramically dated to the middle or late Rincon phase. At Arizona AA:2:61 in Casa Grande National Monument Ambler (1961:82) identified most Sacaton phase houses as oval in plan. The smaller ones seem to be analogous to those at San Xavier.

We may look to the west in the Avra Valley for another possible influence. The unexcavated Blackstone site (Arizona AA:15:1) exhibited up to 100 oval and circular rock alignments with mortar remaining at their bases. No decorated pottery was associated, but Rincon phase ceramics were noted at sites in the vicinity (Tanner 1936). The area near Gila Bend produced a few undistinguished oval houses of the late Colonial and early Sedentary periods (Wasley and Johnson 1965:7-8, 30).

The oval house was not constructed in a deep pit. It was essentially a surface structure with a short entry. A wall groove encircled the floor and entry. The oval shape was irregular and not predictable (Figs. 2.8 and 2.31). Two centerline supports were sometimes present depending on the overall size. The hearth was a shallow basin. Bell-shaped and straight-sided storage pits were the rule. One gains the impression that these were modest structures, varied in plan, not symmetrical as were the later houses.

RECTANGULAR PLAN

The true rectangular plan was an innovation of the late Rincon phase. Tanque Verde phase Houses 13 and 18 at Arizona BB:13:50 were the latest well-executed expression of this concept which was endemic in the early Classic period.

Houses 4 (Fig. 2.27) and 6 at Arizona BB:13:16 (Fig. 2.24), both of the late Rincon phase, previewed this remarkable change. Perhaps by chance only one earlier structure, House 6 at Arizona BB:13:43 (Fig. 2.14), dating to the middle of the Rincon phase, could be properly called rectangular.

Obviously the construction of a large rectangular structure called for more careful planning and selection of materials including well-prepared adobe, the use of caliche mixing basins, and stronger posts and roof vigas. The motivation that produced this new house type was related to the new social, religious, and political influence of the Western Pueblo intrusion in the middle Gila, San Pedro, and Santa Cruz drainages at the start of the thirteenth century.

The plan is a clearly conceived rectangle with the principle variation being the position of the entrance. It varies depending on the time of construction in the transition period between the late Rincon and early Tanque Verde phases.

The whole concept was more rugged and bold than earlier architecture. The wall posts were more regularly spaced and of heavier wood. Two centerline supports were still the rule. The walls were of adobe up to 10 cm in thickness and were either reinforced with an internal line of posts or were sandwiched between an external and internal line of uprights. Caliche-fortified plaster, mixed in the exterior basins, thickly coated the entire floor, not just an area near the hearth as had been the case in earlier times. The hearth itself was larger and deeper with a higher lip than had been the case previously.

Apparently certain cultural forces were at play that permitted a choice in entry details. In two cases, at Houses 4 and 6 at Arizona BB:13:16, the straight-sided entry was chosen. Where the "updated" bulbous entry was desired the thick adobe wall was continued to enclose the vestibule as at House 13 at Arizona BB:13:50. By the time of acceptance of all Tanque Verde traits, the vestibule was dispensed with completely as at House 18 at Arizona BB:13:50 (Fig. 2.32).

Fig. 2.31. Oval plan — Arizona BB:13:43, Unit 1, House 4.

Fig. 2.32. Arizona BB:13:50, House 18 (with House 22 in foreground).

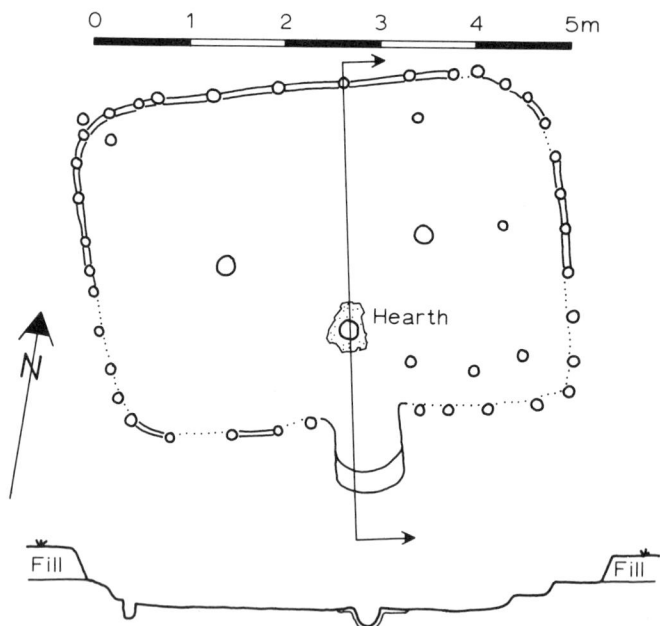

Fig. 2.34. Arizona BB:13:50, Unit 2, House 11. Subrectangular plan: Earlier type with short, straight-sided entry.

SUBRECTANGULAR PLAN

The basic subrectangular plan has well-rounded corners with some houses verging on the elliptical. Three subtypes comprise the bulk of this common Rincon phase house.

A. The earlier type is subrectangular with a short, straight-sided entry (Figs. 2.33, 2.34 and 2.35). Most houses of this type were carefully built of adobe with a high caliche content. The floors show the effects of replastering. An apron of thicker well-sorted caliche generally enclosed the hearth and entry access. Two centerline posts are the major interior supports. The hearths, like those of the rectangular house, are lined hemispherical basins often with a raised collar. The floor area of this type is usually smaller than Type B, discussed below.

B. The later type is subrectangular with a large, bulbous entry, either level or stepped (Figs. 2.36 and 2.37). The construction details are similar to Type A except the construction is sturdier, the design more symmetrical, and the wall posts larger and more evenly spaced. In addition, the hearths are, on the average,

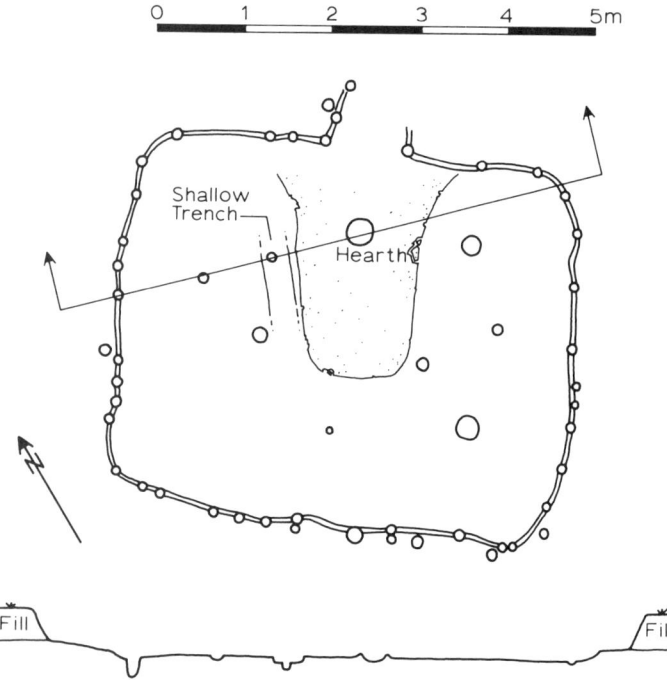

Fig. 2.33. Arizona BB:13:50, Unit 1, House 25. Subrectangular plan: Earlier type with short, straight-sided entry.

Fig. 2.35. Arizona BB:13:50, Unit 2, House 21 (with House 13A in background). Subrectangular plan: Earlier type with short, straight-sided entry.

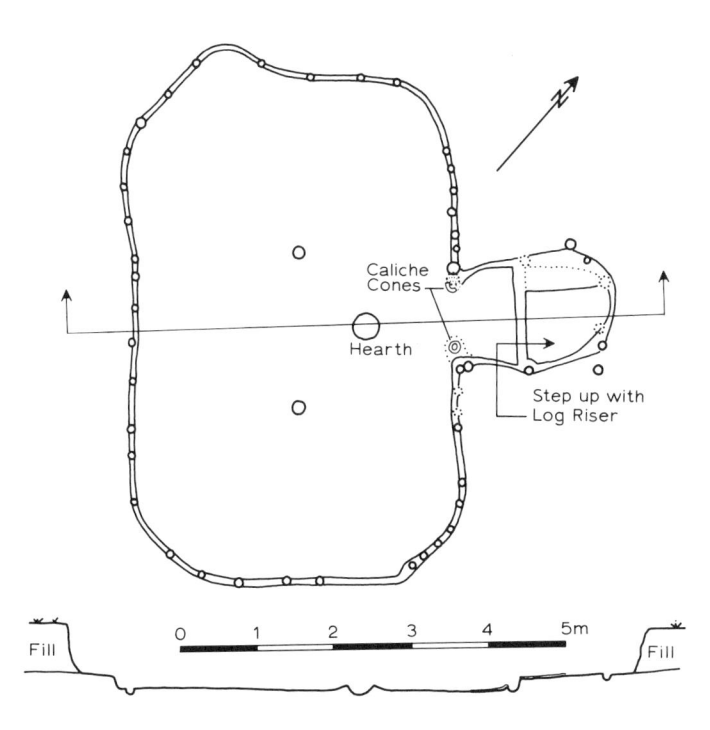

Fig. 2.36. Arizona BB:13:50, Unit 1, House 6. Subrectangular plan: Later type with large, bulbous entry.

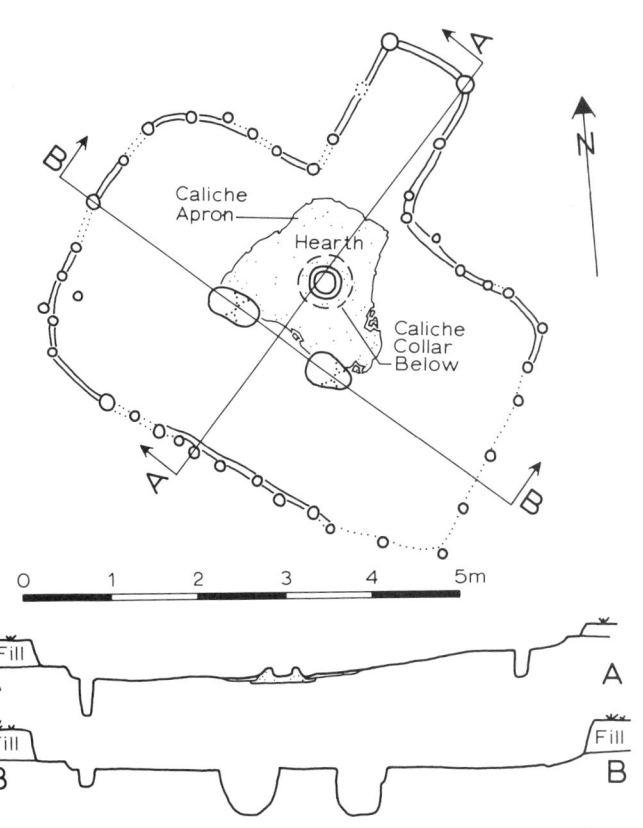

Fig. 2.38. Arizona BB:13:50, Unit 2, House 14. Subrectangular plan: Later type with long, straight-sided entry.

slightly smaller than those in earlier types. The floor of the entry is also covered with many coats of fine caliche plaster. Where the entry encloses a step, a log riser braces the upper part.

There are two sharply defined sizes. For instance, at Arizona BB:13:50 the late type averages 4 by 7 m. In contrast, the contemporary houses at Arizona BB:13:41 only average 3.5 by 5 m.

C. A rare variation of the late Rincon house is subrectangular with a long, straight-sided entry. Otherwise, the construction method is very similar to Type B (Figs. 2.38, 2.39 and 2.40).

It was in the larger houses that the phenomenon of paired, separate adobe cones (with or without interior

Fig. 2.39. Arizona BB:13:50, Unit 2, House 14. Subrectangular plan: Later type with long, straight-sided entry.

Fig. 2.37. Arizona BB:13:50, Unit 2, House 23. Subrectangular plan: Later type with large, bulbous entry.

Fig. 2.40. Arizona BB:13:41, Unit 2, House 3. Subrectangular plan: Later type with long, straight-sided entry.

reed impressions) was discovered. The nature of these rare extra supports will be discussed below. Less common were paired adobe cones set at the entry corner posts as an integral part of the wall screen.

DISCUSSION

The subrectangular house with a short entry was a style preferred in the mid-Rincon phase. It seems to be, on the basis of excavated sites, a Tucson Basin version of the typical Hohokam house usually found with a longer entry. The later bulbous entry type is very similar to the typical Snaketown houses of this period. In fact, the houses at Snaketown could even be divided into two groups based on size (Gladwin and others 1937:62:63).

We have already called attention to the persistence of the Rincon phase up to A.D. 1215. There seems to be a lag in time before the late Sacaton phase style unit became generally accepted in the Tucson area.

Late Rincon-Tanque Verde Transition

The transition period leading to the Tanque Verde phase was short in duration, but was marked by significant ceramic and architectural changes. That the cultural continuity was unbroken could be inferred by the architecture of four houses discussed below.

We have already seen the transformation of House 13 at Arizona BB:13:41 from a typical late Rincon structure to a thick-walled, post-reinforced dwelling of the Tanque Verde phase (Fig. 2.22). Houses 4 (Fig. 2.27) and 6 (Fig. 2.24) at Arizona BB:13:16 fulfill the conditions that would let them be prototypes of the true rectangular, thick-walled Tanque Verde architecture.

At Arizona BB:13:50, the well-built House 3, with an unusual symmetrical ovoid plan, showed the effect of experimentation (Figs. 2.41 and 2.42). Its pit was carefully prepared, the wall reinforcing posts were evenly spaced, the builders selecting posts of an unusually large diameter to support thicker walls and a thicker roof.

The most complete range of Tanque Verde traits was first encountered in House 13A (Arizona BB:13:50) (Fig. 2.6). Here a large rectangular post-reinforced structure with a solid-walled version of the Rincon bulbous entry was revealed. Such a design was common at the Hodges site (Officer 1961:I:26) and was exposed at Arizona BB:14:24 (Zahniser 1966:131) in the Tanque Verde Mountains.

Finally, a distinctive solid-walled structure of puddled adobe was encountered at House 18 (Arizona BB:13:50, Unit 2). A deeper pit was prepared to support the walls (Fig. 2.5). It is analogous to Tanque Verde structures at the two sites mentioned above and at the

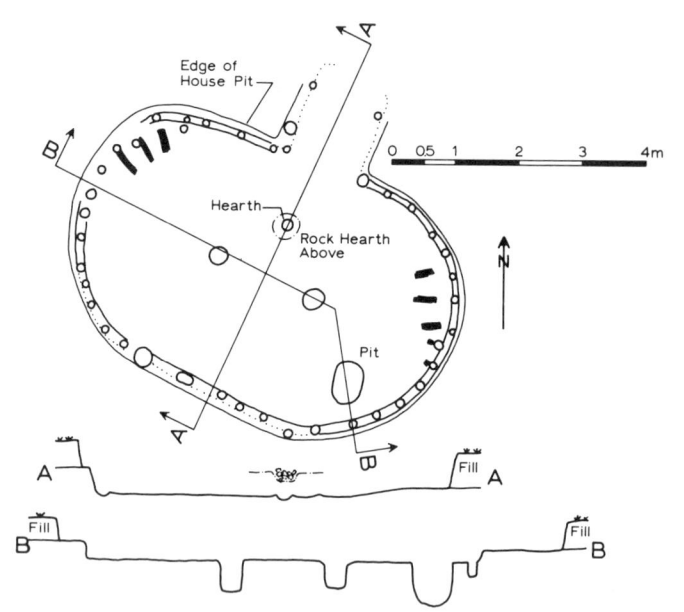

Fig. 2.41. Arizona BB:13:50, Unit 1, House 3. Late Rincon-Tanque Verde transition.

Fig. 2.42. Arizona BB:13:50, Unit 1, House 3. Late Rincon-Tanque Verde transition.

Tanque Verde type site, Arizona BB:14:1 (Haury 1928). Recent work at the Whiptail site (Arizona BB:10:3) shows the same sequence. Similar evolution was also found at Arizona AA:2:61 at Casa Grande National Monument (Ambler 1961:60-83).

Special Architectural Features
THE CURB RIM PLAN

A well-preserved structure (House 5 at Arizona BB:13:16) possessed a curb rim, standing about 10 cm high, that enclosed the house and entry (Figs. 2.28 and 2.43). This house showed traits normally associated with the squared plan of the Rillito phase and others usually associated with the Rincon phase architecture. Some of

Fig. 2.43. Arizona BB:13:16, House 5. Curb rim during excavation.

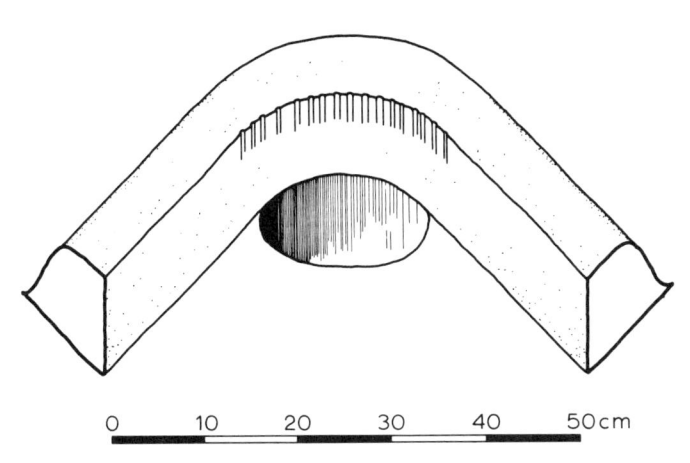

Fig. 2.44. Arizona BB:13:16, House 5. Detail of curb rim.

the latter were fluting around the entry corner posts (Fig. 2.44), and a thick caliche plaster apron reaching from the hearth to the doorway. Its plan, however, made use of four equally spaced major supports. The squared shape and long entry were survivals of an earlier plan.

As for the curb rim, the occurrence of this feature has been sporadically reported from Snaketown (Gladwin and others 1937:62-67); the Hodges site (Officer 1961:I:28-29); and from Paloparado (DiPeso 1956:121-126). In each of these sites the feature occurs in the Sedentary period.

The houses with a curb at the Hodges site were assigned, in most cases, to the Rillito phase. It was suggested that the trait probably continued into the Rincon phase. Therefore, House 5 (Arizona BB:13:16) would seem to prove the hypothesis.

From the same site at Punta de Agua, House 8 (Fig. 2.25), although quite eroded, carried traces of a curb rim in which the wall posts were embedded. By remarkable coincidence, the plan and size were almost identical to House 47 at the Hodges site. Each investigator independently assigned the houses to the Rillito phase.

At House 5 (Arizona BB:13:16) the curb rim construction deserves special mention. Not only were the fluting impressions found at the corner positions, but it is possible that the reeds completely encircled the exterior of the curb. The exterior postholes all lay outside the curb (Fig. 2.28).

ENTRYWAY ADOBE CONES

In the sections above, references have been made to shaped adobe cones, some of which bear fluted impressions on the interior diameter. In each case, the adobe cones were at or near the corner posts of the doorway heading out to the vestibule.

The cones always appeared in pairs in either of the following locations: (1) freestanding and set in from the normal corner posts, thus effectively narrowing the passage; (2) formed around the normal corner posts and integral with the adobe mud comprising the wall screen. In three houses adobe cones or collars survived at the base of the centerline roof supports. No reed impressions accompanied them.

The paired cones were made of selected adobe with a high caliche content which aided their preservation. In fact, where conditions allowed, the cones were cemented to the same higher quality floor plaster. The cones were shaped and smoothed with some standing as high as 12 cm. The interior diameter averaged 10 cm. Each cone tapered from the base to the top with the greatest diameter at floor level ranging from 25 to 30 cm.

The unusual nature of these special cones was realized when it was discovered that four pairs bore fluted impressions on the interior. It seemed logical to assume that these impressions were made by a bundle of reeds or by reeds set around a smaller post. Some of the bundles of reeds penetrated the floor while some did not.

Table 2.3 indicates that five houses had paired, separate cones, although two other units had holes in the correct position, but the cones were eroded. Only two of these houses still possessed the interior fluting on the cones. Two units carried paired integral cones at the normal corner posts; one of these bore reed fluting (Fig. 2.45).

The prime evidence for a bundle of reeds, rather than a post surrounded by reeds, is the multiple fluting on the right hand cone upon entering House 6 (Arizona BB:13:50). The adobe still bears the imprint of an inner bunch of reeds where the clay penetrated the outer layer.

TABLE 2.3
Distribution of Adobe Cones
(All Houses Belong to Rincon Phase)

Site	Paired: Separate	Paired: Integral	Fluted	Plain	Center Posts-Plain	Comment
BB:13:16						
House 6	–	X	X	–	–	–
BB:13:41						
House 4	X	–	X	–	–	–
House 6	–	–	–	–	X	–
House 7	Trace	–	–	–	X	Eroded
House 12	Trace	–	–	–	–	Eroded
House 14	–	X	–	X	X	–
BB:13:50						
House 2	X	–	–	X	–	–
House 6	X	–	X*	–	–	–
House 22	X	–	–	X	–	–
House 23	X	–	–	X	–	–

*Figures 2.46 and 2.47

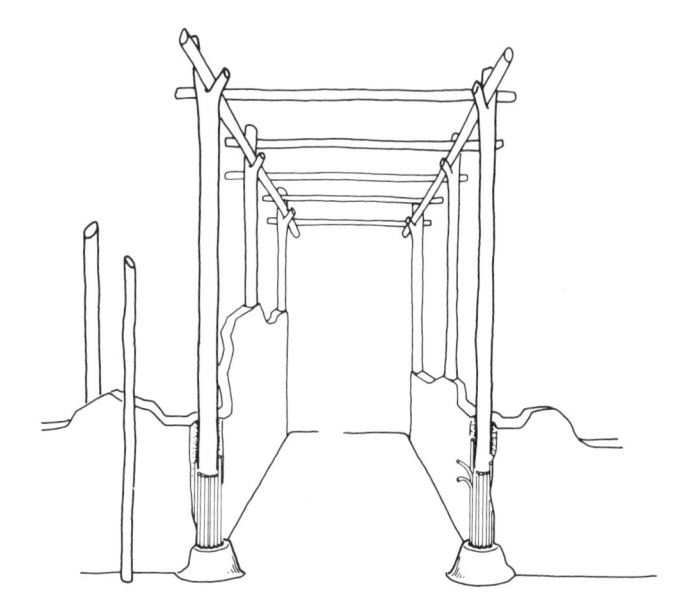

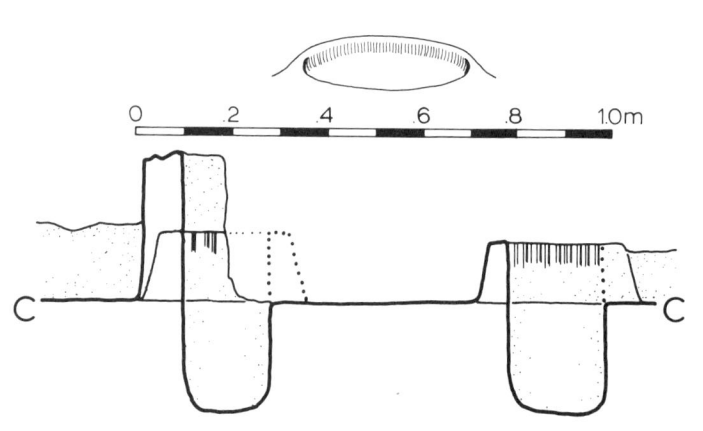

Fig. 2.45. Arizona BB:13:16, House 6. Detail of adobe cones and entry.

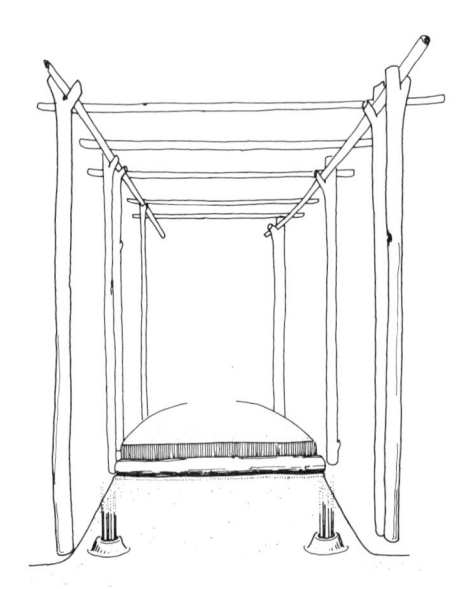

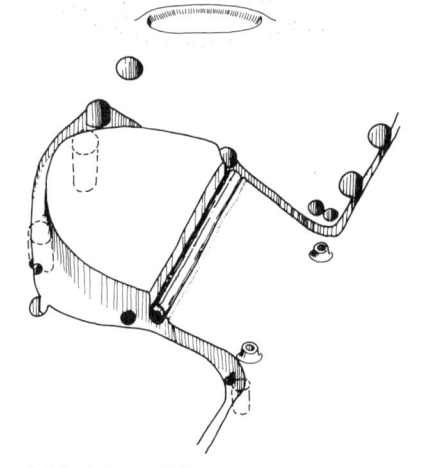

Fig. 2.46. Arizona BB:13:50, House 6. Detail of adobe cones and entry

A tentative reconstruction of the entry of House 6 at Arizona BB:13:16 and of House 6 at Arizona BB:13:50 is presented in Figures 2.45 and 2.46. The distribution of all adobe cones from the Punta de Agua sites is listed in Table 2.3.

One important question can be raised by the presence of paired cones at or near the entry of late Rincon phase structures. Are these reed posts a part of the functional roof support? If not, does this specialized embellishment have only aesthetic value or, perhaps, a ceremonial significance?

Where the cones are separate and lie within the line of the entry passage, the supports do not seem functional since the juncture of the covered entry and the wall screen of the house is supported by posts in the normal positions. However, the same evidence of bundles was found in three houses where the fluting continued around the normal entry corner posts.

The problem of correlating the specialized architecture with a ceremonial use is even more difficult. In the first place, the sure identification of ceremonial structures in the greater Hohokam area has not been possible. One author (DiPeso 1956:222) has ventured the opinion that the largest house within a group is probably the locus of such activity, the logic apparently being that the largest Pima and Papago round houses are used for that purpose.

In contrast, at Punta de Agua the units in question are not necessarily the largest of their group. Yet based on the distribution of the late houses showing adobe cones at three of the sites, the possibility remains that each of the surviving houses could have served a ceremonial function within, not the whole settlement, but each extended family. An evaluation of equating close clusters of contemporary units to a kin structure is reviewed in Chapter 1.

A search of the literature for precedents for fluted adobe cones revealed only one site with similar specialized construction. Two houses at Roosevelt 9:6, a Colonial period site (Haury 1932:43-45) carried traces of related embellishments. House 2 had non-fluted adobe cones at the entry corner posts in the integral position. In addition, in House 12 a bunch of reeds was substituted for posts, but if adobe collars were used, none survived.

In reviewing the site maps from the Hodges site, House 65, a Rincon phase structure, showed postholes in the proper positions for the paired, but separate, type of adobe cone construction.

Unfortunately, the adobe cones, once exposed to the elements, deteriorated rapidly. The photograph of the fluting at House 6 (Arizona BB:13:50) shows the sole survivor (Fig. 2.47).

Fig. 2.47. Adobe cone showing interior fluting from entry of House 6, Arizona BB:13:50.

Identification of Architectural Wood

Through the courtesy of William J. Robinson, Laboratory of Tree-Ring Research, the University of Arizona, the identification of the best preserved charred architectural wood was obtained. Only specimens from Arizona BB:13:50 were examined.

From House 3, the ovoid Rincon-Tanque Verde transitional unit, eleven of the twelve vertical supports were all *Prosopis* sp. One was *Celtis* sp.

One post from House 13 (early Tanque Verde) was also *Prosopis* sp. The late Rincon house, 14, contained both *Prosopis* sp. and *Celtis* sp.

A marked change in species utilization was noted at House 18, the solid-walled Tanque Verde structure. Here seven sections of larger horizontal roof vigas were submitted. Five of these proved to be *Pinus ponderosa* while two were *Juniperus* sp.

It was expected that mesquite and hackberry would have been utilized since they still may be found along the Santa Cruz River. The presence of juniper and ponderosa pine in the latest house at Punta de Agua indicates a major change in cultural preference. The great expenditure of effort that was required to haul logs from either the Catalina or Santa Rita mountains seems out of character with all we know about the Hohokam proper and the indigenous manifestations in the Tucson Basin up to the early Classic period.

Some obvious questions present themselves. What cultural tradition demanded these relatively exotic logs for a house of modest dimensions? Were the dwellers in House 18 originally from a more mountainous region to the north or east of Punta de Agua? It is always tempting to invoke migrations of increments of another population but, in this case, there is not evidence enough to meet the minimum conditions for proof of new arrivals.

However, throughout this report reference has been made to the rapid changes in aesthetics and architecture at the end of the Rincon phase. Perhaps after all, new social and political contacts were having their effect on the older population of southern Arizona. Furthermore, did the use of ponderosa pine and juniper denote any special function for House 18? Specifically, did the unit have a ritual significance which required older and more conservative traits? In this regard, Robinson (private communication) has noted a tendency for this wood to be employed for ceremonial rooms, at the expense of other species, at sites best characterized as representing Western Pueblo culture (Johnson 1965).

SUMMARY

The unpublished Hodges site report (Kelly n.d.) still is the basic source for understanding the phases and the accompanying traits and ceramics for the Tucson area. Of 84 houses at that site, only 4 could, without question, be assigned to the Rincon phase. In fact, of the 84 houses just 38 were given phase provenience. The earlier units suffered from erosion, destruction from the placement of later houses, and from the complication of reverse stratigraphy. As an illustration, the latest period, the Tanque Verde phase, was best represented with 23 houses. As later construction had destroyed most Rincon phase structures, the material traits and ceramics of the Rincon phase depended on the recovery of 56 cremations.

In contrast, at Punta de Agua 8 of 18 cremations belonged to the Rincon phase while 46 of 60 houses related to the Rincon phase. From these data a sequence of architectural changes within the phase was formulated.

Very important to the description of late Rincon houses at Hodges was the lack of houses with bulbous entry units. However, most of the 16 late units at Punta de Agua incorporated this architectural feature.

There is considerable qualitative difference in architecture and ceramics between the middle and late stages in the Rincon phase. That a generous amount of time, perhaps 50 years or more, was involved was confirmed by the series of archaeomagnetic dates (DuBois 1968).

The conclusions point to vigorous activity up to the first part of the thirteenth century. The Rincon phase, therefore, persisted longer than the Sacaton phase, as it is presently understood, at Snaketown. In the process, the end of the Rincon phase would include the proposed Cortaro phase (Haury 1950:16, and Kelly n.d.:III:71-72). Indeed the obsolete Santan phase, a transitional interpolation, covered essentially the same time period.

Further evidence on the developmental stages of the Tanque Verde phase was obtained. The architecture confirms the conclusions put forth by Zahniser (1966:185-186). The transition from the traits of the Rincon phase was rapid and far-reaching. The implication is that major political and social changes occurred as well even though the exact source responsible still eludes us.

The question as to whether the Rillito phase was also out of synchronization with the Santa Cruz phase in the Gila Basin could not be proven, although there is an important clue that might be significant. The characteristic house plan for this phase at Punta de Agua exhibited the squared shape that normally is regarded as a late Pioneer plan along the Gila.

3. THE CERAMICS

INTRODUCTION

The Tucson Basin pottery sequence was originally developed from the material recovered at the Hodges site (Kelly n.d.). It was devised so that types were neatly placed in local phases occupying time periods identical to their Gila Basin counterparts.

Those sherds and vessels of the Pioneer period, found along the Rillito River, are indistinguishable from the pottery originally described in the Gila Basin with one key exception. In Tucson, Snaketown Red-on-buff became Snaketown Red-on-brown since it lacked the slip of the Gila (Kelly n.d.:III:1-10). Therefore, when any reference is made below to early phases of the Pioneer period and their ceramic content, the published types from the Gila Basin may stand for the Tucson types.

At the beginning of the Colonial period at the Hodges site, the local types began to differ sufficiently so that new names and new descriptions became necessary. Following the established criteria, the principal decorated types bear the same names as the phases to which they are equated.

Beginning, then, with the Cañada del Oro phase, and continuing through the Rillito, Rincon, and Tanque Verde phases, an abstract of each appropriate pottery type, based on Kelly's (n.d.) manuscript, prefaces each pottery section. Where supplementary types or data have become known from work at Punta de Agua, the new information appears below the original abstract. The proliferation of ceramic variations in the latter half of the Rincon phase make up the bulk of the new material and are dealt with separately as Late Rincon Red-on-brown.

By way of introduction, a brief review in the form of two quotations presents the basic findings from the work at the Hodges site. These conclusions are still highly relevant to the material discovered in the whole Tucson Basin:

Tucson pottery appears to be intermediate between Hohokam red-on-buff and Mogollon red-on-brown, an ambivalence entirely expectable from its intermediate location. On the one hand it has pronounced Mogollon affinities in its close-grained paste, its polish, its relative absence of slip, its utilization of smudging; and, in certain vessel forms and a preference for geometric ornament. The Gila Basin rose-colored paste with its excessive porosity, its chalky slip, its fugitive pigment, and its mat (matte) surface seems generally foreign to Tucson. On the other hand, shape and ornamentation adhere closely to the Gila Basin patterns (Officer 1961:I:9).

In the last analysis, therefore, our dating rests upon the establishment of local phases stylistically, and presumably temporally, equivalent to those of the Gila Basin (Officer 1961:I:12).

Punta de Agua: Colonial Period
CAÑADA DEL ORO PHASE
Cañada del Oro Red-on-brown

The first marked divergence from the decorated wares of the Gila Basin comes at the beginning of the Colonial period. The Tucson equivalents of the Gila Basin types lean toward Mogollon ceramics with a fine-grained paste, some polish, and an absence of slip. In ornamentation, however, Tucson ceramics are very similar to those of the Gila Basin. The diagnostic motif is the serrated scroll. Some bowl exteriors are faintly scored or incised, but to a much lesser degree than Gila Butte Red-on-buff. The color varies from brown through cream and grey to black. Firing clouds are prominent, but smudging appears not to have been deliberate. The shapes of Cañada del Oro Red-on-brown are similar to those of the Gila Basin. Bowls with flared rims are most prominent.

Compared to the types of the Pioneer period, little mica was used in the paste. The design elements also repeat those of the Gila Basin. When the exterior surface is the chief decorative field, external scoring is more frequent although less common than at Snaketown. Closely spaced trailing lines are the dominant exterior decoration (abstracted from Kelly n.d.:III:19-35).

Only one whole vessel (Fig. 3.1d) and 21 sherds of this type were recovered at Punta de Agua. These were concentrated at Arizona BB:13:16 where the largest Rillito settlement was located. None of this material bears any exterior incising, which indicates that our examples probably date from the early Rillito phase and best represent a transitional type. One incised sherd was noted at Arizona BB:13:43.

RILLITO PHASE
Rillito Red-on-brown

The decorated ceramics of the Rillito phase adhere to the precedents established in the Cañada del Oro phase; the clay, temper, and surface treatment are similar to that of the Mogollon, while shape, motif, and design

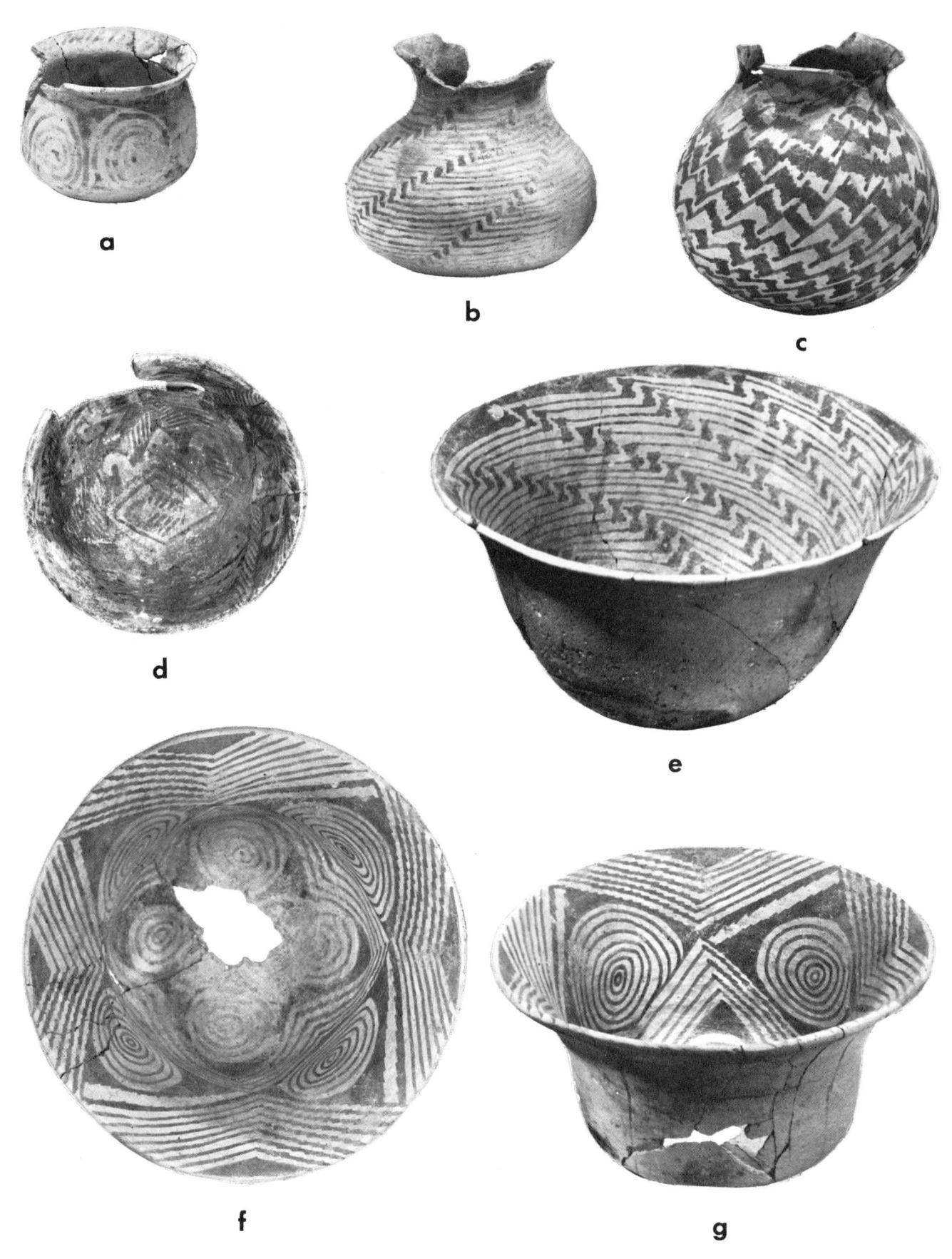

Fig. 3.1. Cañada del Oro and Rillito vessels. *a-c,* Rillito Red-on-brown jars; *d,* Cañada del Oro Red-on-brown bowl; *e-g,* Rillito Red-on-brown bowls (*f* & *g* are two views of same bowl). All vessels figured are from Rillito phase cremation area at Arizona BB:13:16.

Fig. 3.2. Ceramic vessels from a cremation near Arizona BB:13:43. *a,* Rillito Red-on-brown flared rim bowl with animal incorporated in design; *b,* Rillito Red-on-brown jar; *c,* Rillito Red-on-brown plate with animal design; *d,* Fragmentary Rillito Red-on-brown plate. All vessels are from a cremation near Arizona BB:13:43.

placement parallel the Gila Basin types. The vessels are unslipped except for specimens which may bear a self-slip (scumming); there is an increase in polished vessels. Micaceous content is negligible. The bowl exteriors are no longer scored, but exterior trailing lines occur on over 60 percent of interior decorated bowls. Bowls with flared rims and compressed, globular jars are the most popular shapes.

Notably lacking in the Rillito inventory are the more eccentric shapes of the Gila Basin. There are fewer examples of life forms as well. The lack of slip gives the ware a darker surface than Santa Cruz Red-on-buff. The local pigment is deeper red and more permanent than that of the Gila Basin.

Fringing elements are strong in the Rillito phase and occur principally on jars. Crosshatching seems to be confined to bowls. On the whole, vessel shapes are the same as those of the Santa Cruz phase (abstracted from Kelly n.d.:III:36-59).

A more representative sample of Rillito Red-on-brown, especially from burials and trash at Arizona BB:13:16, permits additional comment on the local type (Fig. 3.1). Seven whole vessels from the cremation area, 11 partially restored pots, and the heavy concentration (up to 50 percent) of Rillito sherds in the trash area provide data for some new observations.

The collection was increased by nine partly restorable vessels from Arizona BB:13:50 and one from Arizona BB:13:43. There is no evidence of Rillito occupation at Arizona BB:13:41.

In a group of four vessels salvaged from an arroyo east of Arizona BB:13:43, two bear striking animal representations (Fig. 3.2a,c). They all probably accompanied a cremation.

48 CERAMICS

The first vessel is a deep bowl with a flared rim. The principal decoration is on the exterior and consists of alternating bands. One band is hatched, the other shows, in negative, repeated depictions of an animated animal recalling a roadrunner. It has a long-toothed beak, a feather crest, and a flowing tail. The feet are shown in a striding pattern. The second is a plate with a stylized snake that forms a spiral with its head at the center. The plate had been "killed." A series of pelicans are arranged in a spiral bordering the snake.

From the area of House 7 (Arizona BB:13:16) came an interesting sherd, also with alternating diagonal bands painted on the exterior of a bowl with a small flared rim. In this instance, one band carries, in negative, a repeated series of an animal resembling the coyote. The uppermost outline is inferred from the position of the others lower in the band. Adjacent bands carry diagonal undulating lines. The animal has a curled tail and pointed snout with both ears visible (Fig. 3.3).

It has been suggested that each of the animals on the two bowls is a variation of the same form. There are common elements such as long tails, pointed noses, and stylized feet that apparently were meant to show a beast in motion. A prototype for such figures could exist in Mesoamerican art styles which depict coyotes and jaguars in stone friezes and painted frescos (Vaillant 1966:Plates 23 and 25).

Even though the original description of Rillito Red-on-brown noted the scarcity of mica, a considerable portion of the sherds at Punta de Agua are of a sub-variety with a high mica content and high polish. Most of the sherds are from small hemispherical bowls, some of which bear the traces of a cream wash or scum. Unfortunately, no accurate count of this variety was tabulated; it is perhaps the same as that to which Kelly (n.d.:III:60) assigned the following name and hypothetical origin:

As Picacho Red-on-brown we have designated a small lot of material which intergrades with Tucson Rillito, but which at the same time shows minor divergencies in paste and finish. The ware is cream, and unslipped. A high micaceous content, combined with polish, gives its surface a lustrous sheen. Brush work is consistently precise and well-controlled.... The exact provenience is not known but it may be suspected to have come from some locality intermediate between Tucson and the Gila Basin....

In the laboratory it was noticed that sherds bearing these elements came from a late Rillito or early Rincon provenience. A few of the smallest bowls, with the cream finish, were partly restored and are of Rincon association. The impression was gained that this variety was preferred for bowls which possibly served a special function. Rather than revive the type name, Picacho Red-on-brown, we will consider these sherds to be a variety of early Rincon Red-on-brown, based on their constant association with the more recognizable types of that phase.

The later Rillito types, although of a transitional status, are still readily identified. The whole series has thinner walls and, in general, is more delicate in construction and in design than those of the Rincon phase. The influences of the Gila Basin designs are left further behind and the later local ceramics reflect more Mogollon brownware traits.

Punta de Agua: Sedentary Period
RINCON PHASE
Rincon Red-on-brown

This type was considered a direct outgrowth of the Rillito series. On the whole it is heavier, designs are more cursive and open, and the brushwork is more careless. Smudging appears deliberate and increases in favor. Bowl interiors may be smudged and polished over the decoration. As a result, many sherds appear red-on-gray or red-on-black.

The bowls with flared rims are replaced by a tremendous increase in relatively larger outcurved bowls. The hemispherical bowl continues. A substantial proportion of both bowls and jars were constructed with a shoulder—a condition analogous to the Gila Basin. The low globular jar is quite rare.

Surface slip occurs in about 10 percent of the vessels. It is thin, perhaps a self-slip, but not the chalky slip of the Gila area. Despite the slip, the surface is still polished.

Exterior trailing lines are fewer. The trait, found in about 16 percent of interior-decorated bowls, is more

Fig. 3.3. Coyote design on Rillito Red-on-brown sherd.

common (as expected), on flared rim bowls. The lines are often paired or tripled and are sometimes placed in a zigzag band. In general, Rincon designs are noted for plaited band arrangements, an increase in fringed lines and panels, and an increase in hatched bands and in single scrolls.

In conclusion Kelly (n.d.III:71) found several vessels with a peculiar over-simplification of design verging on the angular. Speculation was offered that such treatment might be a discrete strain on Rincon material that could have contributed to transitional designs leading to the emergence of the Tanque Verde style. A tentative name proposed for this type was Cortaro Red-on-brown (abstracted from Kelly n.d.:III:62-83).

A final quotation (Kelly n.d.:III:72) shows that the rapid changes in ceramic styles and the explanation of the cultural factors involved are still open to question:

It may be noted that the same stylistic hiatus holds for the Gila Basin. It is a far cry from Sacaton to Soho, and the break parallels precisely the situation at the Hodges site. This doubtless means that the Classic complex was not evolved on the spot, either at Tucson nor at any of the Gila Basin sites so far excavated.

At Punta de Agua the Rincon phase is the most extensive. This wealth of material enables a more detailed assessment of the internal growth during the phase. This is different from the situation at the Hodges site where Rincon ceramics are limited to those pieces accompanying cremations.

The number of whole vessels suitable for illustration is still distressingly small. The photographs of the most representational vessels of the early, middle, and late Rincon stages are selected from 20 whole and 55 partly restored pots (Figs. 3.4 and 3.5). Many of the latter are

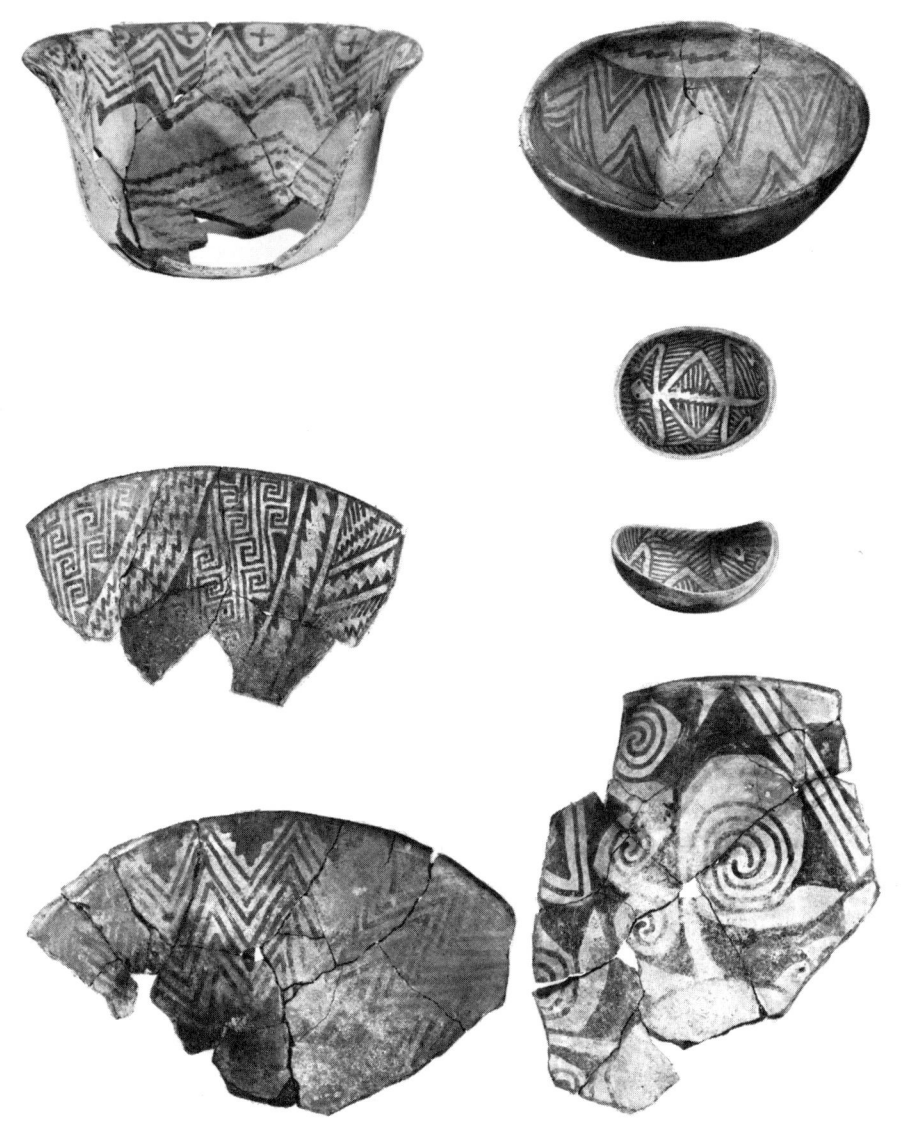

Fig. 3.4. Rincon Red-on-brown bowls. Small bowl at right center is shown in both plan and side views.

50 CERAMICS

Fig. 3.5. Rincon Red-on-brown jars.

so fragmentary or in such poor condition, usually from secondary fires, that they are useless for illustrations. The most useful examples are the well-preserved mortuary vessels from the burial zone at Arizona BB:13:16 (Fig. 3.6). There is a marked increase in the prevalence of decorated scoops.

At Punta de Agua the ceramics of the Rincon phase are a heterogeneous mixture. As postulated by seriation and confirmed by architectural association, Rincon Red-on-brown clearly shows its evolution from transitional Rillito Red-on-brown to the described Rincon style and, finally, to the angular late Rincon types that presage the development of Tanque Verde Red-on-brown.

The varieties included in Rincon Red-on-brown deserve mention.

1. The early types repeat Rillito designs, but the vessels become larger, thicker and new characteristic shapes dominate.

2. A considerable portion of early and mid-Rincon vessels have a whitish slip and designs that are definitely an attempt to recreate the effect of Sacaton Red-on-buff.

3. As noted, a recognizable number are highly micaceous and well polished. A surface sheen is present with or without a creamy slip. This technique is confined to small hemispherical bowls.

4. Six sherds of a thick, coarse-tempered, decorated type with a whitish slip or wash do not fit this pattern. Ordinarily, such a small sample might be overlooked, but the anomalous sherds are so distinctive that external relationships were pursued. It was found that at Valshni Village (Withers 1941:45) a similar intrusive type occurred.

As such a large quantity of the distinctive Late Rincon Red-on-brown was excavated a separate analysis of the new angular designs and newly introduced shapes was performed. These data will be presented in a subsequent section of this chapter.

The general conclusion which can be reached here is that certain ceramic and architectural innovations spread over a wide area of southern Arizona give in-

Fig. 3.6. Rincon Red-on-brown mortuary vessels.

dications of rapid social change, and, if carefully delineated, might show the beginnings of the local response to intrusive Western Pueblo culture.

Since the time that these intermediate phases were advanced, an intrusive Western Pueblo site on the middle Gila near Bylas has been reported (Johnson and Wasley 1966). This settlement, delineating the Bylas phase A.D. 1100-1200, assumes real importance in tracing a route or direction for many of the changes in pottery and the settlement pattern in the Tucson area. There is now proof, for example, that the pottery type San Carlos Red-on-brown was the main decorated pottery by A.D. 1150 at Bylas.

TANQUE VERDE PHASE

No abstract of the original description of Tanque Verde Red-on-brown (Kelly n.d.) is presented as later published works have made the details available.

Zahniser (1966:176-186) has presented an excellent summary of the different proposals for establishing the time of the introduction of Tanque Verde Red-on-brown, its life span, and the length of the Tanque Verde phase. The same author summarized the Tanque Verde phase and proposed the inclusive dates of A.D. 1100 to 1300. However, when the new evidence from Punta de Agua, in the form of preliminary archaeomagnetic dates (DuBois 1968) is considered, a beginning date for the Tanque Verde phase at about A.D. 1200 would be more exact. In other words, the persistence of the Rincon phase in the Tucson area, with the associated late Rincon pottery and architecture, continued through the latter part of the twelfth century.

Tanque Verde Red-on-brown pottery, therefore, made its appearance about A.D. 1200 and persisted through the whole Classic period or to A.D. 1400 and probably later. In fact, the later history and isolation of area variations of Tanque Verde Red-on-brown still await more analysis (Danson 1957:220-223; Kelly n.d.:IV:83-112; Scantling 1940:27-30). From the present state of our knowledge, it may be concluded that the development of Tanque Verde Red-on-brown was a rapid process in a time of major cultural change.

As far as the late Tanque Verde ceramics are concerned, we subscribe to the following apt remarks by Kelly (n.d.:IV:110-111).

... the most striking Tanque Verde resemblances are found not in Casa Grande red-on-buff ... but in San Carlos red-on-brown. In certain typical shapes and in design ... the resemblance amounts to virtual identity except for the fact that San Carlos vessels invariably are smaller ... and that the designs ... are more delicate.

After noting that San Carlos lacks interior borders in bowls and jars, Kelly stated:

These precise resemblances bespeak a common origin. ... In fact, in Tanque Verde red-on-brown, in San Carlos red-on-brown, and in Casa Grande red-on-buff, there is evidently a tripartite manifestation of essentially the same decorative complex ... the relationship must have been rather direct. ... Consistently smudged interiors and pre-occupation with the geometric (on San Carlos and Tanque Verde) suggest Mogollon ancestry.

Early Tanque Verde Red-on-brown

When studying pottery created at the juncture of two phases, one would expect evidence of experimental designs and new shapes that mark the transitional period.

These conditions are fulfilled by the data presented next. Examples of Early Tanque Verde Red-on-brown exhibit basic qualitative changes in shapes, design elements, clay, temper, and thickness. The development of Tanque Verde Red-on-brown might be considered the culmination of the old regional Sonoran Brownware tradition (Ezell 1955:369). The late Rincon types were transformed into something new.

Three fragmentary Early Tanque Verde Red-on-brown jars (Fig. 3.7a, b, and d) were found in the following transitional proveniences: Cremation 3 (Arizona BB:13:50), House 13 (Arizona BB:13:41), and House 18 (Arizona BB:13:50). Two Early Tanque Verde

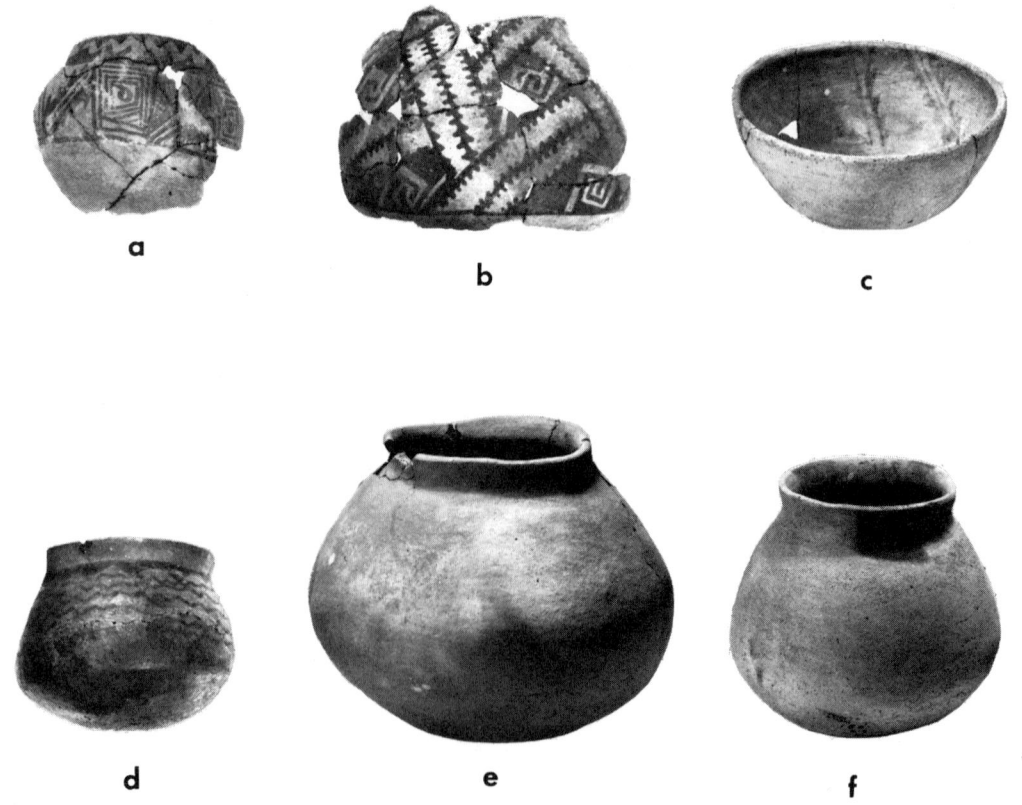

Fig. 3.7. Early Tanque Verde Red-on-brown vessels and Tanque Verde plainware jars. *a, b, d,* Fragmentary Early Tanque Verde Red-on-brown jars; *c,* Early Tanque Verde Red-on-brown bowl; *e, f,* Early Tanque Verde Plainware jars. (*a & f* from Cremation 3 at Arizona BB:13:50; *c* from Cremation 1 at Arizona BB:13:50).

Fig. 3.8. Early Tanque Verde Red-on-brown: Plans of two bowls. *a*, From House 4, Arizona BB:13:16; *b*, From Cremation 1, Arizona BB:13:50.

Red-on-brown bowls (Fig. 3.8a and b) were located in House 4 (Arizona BB:13:16) and in Cremation 1 (Arizona BB:13:50) respectively. The interior design on the latter may be poorly discerned in the photograph (Fig. 3.7c).

The shape of two Early Tanque Verde plain jars (Fig. 3.7e and f) from Cremations 2 and 3 (Arizona BB:13:50) presaged the common form of the Tanque Verde phase proper. In addition over 20 jar sherds of this type were distributed throughout the five sites (Fig. 3.9). The restorable bowls included three shapes: hemispherical, incurved and, recurved. The jars have low, rounded shoulders and relatively straight collars. The association of most of these vessels with early Tanque Verde

Fig. 3.9. Early Tanque Verde Red-on-brown sherds.

architecture and with the Tanque Verde cremations confirmed the dating.

The broad line work, simplified design elements, and characteristic tan slip of normal Tanque Verde types (but of a crude experimental nature) made recognition possible. The jar designs do present good evidence to back up the hypothesis that it was upon this form that the Tanque Verde elements were first synthesized. It must be remembered that the popular types of bowls at this time were the interior decorated forms with late Rincon angular elements and that these persisted into Tanque Verde times. The bowl from Cremation 1 (Arizona BB:13:50) was of this type (Fig. 3.7c). In particular, the shapes and simplified design elements reflect an intermediate position between the late Rincon introductions and the more common late Tanque Verde styles.

Tanque Verde Red-on-brown

Only five sherds of the described type were found. Two were surface finds and the others came from mixed trash deposits. In unexcavated portions of Arizona BB:13:16 and BB:13:49 there was a thin veneer of Tanque Verde debris on the surface. Near Arizona BB:13:43 the outline of architectural foundations and surface sherds points to occupation in the late Tanque Verde phase.

Topawa Red-on-brown (Tucson Variety)

The prototype of this type was found at and near Valshni Village west of the Baboquivari Mountains on the Papago Reservation (Withers 1941:32-34). To our knowledge it has not been reported in any quantity at major sites either in the Gila Basin or in the Santa Cruz drainage. It was present at Ventana Cave (Haury 1950:347-348) although it was difficult to distinguish it from Tanque Verde Red-on-brown.

For the reconstruction of cultural events in southern Arizona, Topawa Red-on-brown has significance for the following reasons: (1) it was described as a distinctly local development from the antecedent Vamori Red-on-brown and showed strong influence from the Tucson area (Withers 1941:51); (2) it was considered an obvious forerunner of Tanque Verde Red-on-brown (Haury 1950:10); and, (3) it was the only type to carry both interior and exterior decorative elements. Such an arrangement was later formalized into the principal characteristic for identifying Tanque Verde Red-on-brown bowls. Thus, Topawa Red-on-brown seems to fit the technical stage that Kelly (n.d.:III:71-72) logically felt was missing at the Hodges site. It is a type bridging the gap between interior decorated Late Rincon Red-on-brown and exterior decorated Tanque Verde Red-on-brown bowls. The latter usually possesses a continuous band of elements on the interior of the rim. Perhaps this decorative element was a conscious holdover from earlier emphasis on exclusive interior painting.

The small collection, about 26 sherds, all from bowls, of Topawa Red-on-brown from Punta de Agua apparently was locally made. The type specimens from Valshni Village are harder, thicker, and more carelessly decorated with a more highly polished surface than the sherds recovered from Punta de Agua. The paste, temper, and slip of the local specimens are similar to Rincon Red-on-brown.

Practically all the sherds were discovered in three specific proveniences, each of which was far removed from the others. These were in and near House 12 (Arizona BB:13:41), in Test 89, a work shelter (Arizona BB:13:16), and from the floor and fill of neighboring Houses 2 and 3 (Arizona BB:13:50). Perhaps this can be explained as the localized products of potters who had recently come from the Valshni area and joined the Punta de Agua community. The decorative elements on the Punta de Agua sherds show more precision and variation than those of the prototype. Best examples of interior decoration appear in Figure 3.10. Many of the bowls have an everted rim, a feature of Tanque Verde Red-on-brown. The exterior pattern on some bowls recalls the simplified angular elements on the small, hemispherical and incurved late Rincon bowls (Fig. 3.11). This combination of traits has been traced ultimately to the decorative pattern on San Carlos Red-on-brown. Thus, it appears that the development of Topawa Red-on-brown in combination with the spread of San Carlos Red-on-brown most likely played an important part in the emergence of Tanque Verde Red-on-brown in the Tucson Basin. Under exactly what sociocultural conditions the changeover occurred still cannot be satisfactorily reconstructed.

The appearance of the Topawa style in association with late Rincon architecture tends to corroborate the end date of the Topawa phase at about A.D. 1250 (Haury 1950:9). The range of archaeomagnetic dates for two late Rincon houses (Houses 2 and 22 at Arizona BB:13:50) and one Tanque Verde phase unit (House 18 at Arizona BB:13:50) encompasses the years A.D. 1210 to 1240 (DuBois 1968).

PLAINWARE

The plainwares found in the Tucson area and along the Santa Cruz River, with one exception noted below, could not be classified. As with local decorated wares, the discussion of the evolution of plainwares uses as a reference the work by Kelly (n.d.:IV:129-147) at the Hodges site.

Fig. 3.10. Topawa Red-on-brown sherds: Interior design.

Fig. 3.11. Topawa Red-on-brown sherds: Exterior design.

By way of preface, it should be noted that Kelly (n.d.:IV:129) found the analysis of local plainwares to be so unsatisfactory that she wrote:

We have preferred not to designate the local plainware by any particular name. ... The series is too varied to be included under one caption. But, at the same time, differences from phase to phase are not sufficiently marked to justify separate ware groupings. ... The general run of Tanque Verde intergrades with the plainware of previous phases.

The only named plainware in the Tucson Basin was from the late Classic period. It was uncovered during tests at the University Indian Ruin and was called Gila Plain (Tucson variety). A description of this type was published by Danson (1957:229-231). It is well to note that significant qualifying remarks accompanied the description. For instance:

It is difficult, if not impossible, to differentiate the Classic plain ware from that of the Sedentary period. ... This is the late variant of the locally made plainware, which in turn is a variant of Gila Plain. ... This type represents but one part of an unbroken continuum of plain wares found in the Tucson area (Danson 1957:230-231).

The work at San Xavier corroborated this suggestion that the plainware intergrades through time and can not be easily distinguished by temporal position. Even though nothing earlier than Colonial period wares were discovered, a résumé of the plainware from the Snaketown phase at the Hodges site sets the stage for a review of the characteristics that might be helpful in generally dating plainwares.

At all the sites tested or excavated at Punta de Agua, a total of about 90,000 plain sherds were recovered. This estimate was derived from the weight of the processed sherds. A series of sherds from each site was weighed and then the number per pound was counted. Two different counts were established, each depending on the average size of sherds. The greater part of the plainware total was determined at 25 sherds per pound. The remainder averaged 20 sherds per pound. This method followed a similar practice established at salvage projects on the Gila River Indian Reservation (Johnson 1964:153), at the Bylas sites (Johnson and Wasley 1966:224), and at the Fortified site at Gila Bend (Greenleaf in press).

The following descriptive sections are abstracted from Kelly (n.d.) and refer to her work at the Hodges site.

Snaketown Phase

From a small series of sherds an extreme range of variation existed. Practically the only common denominator is the consistently granular paste. The ware is non-micaceous, the surface finish varies considerably, and there is little polish. The surface color ranges from grey to brown to black and invariably firing clouds are present. The ware has a reddish cast varying from pink to maroon (Kelly n.d.:IV:132).

Cañada del Oro Phase

The data again come from a small series, but there is a heritage from the Snaketown phase in shape and reddish cast. The most pronounced new attribute is the increase in mica content in the paste. As a result of increased mica content, the surface presents a sheen with a grainy, rather than closed pore, appearance. Jars also show a new treatment—the technique of vertical wiping. The paste and vessel forms show no major changes. There is, however, an indication of the so-called thin-walled mortuary vessels of the Rillito (and Santa Cruz) phase (Kelly n.d.:IV:134).

Rillito Phase

A larger sample of Rillito vessels leads to a more confident inventory for the phase. There is little marked change from the Cañada del Oro phase. Most of the plainware remains heavily micaceous with exterior color as variable as in the preceding phase. Several bowls and jars have uniform black interiors that must be the result of deliberate smudging. As expected, there is a greater range of shapes. Legged vessels make their appearance.

A distinct group of small bowls and jars, usually found in cremations, seem to be especially prepared as mortuary vessels. The presence of this type has an analogy in Santa Cruz Buff, the special type of the Gila Basin with the same function. These mortuary vessels exhibit possible conservative attributes such as thin walls, vertical wiping on jars, and an exterior rose-colored cast. The local ware is not slipped (Kelly n.d.:IV:138).

The material from the Punta de Agua sites reveal that there was a greater range in the plainware of the Rillito phase. On one hand, the paste includes minute particles of mica with a resultant smooth sheen on the surface; on the other hand, a smaller proportion have larger flecks of mica throughout. The surface, therefore, is not smooth, but has a pitted surface caused by the high content of mica. This variety more closely resembles the Gila Plain of the Gila Basin (Fig. 3.12a-e).

In addition, another variety of what is best called a crude, sand-tempered ware first appeared in Rillito times. For instance, the cover bowl in Cremation 2 at Arizona BB:13:16 is of this type. However, most of the crude sherds were found in association with Rincon phase houses (Fig. 3.12f).

Fig. 3.12. Four plainware bowls and two plainware jars. *a-c*, Rincon plainware with mica temper; *d, e*, Rillito plainware with mica temper; *f*, Crude sand-tempered bowl from Cremation 2 (Rillito phase).

This variety consists primarily of low hemispherical bowls, roughly made, with indentations and scraping marks. Similar crude ware has been written off as children's work or experimentation. No new insight can be added to account for its presence.

Rincon Phase

The plainware of the Rincon phase continued the trend toward greater variation. The ware becomes thicker and is markedly less micaceous than that from the preceding phase. Generally, the surface is well smoothed and has lost the grainy appearance that is a concomitant of mica inclusions.

There is a wide range of color, but the norm is a light tan. Firing clouds are prominent on all shapes. Interiors of many plain bowls are darkened, but cannot be called deliberately smudged, although the decorated bowls are consciously smudged and polished.

In Rincon times the hemispherical bowl was introduced and rapidly became dominant by the end of the phase. The decorated outcurved bowl of late Rincon design became an important component of the Tanque Verde phase along with its plainware counterpart.

At the Hodges site the recovery of a smaller number of sherds from specially created funerary vessels indicated, perhaps, that this cultural trait was being eclipsed by other burial practices (Kelly n.d.:IV:139-140).

The Rincon phase at Punta de Agua may be characterized by a number of distinct varieties. One of these, the micaceous variety, was reserved for the smaller, more delicate, bowls and jars which had a Rillito heritage.

In the associations considered late Rincon at the Punta de Agua sites, much of the plainware shows an increase of larger mica particles in the temper. The handling of the constituents seems to indicate a renewed preference for micaceous vessels. The ollas are well smoothed and often carefully polished, with the burnishing strokes clearly visible (Fig. 3.13). This late ware is practically indistinguishable from the dominant plainware of the Tanque Verde phase. The evidence from the late Rincon phase, a transition time, shows that there was a continuum from the Sedentary through the Classic periods.

Tanque Verde Phase

The key innovations noted at the Hodges site are lipped jars, handled jugs, and boot-shaped vessels. One variety of plainware is thicker, non-micaceous, smooth-

58 CERAMICS

ed, but with little polish. Surface color ranges from dark brown to tan.

Several vessels are fashioned of a paste with high mica content, which suggests a survival of earlier styles (Kelly n.d.:IV:142-144).

At the Punta de Agua sites few sherds and only two whole plain vessels were found, making further remarks about the Tanque Verde plainware impossible (Fig. 3.7e, f). The only observation that can be made is that a range of types exists which depend, for their individual identities, on the amount of mica in the paste.

In the Tucson area we are probably looking at locally made ceramics, the differences in pastes reflecting the minerals found in local sources. For instance, the Tanque Verde material from sites along Rincon Creek and Agua Caliente Wash are all heavily micaceous. The varieties of Tanque Verde phase types found to the west are much less so. The decorated types exhibit exactly the same variations.

The renewed preference of mica temper would seem not to be a conscious effort to recreate the micaceous style of Rillito and early Rincon plainware, but rather the result of experimentation with available clay and temper sources.

REDWARE

At Punta de Agua and in most of the Tucson district, locally manufactured redware had its start near the end of the Rillito phase (Kelly n.d.:IV:119-120). In the rapidly evolving Rincon phase, with emphasis on new local varieties of decorated wares, a well-defined style appeared which has been called Rincon Red.

For a considerable time it has been noted that there was no finely developed redware in neighboring areas to which temporal and technological precedence could be given. Of course, in the Mogollon district, the distinctive San Francisco Redware (Haury 1936:28-31) had a long life. At Snaketown and in sites along the San Pedro River it was the principal intrusive redware. In the Sacaton phase at Snaketown a local variety, Sacaton Red, made its appearance in modest numbers.

Fig. 3.13. Two Rincon phase plainware bowls and two plainware jars.

Its origin could not be traced to Vahki Red, which died out by the Colonial period.

In contrast to the Gila Basin, in the Tucson area Rincon Red formed a larger percentage of the inventory, was technically more developed, and was represented by a greater range of shapes than Sacaton Red. Neither of these wares was purposely smudged on the interior.

In looking for antecedents to Rincon Red, we find that Valshni Red, from the Papaguería (Withers 1941:34-36) bears the closest relationship in technique and in temporal placement. Valshni Red, itself without immediately apparent progenitors, was introduced in the Vamori phase, or roughly about A.D. 800. Valshni Red finally evolved into the widespread Sells Red (Scantling 1940:30-33) of the Classic period. After Ekholm (1942:75-77) described a sophisticated redware complex located near the Sinaloa-Sonora border, in what he labeled the Huatabampo district, Haury (1950:17-18) showed that Ekholm's Guasave Red and Valshni Red were almost indistinguishable. As other Guasave traits (modeled spindle whorls, and a mano with overhanging ends) appear at this time, the Huatabampo area may be the ultimate source for Rincon Red as well.

In fact, Rincon Red, Valshni Red, and Dragoon Red seem to be the only local varieties of the same complex. They antedate Gila Red (Haury 1945:80-100) but do not seem related to Sacaton Red (Gladwin and others 1937:202-204). It is possible that there is a southern component in the development of Gila Red and that it resulted from a blend of Mogollon and Rincon redware traditions.

At the Hodges site, Kelly (n.d.:IV:119-120) noted that a few redware sherds occurred in the local Snaketown phase. The sample was varied (some of questionable provenience), and no attempt was made to assign any name to such a small sample. However, of real significance to us was the recovery of one restorable bowl with a maroon interior. The exterior was unslipped, but was fire blackened. It was described as horizontally wiped on the exterior and there was a suggestion of interior dimpling. At Punta de Agua, parts of two vessels fitting this description were found in early Rincon associations.

The whole Colonial period at Hodges produced only two sherds, which emphasizes the fact that redware was not a Colonial characteristic.

Intrusive Redware

From the Gila River area, a small quantity of Sacaton Redware came to the Punta de Agua sites; however, the most common intrusive is identified as Sells Red. It was, moreover, found in contexts assignable to the late Rincon phase (about A.D. 1200) and, perhaps, indicates that Sells Red formed a larger component of the Topawa phase than previous work indicated.

Nothing identifiable as Dragoon Red (Fulton and Tuthill 1940:45) or San Francisco Red (Sayles 1945:39) was found in the tests at the Punta de Agua sites. Since these were the predominant types at Tres Alamos in the San Pedro Valley in the Colonial and Sedentary periods (Tuthill 1947:63), their absence only points up the lack of communication before the Classic period between settlements on the San Pedro and Santa Cruz rivers.

Local Redware
RINCON RED

Rincon Red is characterized by a coarse, granular, sand-colored paste, and is generally non-micaceous. The vessels may be highly polished on either the exterior, interior, or both surfaces. No interior smudging occurs. The slip is a clear, deep red. Weathering causes it to become powdery and fugitive and it may pit or flake. As a result of original firing, the exteriors vary from tan to red with fire clouds usually present.

The polishing or burnishing marks are almost invariably horizontal and are prominent, especially on the exteriors—less so on the interiors. The polishing patterns, so noticeable on Gila Red, are not visible on Rincon Red.

At the Hodges site the bowls are both outcurved and hemispherical. Some bowls have Gila shoulders and flaring rims. There is an example of a shouldered bowl with an incurved rim. Scoops may have been present; no jars were recovered.

Rim treatment can be added to Kelly's description of Rincon Red. By far the overwhelming majority of rims are direct and rounded. The same holds for those vessels with flared or sharply everted rims. A few squared or flattened rims also appear. In such cases, the thickness of rim usually exceeds that of the wall of the pot (Kelly n.d.:IV:121-124).

The original description of Rincon Red holds up well when the Punta de Agua material is added to the inventory. A seed jar and a flared-rim jar with a high collar are new shapes.

Kelly (n.d.:IV:123) in the original description of Rincon Red mentioned that, with more data, it might be possible to isolate a second local redware type which was less highly polished and more micaceous. At Punta de Agua a small sample of redware sherds meeting this description was identified. Most sherds came from deep, hemispherical or straight-sided bowls exhibiting good polish. Some of this group had relatively thin side walls. Unfortunately, these sherds did not have good association with burials or architecture, but did come from Arizona BB:13:16 where the proportion of Rillito material was high. In the final analysis, it is not possible to assign the more micaceous ware definitely to an earlier phase.

In the Tanque Verde phase at the Hodges site, although represented by a heavy occupation, no redware was found which showed evidence of a Rincon heritage. The redwares of this phase are of two intrusive types, San Carlos Red and another that "strongly suggests" Gila Red.

At Punta de Agua from the trash and fill within and outside of the early Tanque Verde phase units, numerous sherds of Rincon Redware were identified. No sherds with interior smudging were found.

It seems strange that no continuity from Rincon Red to another local variety of the Classic period has been demonstrated in the Tucson area. The report from the work at the University Indian Ruin (Hayden 1957) clearly shows that, aside from a problematical group called "other red," which could relate to Santan Red (Hayden 1957:124-125), the redwares are intrusive. There is some equivocation regarding the status of Gila Red, however, since it is not treated as intrusive in the percentages.

VARIETIES

(1) Four rim sherds come from Rincon bowls that were slipped only on one side. Three are slipped on the interior. The red is carried up and over the rim and down the exterior for about 5 mm. On the fourth the process is reversed. (2) Two sherds are slipped with maroon paint on the interior. Dimpling of the surface is evident. These are discussed in the introduction to this section where it is shown that they could not be assigned to a phase earlier than Rincon. (3) Three red sherds cannot be equated with any known type. They carry a fugitive slip of orange-red cast. The rim of one is flattened.

LATE RINCON CERAMICS
Rincon Red-on-brown

The presence of jar and bowl sherds bearing angular designs exclusively has already been noted. The new type and its components are reviewed here. No photographs of this type are included. The sherds are badly eroded and often secondarily fired obscuring the decoration. Therefore, for more clarity this unusual decorated style is depicted in drawings. Before describing the distinctive late variety of Rincon Red-on-brown which offers new insight to the cultural factors affecting the transition to the Tanque Verde phase, it is well to introduce a quotation from Kelly (n.d.:III:71-72) regarding ceramic continuity at the Hodges site:

... on the basis of a few sherds, but largely upon theoretical grounds, Mr. Gladwin (the excavations were under the auspices of the Gila Pueblo in 1937-1938) envisaged a phase, designated as Cortaro, which would bridge the gap between the more or less curvilinear style of Rincon and the essentially angular treatment of Tanque Verde, between Rincon interior bowl decoration and Tanque Verde exterior ornamentation. Hypothetically, this would be an interior decorated bowl, its design verging on the Tanque Verde angular. Logically, there is need of such a transition. But we found few sherds of such description, and only one restorable vessel.

These thoughts evidently led Haury (1950:Fig. 2) to include a tentative Cortaro phase, with an approximate end date of A.D. 1250, in the Tucson sequence. This proposed phase has suffered from the same neglect as the proposed Santan phase of the Gila Basin, which was orginally conceived by Gladwin (Gladwin and others 1937:33, 170, 216, and 264). The Santan phase, at the end of the Sedentary period, was still proposed by Haury in 1945 (1945:13, 204, and 212) although it has never been well understood.

In association with late Rincon houses at three of our sites (Arizona BB:13:16, BB:13:50, BB:13:41) and in the trash mounds at Arizona BB:13:49, a large series of sherds and a few partly restorable vessels were easily distinguished from the essentially curvilinear Rincon Red-on-brown.

These newly discovered designs bear some relationship to the few late Sacaton Red-on-buff vessels illustrated by Haury (Gladwin and others 1937:178, Plates CLXIIIb, CXLIXf, and CLIr,s). However, the decorative elements are even more complex with extremely stylized layouts.

Equally as diagnostic as the new angular designs is the introduction of new shapes. These seem to be indicative of a specialized regional development that lasted until about A.D. 1200 and resulted in the divergence of late Rincon types from Sedentary vessels of the Gila Basin. To a large extent this regional specialization introduces the widespread Tanque Verde horizon.

BOWLS WITH INTERIOR DECORATION

Hemispherical: Interior decoration (Figs. 3.14 and 3.15). The most common bowl of the Rincon phase is hemispherical and ranges from small to medium. It is exclusively decorated on the interior. Offset quartering is the most popular arrangement. The flattened rim is invariably painted. As in all of these late varieties, the brown slip assumes a more tan coloration. This type in-

Fig. 3.14. Late Rincon Red-on-brown: Interior decoration on two hemispherical bowls.

[61]

62 CERAMICS

Fig. 3.15. Late Rincon Red-on-brown: Interior decoration on hemispherical bowl sherds.

tergrades with a similar interior decorated variety that forms a major sub-group within the Tanque Verde Red-on-brown series. The Tanque Verde variety may be distinguished by certain characteristics such as: (1) a return to mica as a tempering material, (2) better polishing on interior and exterior, (3) a greater incidence of intentional interior smudging, and, (4) an even more formalized arrangement of the design and hatched serrated panels.

Outcurved: Large, interior decoration (Fig. 3.16). The occurrence of large outcurved bowls with exclusive interior decoration increases and they form, with the hemispherical shape, the principal component of late Rincon ceramics. The same decorative features are found as are on the hemispherical bowls.

BOWLS WITH EXTERIOR DECORATION

A lesser number of rim sherds indicate that a true hemispherical shape was also produced. Furthermore, sherds in the collection show that the small incurved bowl may have a low shoulder.

Incurved: Small. A newly introduced, small, slightly incurved bowl usually with thickened rim and with exclusive exterior decoration becomes a key diagnostic trait of the late Rincon phase (Fig. 3.17). There was no indication of this preferred form in the first part of the Rincon phase. Many of the sherds provide evidence of intentional smudging of the interiors, but the exterior is not highly polished. The rims are usually painted. The transfer of the decoration to the exterior and the resulting convex surface led to a noticeable change in

Fig. 3.16. Late Rincon Red-on-brown: Plan view of interior decoration on large, outcurved bowl.

Fig. 3.17. Late Rincon Red-on-brown: Exterior decoration on small, incurved bowl sherds.

[63]

64 CERAMICS

Fig. 3.18. Late Rincon Red-on-brown: Exterior decoration on recurved bowl sherds with flared rims.

the choice of design elements. Pendant and opposed triangles, filled with broadline hatching, and serrated triangles are the dominant elements. The relationship of the small incurved bowl with its most probably antecedent, San Carlos Red-on-brown, will be discussed below.

Recurved: Flared rim. Also new to late Rincon time are a series of rounded bowls with a flared and recurved rim treatment. All bear exterior decoration. About half are smudged internally with noticeable burnishing marks. Most rims are painted (Fig. 3.18).

This type includes a small variety with a shorter recurved rim while the more common large type has a flared rim. The designs on the latter bear clear resemblance to the elements found on the late Rincon jars that are described below. The designs on the smaller variety are composed of simpler elements since the field of decoration is quite limited.

BOWLS WITH INTERIOR AND EXTERIOR DECORATION

From the various sites at Punta de Agua comes a small group of hemsipherical bowl sherds with the principal design on the interior, but which also show a simple decoration on the exterior, usually pendant from the rim. The external elements are short, parallel, trailing lines or vertical wavy lines. These sherds are not illustrated. Most sherds have smudged and polished interiors. Such a combination of decorated surfaces appears to be the first indicator of the transfer of the principal decoration to the exterior, an arrangement which is a major component of Tanque Verde Red-on-brown bowls.

The appearance of the small incurved bowl together with the recurved type at Punta de Agua satisfies the hypothesis that the material culture was in transition. Both these vessel forms comprised a major part of the early Tanque Verde phase at the Hodges site (Kelly n.d.:IV:83).

JARS

The late Rincon decorated jar sherds indicate that this form was in an experimental or, better, a transitional stage. A distinct group of jar sherds, with the characteristic angular decoration, can be separated. Upon closer inspection most shapes with the late Rincon designs have a low recurved or sharply returned rim to the exclusion of the flaring rim variety. Where shoulders are observed, they are less acute than those used for earlier Rincon jars which echoed the familiar Sacaton shoulder. Futhermore, the late Rincon shoulder generally is placed below the point of maximum diameter. This trait became diagnostic for the jars of the Tanque Verde phase (Kelly n.d.:IV:84).

Recurved: Flared rim (globular and shouldered varieties). This diagnostic form appears in both large and small jars, which may or may not have been constructed with a low shoulder. The rims are painted, but the collar is not decorated. The top of the decorated zone is introduced by one or two horizontal framing lines. The choice of angular patterns is the same as those used on the late Rincon bowls. However, the convexity of the jar surface gives even more freedom of expression. The result is more often space and greater use of hatched fillers, often within opposed triangles (Fig. 3.19).

Recurved: Low, flared rim. This variety has a short and acute recurved rim section. One restored low shouldered jar provided a fine exhibit (Fig. 3.20). The decoration in broad horizontal bands is rare. The other illustrated rim sherds of this form tend to bear vertical or diagonal panels. The rim is usually painted. The top framing line may be omitted. Just one of these jars has decoration on the interior of the rim consisting of a series of three short, vertical, wavy lines. From the sample collected, these jars seem to be generally smaller than the more numerous recurved rim form mentioned above.

In the Tanque Verde phase at Hodges (Kelly n.d.:IV:87-88) jars with the same globular shape, often with a low shoulder, but carrying a short collar (synonymous with the low recurved rim) are characteristic. Once again the transitional nature of the late Rincon phase is emphasized by the introduction of a form that only needed a more vertical collar to be accepted at a later date.

Fig. 3.19. Late Rincon Red-on-brown: Recurved jar sherds with flared rims (globular and shouldered varieties).

Fig. 3.20. Late Rincon Red-on-brown: Recurved jars with low, flared rims (one restored, two sherds).

PITCHERS

Only one fragmentary handle from a late Rincon pitcher (?) was recovered. The shape of the vessel could not be determined.

Summary

The angular or geometric elements of design which identify the late Rincon ceramics may be listed as follows: (1) interior decorated bowls dominated by bold, simplified, offset, quartered patterns in combination with opposed triangles with neat parallel hatching; (2) exterior decorated bowls showing a preponderance of opposed triangles bordered by hatched, serrated panels or solid, serrated borders, the design being commonly interrupted by large, open, diagonal panels; (3) jar designs which carry these elements to their natural conclusions (with more area to cover, large triangles are filled with fine, nested chevrons, in addition to opposed triangles enclosing hachures).

Some jars, and a few bowls, have diagonal bands consisting of a series of squared or interlocked scroll elements, a carry-over from early Rincon times. A smaller proportion of each shape has fillers of wavy lines.

Notable for their absence are: (1) crosshatching, (2) solid areas, and, (3) horizontal bands. A remarkable exception is the jar in Figure 3.20.

The whole effect of the late Rincon design is an overwhelming use of well-executed, fine and broad parallel lines in a great number of combinations. The principal decorated panels are separated by an obvious desire for large open areas.

The introduction of the exterior decorated, thin-walled bowls with interiors smudged and polished, seems to be directly related to the development of San Carlos Red-on-brown. It is now understood that by A.D. 1200 this type was a major component at the Bylas, Arizona sites (Johnson and Wasley 1966:242). The designs, shapes, and thin walls are startlingly similar.

It is more difficult to find good prototypes for the jar designs. To a large degree the elements may be found in some late Sacaton Red-on-buff vessels. More hatched bands and zones are found on Casa Grande Red-on-buff (Haury 1945:55-62), but the shapes are dissimilar. All this points to the possibility that the distinctive late Rincon designs, particularly those on jars, provide the continuity from which the standard Tanque Verde style of exterior decoration evolved. This proposed sequence implies that the formal Tanque Verde elements were first devised on jars where more experimentation was possible.

An interesting insight into a probable aesthetic continuity from late Rincon through the Tanque Verde phase is provided by the discovery of large outcurved bowls, with angular interior decoration, as an important component at Tanque Verde sites. Evidence from the Whiptail site near Agua Caliente Wash (Arizona BB:10:3) confirms the popularity of this form, conceived in the Rincon phase, coexisting with the typical Tanque Verde Red-on-brown exterior decorated hemispherical bowls with interior band.

RINCON POLYCHROME
Introduction

Since about 1934 occasional pieces of an unidentified polychrome have been recovered from various sites extending from Cashion on the Gila River (Arizona A:11:9) to as far south as Paloparado (Arizona DD:8:12). The majority of the finds clustered within the Tucson district.

Although various temporary names have been used by local archaeologists to describe the samples, no previous study of this material has been attempted. The earliest known reference is from Arizona AA:12:36, near the community of Rillito on the east side of the Santa Cruz River. The fact that a "strange polychrome" was discovered was noted by Getty (1934).

The first, brief description of this polychrome may be found in Kelly (n.d.:IV:149, footnote 4) where the author refers to an unidentified polychrome:

Black-and-white-on-red fragments, pigment fugitive. Probably two wares are represented. One sherd is decorated interior and exterior with large white motif, apparently a key or fret, edged in black. The two others apparently are deep bowls with semi-flaring rims. The exterior of one is chevron hatched, the component lines alternately white, black. The other has an exterior interlocking fret, one arm of which is black, the other, white. In addition it has a diagonal white bank, overpainted in black with a series of small T-shaped elements. Both the latter sherds have small black triangles pendant from the interior rim.

The name, Rincon Polychrome, has been assigned to these pieces by the writer. The Hodges collection has now been supplemented by 15 sherds from Punta de Agua as well as by sherds located in survey and excavation collections in the Arizona State Museum. In addition, two restored hemispherical bowls were loaned by the Amerind Foundation. A complete list of these and all other known Rincon Polychrome sherds, and their proveniences, is presented in Appendix B.

Where there were data on the chronological position of Rincon Polychrome, the consensus points to the late Sedentary period, that is, the late Sacaton and late Rincon phases. It is possible, from evidence at the Punta de Agua site (Arizona BB:13:50) that some of the vessels may have been used in the early Tanque Verde phase. The relative placement of this new type has been greatly aided by a series of archaeomagnetic dates from Arizona BB:13:50 (DuBois 1968).

Although the name, Rincon Polychrome, was chosen rather arbitrarily, in light of the following facts it appears to have been a good choice: (1) the preponderance of sites with the new type are in the Santa Cruz drainage near Tuscon; (2) previously published types—Rincon Red-on-brown and Rincon Red—occur in the same area and in association with the polychrome; (3) the Rincon phase embraces the period in question; and, (4) a preferred geographical locus is created.

General Description

Rincon Polychrome was created by applying black and white designs on a slipped and polished redware. In general, the pottery utilized was constructed of the same materials and was finished in the same manner as Rincon Redware. The paste, temper, color of slip, and surface finish were identical. All shapes common to Rincon Red, as well as the low-shouldered, incurved jar form, were utilized. Fine mica particles, however, were notably absent from the polychrome vessels, whereas a variety of Rincon Red exhibited more use of mica.

The red slip (from hematite) tended to assume a rosy cast after firing and has been commented on previously by one investigator (Zahniser 1966:145). The dull white to cream-colored paint was applied first. It formed the base for the panels and for the broad intervening strips. Rarely, narrower white lines were incorporated into the design. The white paint was quite fugitive and tended to flake, thus exposing the red beneath. It also tended to turn darker or more cream to tan color through use and exposure.

An organic black paint was used to edge or frame the strips and panels, and to create the design elements within the sections of the panels. The black paint was often transformed to a dark brown or maroon color as a result of primary oxidation in the original firing or of secondary oxidation after a house fire. Therefore, the combination of the two changes in the original colors sometimes obscure the true nature of the polychrome. For instance, one survey disclosed "nine bowl sherds with red slipped interiors and red-on-brown painted exteriors.... The exteriors of two ... have a light brown slip.... The exterior designs in each case have been eroded beyond recognition. Technically, this ware is a polychrome because the two reds are of different shades" (Frick 1954:64).

Certain variations from the basic description of Rincon Polychrome occur. One bowl, a large outcurved type, was slipped only on the interior where the main decoration was placed (Fig. 3.21d). Some of the larger incurved jars with wider orifices have the slip carried down the interior surface as far as the low shoulder.

The principal field of decoration, for all shapes, is the exterior surface. The designs stop at the shoulder or at the point of sharp curve leading to the rounded base. Two bowls, on the contrary, have the main design on the interior. Furthermore, flared rims on bowls often have an interior black-on-white horizontal band just below the rim or have black pendant triangles around the interior.

68   CERAMICS

Fig. 3.21. Rincon Polychrome: Sherds. *a, b,* Low shouldered bowl sherds from same vessel (House 3, Arizona BB:13:50); *c,* Incurved jar sherd (Arizona BB:14:24); *d,* Shallow, outcurved bowl, exterior unslipped (House 20, Arizona BB:13:50).

FORMS

Forms are limited to four types of bowls and one type of jar. The bowl shapes may be defined as:

1. hemispherical, direct rim that may be thickened (Figs. 3.22a and 3.23a).
2. low shouldered, rounded base, flared rim (Figs. 3.21a, 3.22b and 3.23b).
3. shallow, outcurved direct rim (Fig. 3.21d).

The jars have a low shoulder and are incurved with no neck and a rounded base (Fig. 3.22c).

Shoulders. A significant fact is that all Rincon Polychrome jars (whole or in sherd form), were of the incurved shouldered type. It is a distinctive shape in which the angular shoulder was placed about three-quarters of the distance down from the direct rim.

The size of the jars varied so that, in the large examples, the orifice was wide enough to enable the potter to run red slip down the interior. (Two good specimens of bowls with the same low shoulder, relatively straight sides and with flaring rims make impressive vessels.) The same shouldered bowls also were found in the Rincon Red inventory.

Rims. As noted, all polychrome jars had direct rims, not recurved as in the Sacaton Red-on-buff and Rincon Red-on-brown examples.

The shape of the rims varied on bowls. As far as the shouldered bowl is concerned, the rims were flaring and offered an opportunity for interior decoration. Most examples were hemispherical with direct rims. A few had slightly everted rims. One notable variation was one hemispherical bowl which had a thickened rim by the addition of a thicker, or extra, coil.

DESIGNS

The principal designs on Rincon Polychrome usually were on exterior red slipped and polished surfaces and all were characterized by diagonal or vertical white panels, and broad or narrow white strips, all framed by thin black lines. The white background was painted first, then black framing lines and interior sectioning lines were drawn. Within the irregular sections thus created, small serrations or short "T" shaped elements could be added as fringing designs. The potter then completed the interior of the panels with familiar repeated designs including interlocked scrolls or hatching. Generally, a

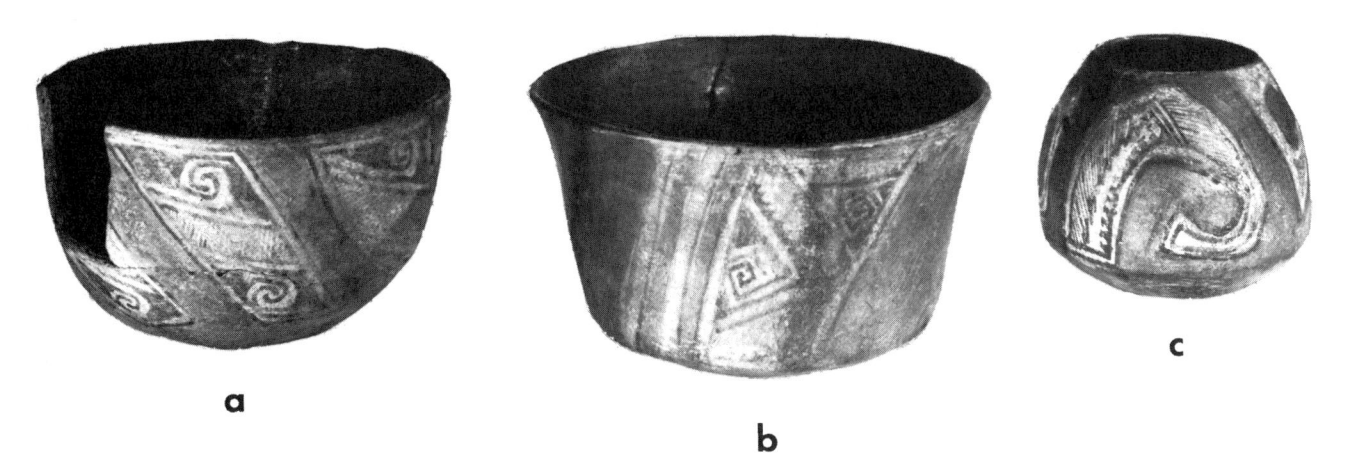

Fig. 3.22. Rincon Polychrome: Two bowls and one jar. *a*, Hemispherical bowl with direct rim; *b*, Low-shouldered bowl with rounded base and flared rim; *c*, Low shouldered jar with no neck and rounded base.

Fig. 3.23. Rincon Polychrome: Hemispherical bowl and low shouldered bowl. *a*, Hemispherical bowl with direct rim; *b*, Low shouldered bowl with everted rim.

70 CERAMICS

Fig. 3.24. Rincon Polychrome: Sherds. *a,* Alternate black and white lines in nested chevrons: bowl; *b,* "S" fret: bowl; *c, d,* Broad, diagonal strips: bowl; *e, f,* Diagonal panels: jars.

secondary black framing line enclosed the larger panels and strips.

The narrow strips, edged in black, bore no interior design elements. Usually these narrow components were placed parallel to the main diagonal or vertical panels so that they formed an external border or balancing effect. One hemispherical bowl carried a fret composed of a black-edged white strip on both the interior and exterior surfaces.

An exception to the general rule of design was one vessel that had the main design composed of alternate black and white lines in nested chevrons (Fig. 3.24a).

Large triangles, decorated in the normal manner, were used between curved panels on the illustrated incurved jar (Fig. 3.25a).

In summary, the overall concept gave the effect of bold use of open, widely spaced, simple major design elements. The larger and smaller components generally were repetitive around the interior or exterior circumferences.

The use of panels in conjunction with certain vessel forms often dictated that the panels or strips become curved at the lower end. This variation was observed on interior bowl designs. Often the lower end of exterior

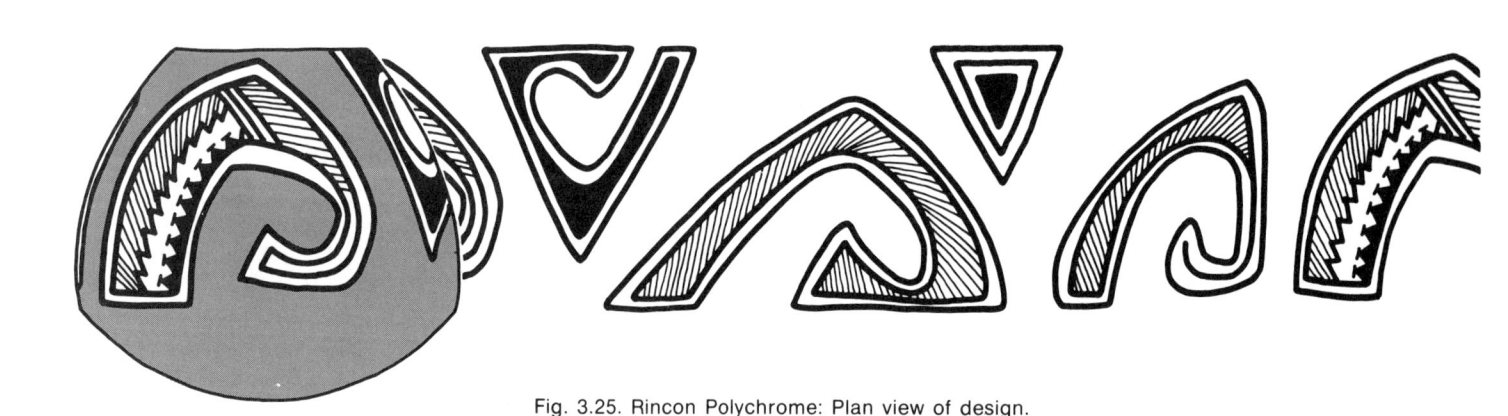

Fig. 3.25. Rincon Polychrome: Plan view of design.

diagonal panels was narrowed, or pinched off, when it approached the shoulder where the limit of the design occurred.

The rims of bowls generally were painted black. A few were left unpainted. When a bowl had a flaring or everted rim, interior decoration in the form of small black pendant triangles or a narrow black-on-white band was applied. One hemispherical bowl, with an "S" fret design on the exterior and a similar design on the interior, had a white rim. On jars the rim was unpainted. It is important to understand that only one form of jar, shouldered and incurved, has been discovered.

Principal Design on Exterior of Bowls

Panel, diagonal (Figs. 3.22a, b and 3.23a, b). Often, at the point where the panel neared the shoulder or point of greatest curvature, it was pinched off or tapered. Panels were sectioned and filled with repeated elements. Panels could have single or double black framing lines.

Panel, vertical (Fig. 3.21a, b). Each panel stopped at the shoulder or point of greatest curvature. Panels were sectioned and filled with repeated elements.

Strip, broad—diagonal or vertical (Figs. 3.21d and 3.24c, d). A strip is more narrow than a panel, but could be sectioned and decorated with similar repeated elements.

Strip, narrow—diagonal or vertical (Figs. 3.22b, 3.23b, and 3.24c). One or two parallel strips with black framing lines but without interior elements could accompany and complement the main panels.

"S" Fret (Fig. 3.24b). One hemispherical bowl carried as principal decoration on interior and exterior, a white "S" fret edged in black.

Fret, interlocking (Fig. 3.24d). This design occurred in conjunction with decorated broad strips. The frets were alternate black and white strips placed directly on the red slip. An interior band of black triangles was pendant from the rim on the same bowl.

Chevrons, alternate narrow black and white lines (Fig. 3.24a). One bowl with everted rim was decorated in this manner. A band of black triangles was placed on the interior of the rim.

Principal Design on Exterior of Jars

Panel, diagonal (Figs. 3.21c, and 3.24e, f). The overall concept was similar to bowl panels. The design stopped at the shoulder. The collected samples have no strips balancing the main panel.

Panel, hooked (Fig. 3.25). This element occurred together with the following on the same vessel.

Triangle, decorated. One complete jar (Figs. 3.22c and 3.25) had large pendant triangles each with original interpretations of familiar motifs.

Principal Design on Interior of Bowls

Strip, broad—diagonal or vertical. (Not illustrated.)

Strip, broad—curved. (Not illustrated.)

Strip, narrow—straight. One large outcurved bowl (exterior unslipped) had a straight white strip with repeated black fret (Fig. 3.21d).

One hemispherical bowl from Arizona AA:12:36 carried both diagonal and curved strips as part of an intricate composition. Diagonal strips were apparently placed, alternately, between broad curved strips. The diagonal strips carried simple framing lines while the curved units bore repeated elements. From the fragments remaining, it appears that the diagonal strips commenced at the rim while the curved strips formed an intricate arrangement below the rim.

Secondary Design on Interior of Bowls

Strip, narrow. The hemispherical bowl with exterior black framed strips arranged into an "S" fret design also carried an interior design of the same order (Fig. 3.24b).

Band, triangles pendant from rim. (Not illustrated.)

Band, horizontal with repeated elements pendant from rim (Fig. 3.23b). Only on bowls with flaring and everted rims do we find bands of repeated solid elements or a continuous black-on-white band with characteristic small repeated elements. The shouldered restored bowl in Figure 3.23b demonstrated this combination, although it is not visible in the photograph.

Elements

The decorative elements that appear in Rincon Polychrome were used in the sections of panels and large triangles, on the broad strips and on interior horizontal bands.

Scroll, interlocked, curvilinear (Fig. 3.22a and 3.23a). This was a common motif often balanced with solid black elements.

Scroll, interlocked, angular (Fig. 3.22b and 3.23b). Occurred under same conditions as curvilinear scroll.

Scroll, single (Fig. 3.24e). One example appeared as a triangular filler of a diagonal panel.

Serrated framing or border lines. Often with "T" shaped elements. Found in series within framing lines of panels (Figs. 3.23b, 3.24d, e, and 3.25).

Fringed borders of short parallel hatching (Figs. 3.21a, b, and 3.23b). Usually found on the interiors of framing lines that sectioned the panels.

Framing lines, single or double (Figs. 3.21a, b, 3.23a, b and 3.24e).

Hatching. Often filling the decorated space of broad strips (Fig. 3.24e).

Frets, Independent. Usually repeated on broad strip or re-occurring in a more complex design on the panels (Fig. 3.21d).

Frets, interlocked (Fig. 3.24d).

Meanders. Examples fill diagonal panels (Figs. 3.21c and 3.24f).

Zigzag (or wavy) repeated lines. The best examples fill a complete panel (Fig. 3.23a).

Chevrons (Fig. 3.24a).

Discussion

We have seen that a basic redware already existed in the area that yielded the rare Rincon Polychrome. In contrast, there was apparently no antecedent for the creation of a polychrome type utilizing black-on-white decorations on the redware. Using present chronologies, the well-known varieties of Gila Polychrome made their appearance about 50 to 100 years later in this part of the Southwest (Breternitz 1966:76-77).

Looking closer to home, we find not only that most of the individual elements used on Rincon Polychrome but also the vertical and diagonal panels were found in some designs on late Sacaton Red-on-buff and on late Rincon Red-on-brown. The panels, however, were not as discrete nor did they form the principal design as they did on Rincon Polychrome.

The illustrations from Snaketown (Gladwin and others 1937:Plates CXLII, CXLIX) show low shouldered bowls with flaring rims and shouldered incurved jars with variations of vertical panels. Diagonal panels were less obvious but were part of the design on shouldered incurved jars. It is perhaps significant that these two forms comprised a distinctive part of the Rincon Polychrome bowls and all of the identified jars.

In contrast, certain Rincon Polychrome design elements such as the hooks and curved broad strips have no local precedents. It is possible that the Casas Grandes district in Chihuahua might contain certain ceramic attributes that were reflected in Rincon Polychrome. The existence of Escondida Polychrome (synonym: Animas Polychrome) from A.D. 1080 to 1340 in association with Gila and Tonto variants has been published (Lindsay and Jennings 1968:6). If this chronological placement holds up, some of the designs on Rincon Polychrome and the concept of black-on-white decoration on a red-slipped ware may have a southern connection.

The hooked design (a variant of the "birdwing"?) and broad meandering strips were common to both Animas and Tonto Polychromes. The decorations are most often found on low squat jars. Such an influence was clear on the Rincon Polychrome jar (Fig. 3.22c) and on the interior decorated bowl (not illustrated).

Traditionally, the appearance of a series of local redwares (Rincon, Valshni, and Dragoon) in southern Arizona in the eleventh and twelfth centuries had been related to the highly developed Guasave Redware (Ekholm 1942:74-77) from northern Sinaloa and the Huatabampo complex from the Mayo River. Such thinking was bolstered by the appearance of a cluster of other material traits in the same area. Modeled spindle whorls and overhanging manos apparently accompanied the new redware. More direct economic, political, and religious connections with Sinaloa and more southern centers on the west coast of Mexico should be investigated as research grows.

The possible derivation of the origins of Rincon Polychrome from the Huatabampo complex is as tenuous as the problem of a Chihuahua relationship noted above. Even though the surmised connection between Guasave Redware and Rincon and Valshni redwares appears quite logical, no direct prototype of a polychrome encompassing black-on-white designs on a fully slipped redware is found in the Guasave area. Most of the Sinaloa polychromes were composed of red, black, and white elements on a buffware.

However, there exists one clue. A series of eight vessels were isolated by Ekholm (1942:77-79) under the title Amole Polychrome. Generally the interiors of bowls were slipped red. Furthermore, the most common motif is a stepped *Grecque*. Perhaps the hooked designs on Rincon Polychrome may be a simplification of the stepped *Grecque*. Therefore, the designs on the jar in Figure 75 might have an alternative antecedent.

The interior decorated bowl (not illustrated) from Arizona AA:12:36 echoes the same concept.

Finally, even from a relatively small collection, there was a considerable range in the decorative treatment on Rincon Polychrome. We have already quoted Kelly (n.d.:IV:149:footnote 4) to the effect that two types were probably present; however, it can be safely inferred that all the examples described do properly represent one type. At first glance, the disparate design elements seemed to reflect different traditions, yet all the major elements (interior and exterior) may appear in combination with each other. For instance, interior pendant triangles occurred with normal panels and with the nested chevron pattern. The bowl with white frets (bordered in black) both on interior and exterior (with white painted rim) also was unusual, but the narrow strips found adjacent to large panels (Fig. 3.22b) were composed in the same manner as the frets. In other words, the elements are not mutually exclusive.

Therefore, Rincon Polychrome would best be understood as the end result of local decorative experiments upon the local redware. Broad panels and filler elements were borrowed from the contemporary Hohokam painted types. Some new designs (the frets) reflect knowledge of St. Johns Polychrome (Carlson 1970:31-41).

INTRUSIVE CERAMICS
Introduction

The four settlements at Punta de Agua as well as the trash mound area (Arizona BB:13:49) located north of the historic mission produced some intrusive sherds. Previously, it has been shown that Arizona BB:13:49 represented a more homogeneous collection relating to the late Rincon-early Tanque Verde transition.

The foreign sherds from each site are listed in Table 3.1. The culture areas contributing these specimens are listed below in the order of specimen frequency:

1. Gila Basin
2. Papaguería
3. Mimbres district
4. San Pedro Valley (Dragoon series)
5. Trincheras district
6. Tonto-Roosevelt
7. El Paso area

Gila Polychrome

Before continuing the discussion of intrusive pottery, the problem of the presence of eight Gila Polychrome sherds must be considered. All the examples came from trash and fill at Arizona BB:13:16. No good cultural or temporal associations could be established. It is felt that these sherds came from later houses lying outside the

TABLE 3.1
**Intrusive Ceramics Listed by Provenience
Ariz. BB:13:41**

Provenience	Santa Cruz Red-on-buff	Sacaton Red-on-buff	Mimbres Black-on-white	Unidentified Whiteware	Dragoon Red-on-brown	Trincheras Purple-on-red	Sells Red	Topawa Red-on-brown (Local variety)
House 11 Fill	–	–	1	–	–	–	–	–
House 6 Fill	–	–	–	–	–	1	–	–
Test 5	–	–	–	–	1	–	–	–
House 2 Floor	–	–	–	–	–	–	–	1
House 4 Fill	–	–	–	–	–	–	–	1
House 12 Floor	–	–	–	–	–	–	–	1
Trench 29	–	–	–	–	–	–	–	2
Trench 30	–	–	–	–	–	–	–	1
General Excavation	–	–	–	–	–	–	–	1
Trench 14, L. 1	–	–	–	–	–	–	1	–
Trench 26	–	–	–	–	–	–	1	–
House 9 Fill	–	–	–	1	–	–	–	–
House 8 Floor	–	–	–	–	–	–	–	–
SITE TOTAL			1	1	1	1	2	7

(continued)

TABLE 3.1 (continued)
Intrusive Ceramics Listed by Provenience
Ariz. BB:13:16

Provenience	Santa Cruz Red-on-buff	Sacaton Red-on-buff	Hohokam Buffware	Mimbres Black-on-white	Gila Polychrome†	Dragoon Red-on-brown	El Paso Polychrome	Nogales Polychrome	Sells Red	Topawa Red-on-brown (Local variety)
Test 11	–	–	–	–	1	–	–	–	–	–
House 4, Fill	–	–	–	–	2	–	–	–	–	–
Test 6	–	–	–	–	1	–	–	–	–	–
Test 13	–	–	–	–	1	–	–	–	–	–
Broadside 11	–	–	–	–	1	–	–	–	–	–
Trench 14, Level 2	–	–	–	–	1	–	–	–	–	–
Trench 14, Level 1	–	–	–	–	–	–	–	1	–	–
House 5, Fill	–	–	–	–	–	1	1	–	–	–
Trench 12, Level 1	–	–	–	1	1	–	–	–	–	–
Trench 21, Level 1	–	–	–	–	–	–	1	–	–	–
House 6, Fill	–	–	–	–	–	–	–	–	1	1
Test 11	–	–	–	–	–	–	–	–	–	1
House 9, Floor	*	–	–	–	–	–	–	–	2	1
Test 16	–	–	–	–	–	–	–	–	1	–
Test 24	–	–	–	–	–	–	–	–	1	–
Trench 17, Level 1	–	–	–	–	–	–	–	–	2	–
Trench 18, Level 2	–	–	–	–	–	–	–	–	1	–
Test 89	–	–	–	–	–	–	–	–	–	6
Trench 23, Level 1	–	–	–	–	–	–	–	–	4	–
Test 103	–	–	–	–	–	–	–	–	–	–
Test X	–	–	–	–	–	–	–	–	–	1
SITE TOTAL	27	30	9	1	8	2	1	1	12	10

*10 sherds from one vessel
†Gila Polychrome has no good provenience.

Ariz. BB:13:43

Provenience	Santa Cruz Red-on-buff	Sacaton Red-on-buff	Hohokam Buffware	Casa Grande Red-on-buff	Mimbres Black-on-white	Unidentified Whiteware	Roosevelt Black-on-white	Dragoon Red-on-brown	Nogales Polychrome	Sells Red	Topawa Red-on-brown (Local variety)
General Excavation	–	–	–	–	1	–	–	1	–	–	–
House 4, Fill	–	–	–	–	1	–	–	–	–	–	–
House 2, Subfloor	–	–	–	–	–	1	–	–	–	–	–
Cache 2	–	–	–	–	–	–	–	–	1	–	–
House 1, Fill	–	–	–	–	–	–	–	2	–	–	–
SITE TOTAL	–	6	10	–	2	1	–	3	1	–	–

Ariz. BB:13:50

Provenience	Santa Cruz Red-on-buff	Sacaton Red-on-buff	Hohokam Buffware	Casa Grande Red-on-buff	Mimbres Black-on-white	Unidentified Whiteware	Roosevelt Black-on-white	Dragoon Red-on-brown	Nogales Polychrome	Sells Red	Topawa Red-on-brown (Local variety)
House 2, Fill	–	–	–	1	5	–	–	–	–	1	4
House 3, Floor	–	–	–	–	1	–	–	–	–	1	3
Test 7	–	–	–	–	1	–	–	–	–	–	–
House 20A, Fill	–	–	–	–	2	–	–	–	–	–	–
SITE TOTAL	3	80	42	1	9	–	–	–	–	2	7

Ariz. BB:13:49

Provenience	Santa Cruz Red-on-buff	Sacaton Red-on-buff	Hohokam Buffware	Casa Grande Red-on-buff	Mimbres Black-on-white	Unidentified Whiteware	Roosevelt Black-on-white	Dragoon Red-on-brown	Nogales Polychrome	Sells Red	Topawa Red-on-brown (Local variety)
Mound I	–	–	–	3	2	–	2	–	–	–	1
Mound II	–	–	–	–	1	–	–	–	–	–	–
SITE TOTAL	–	7	4	3	3	–	2	–	–	–	1

right-of-way—between Arizona BB:13:16 and Arizona BB:13:50.

More important to our discussion, however, is whether the Gila Polychrome sherds should be considered intrusive or local. It has been shown that Gila Polychrome was widely made throughout the Southwest (Danson and Wallace 1956:180-183). Furthermore, Wallace (1957:214-217) described a variety of Gila Polychrome from the University Indian Ruin.

Two sherds of Gila Polychrome from the fill of House 4 (Arizona BB:13:16) are similar to those from the University Ruin. Mica flecks are clearly visible on the interior and exterior surfaces. The six remaining sherds from Arizona BB:13:16 lack mica. They could have been made locally, perhaps at Martinez Hill or at the small Tanque Verde phase sites nearby.

All eight sherds were from bowls; rims were absent. None of these examples provide any absolute chronological significance. However, since the transition to the Tanque Verde phase at Punta de Agua occurred about A.D. 1215, the Gila Polychrome sherds may date from any time after that period.

As noted, the earliest, but short-lived, polychrome with black-on-white designs on a local redware (Rincon Polychrome) did not, to our knowledge, continue to be made after the first part of the thirteenth century.

Gila Basin Types

Casa Grande Red-on-buff, Sacaton Red-on-buff, and Santa Cruz Red-on-buff were the only types identified from the Gila Basin. As expected, they comprised the bulk of the intrusive pottery. Their distribution throughout the sites at Punta de Agua fits quite well the proposed time range and internal development based on the architecture and stratigraphic evidence. For example, the site showing the earliest settlement (Arizona BB:13:16) contained the greatest number of Santa Cruz Red-on-buff sherds, while just five were identified at the other four sites.

This evidence reinforces the supposition that the villages excavated owed their existence to the rapid establishment of new communities in the Rincon phase. The relative scarcity of Sacaton Red-on-buff in the late Rincon houses at Arizona BB:13:50 testifies to the growing independence of the Tucson Basin settlements after A.D. 1150.

Casa Grande Red-on-buff was found only in trash mounds at the transition site (Arizona BB:13:49) and at House 2 (Arizona BB:13:50); three sherds at the former and one at the latter.

76 CERAMICS

Papaguería Types

The discovery of 25 sherds of the distinctive Topawa Red-on-brown type has created a second unresolved problem. The paste and temper of the sherds are indistinguishable from the other types of the Rincon phase. It was noted above that the pieces might be a local variety.

The Topawa finds tended to cluster in three distinct zones. The first zone comprised the late Rincon Houses 2 and 3 at Arizona BB:13:50. The second zone was found in and near Houses 2 and 4 at Arizona BB:13:41. The final zone centered on House 9 at Arizona BB:13:16. All except the last are perfect examples of late Rincon structures.

This highly selective distribution must have some significance bearing on the nature of contact or closeness of kin between some of the groups near Valshni Village and at Punta de Agua. Moreover, if the characteristic trait of interior and exterior decoration proves to be the direct source for the same combination in a large proportion of Tanque Verde Red-on-brown or proves to be a major component in the same type's evolution, then we are closer to explaining the rapid development of Tanque Verde Red-on-brown and the direction of influence, as well as the cultural units responsible.

Sells Red was the next most common type from the Papaguería. It generally accompanied Topawa Red-on-brown at each of the site locations. The association of these two types was reassuring and offered sure ground for the speculation just mentioned. The types form the major decorated wares of the Topawa phase which was estimated to last until A.D. 1250 (Haury 1950:9).

Mimbres District

Sixteen sherds of Mimbres Black-on-white were found at the Punta de Agua sites. Each site contained at least one piece, but of more use to us for establishing relative dating, was the appearance of nine sherds in two late Rincon houses at Arizona BB:13:50. From the floor of Houses 2 and 3, Mimbres Black-on-white (Fig. 3.26a,

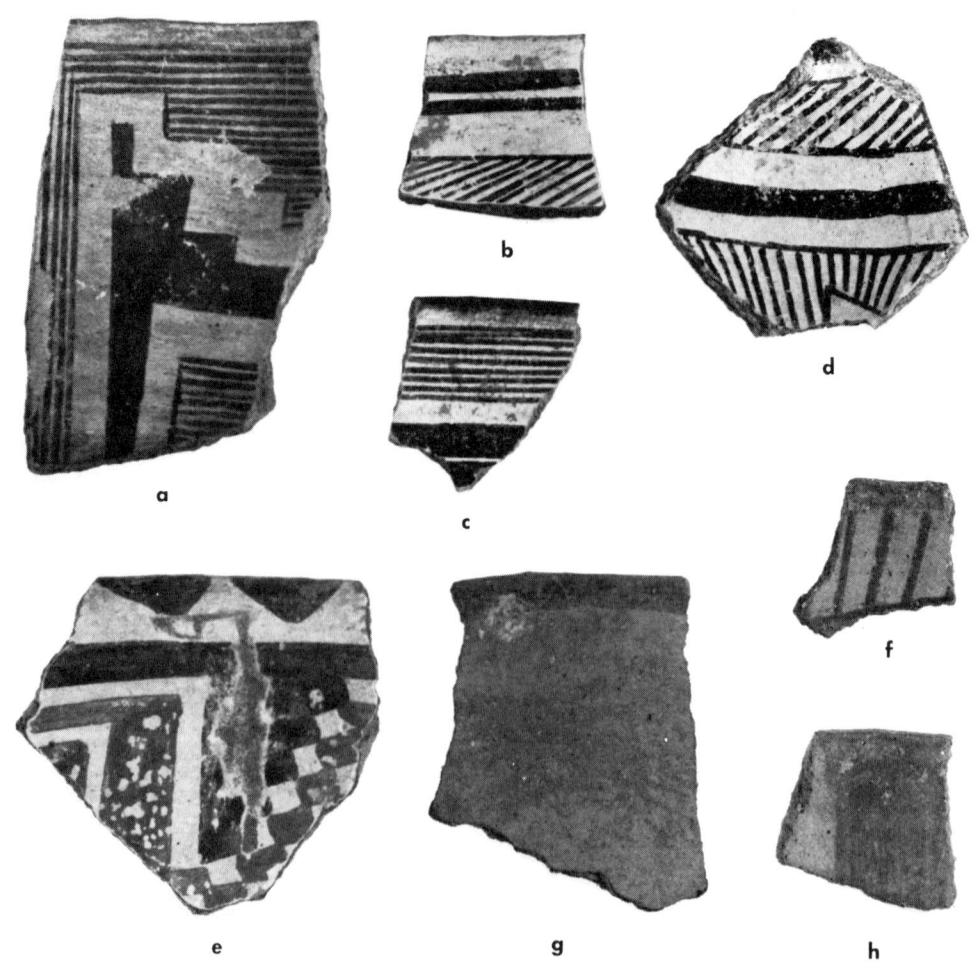

Fig. 3.26. Intrusive ceramics. *a, b, c,* Mimbres Black-on-white; *d,* Roosevelt Black-on-white; *e,* Nogales Polychrome; *f,* Trincheras Purple-on-red; *g, h,* Dragoon Red-on-brown.

b, c) was in direct association with Topawa Red-on-brown and also with Rincon Polychrome. The other important finds were in late Rincon proveniences at Arizona BB:13:49 where Roosevelt Black-on-white appeared in the same trash mound.

The problem of the Mimbres cultural dispersal from its heartland at the end of the twelfth century is receiving more attention. New data on possible intrusive Mimbres sites on the San Pedro River have been published by Hammack (1971:16). In any event, the quantity of Mimbres Black-on-white at the Punta de Agua sites indicates that more contact was maintained with that area than any other outside of the adjacent Gila River and Papaguería zones.

San Pedro Valley (Dragoon Series)

Six sherds of Dragoon Red-on-brown (Fulton and Tuthill 1940:40-44) were recovered. This series was recently reviewed by Hammack (1971:16) at sites on the San Pedro River. The finds were dispersed among the three sites that were architecturally associated with the early part of the Rincon phase. None of the sherds had good provenience, but three were located near House 1 at Arizona BB:13:43 (Fig. 3.26g, h).

Trincheras District

Two Nogales Polychrome sherds (Fig. 3.26e) and one Trincheras Purple-on-red (Fig. 3.26f) comprised the total intrusive material from the south. No information could be gained from their locations since direct association and good provenience were lacking. The general location of the Nogales Polychrome sherds indicated an early Rincon date, while the single Trincheras Purple-on-red (rim painted only) was in the later architectural zone.

Tonto-Roosevelt District

Two Roosevelt Black-on-white sherds were found in the trash mounds at Arizona BB:13:49 (Fig. 3.26d). This was not unexpected as this transitional site was accumulating during the first part of the thirteenth century. Roosevelt Black-on-white has been assigned dates of A.D. 1200-1350 (Pomeroy 1962).

El Paso District

One El Paso Polychrome sherd was found in the fill near House 5 (Arizona BB:13:16). The house and other pottery in association related to the last half of the Rincon phase. (Not illustrated.)

4. CERAMIC ARTIFACTS

The inventory of ceramic artifacts includes items fashioned from clay and then fired. The familiar examples are modeled spindle whorls, human figurines, and animal effigies. Another category covers the secondary uses of sherds that were ground and polished into spindle whorls, discs, and eccentric shapes.

Two of the human figurine heads were especially deserving of further attention and are mentioned in detail below.

MODELED SPINDLE WHORLS

Eight whole and fragmentary modeled whorls were recovered from the Punta de Agua sites (Fig. 4.1g-n).

They are listed below using terminology developed by Haury (1945:115-117). The provenience, in each case, was in association with late Rincon phase structures.

Site	Provenience	Type	Phase
BB:13:50	House 1 floor	Pulley-shaped	Rincon
	House 22 floor	Pulley-shaped	Rincon
	House 23 floor	Ellipsoidal	Rincon
BB:13:16	House 4 floor	Pulley-shaped	Rincon
	House 6 fill	Biconical	Rincon
BB:13:41	Trench 10 fill	Discoidal	Rincon
	House 6 floor	Ellipsoidal	Rincon
	House 6 fill	Pulley-shaped	Rincon

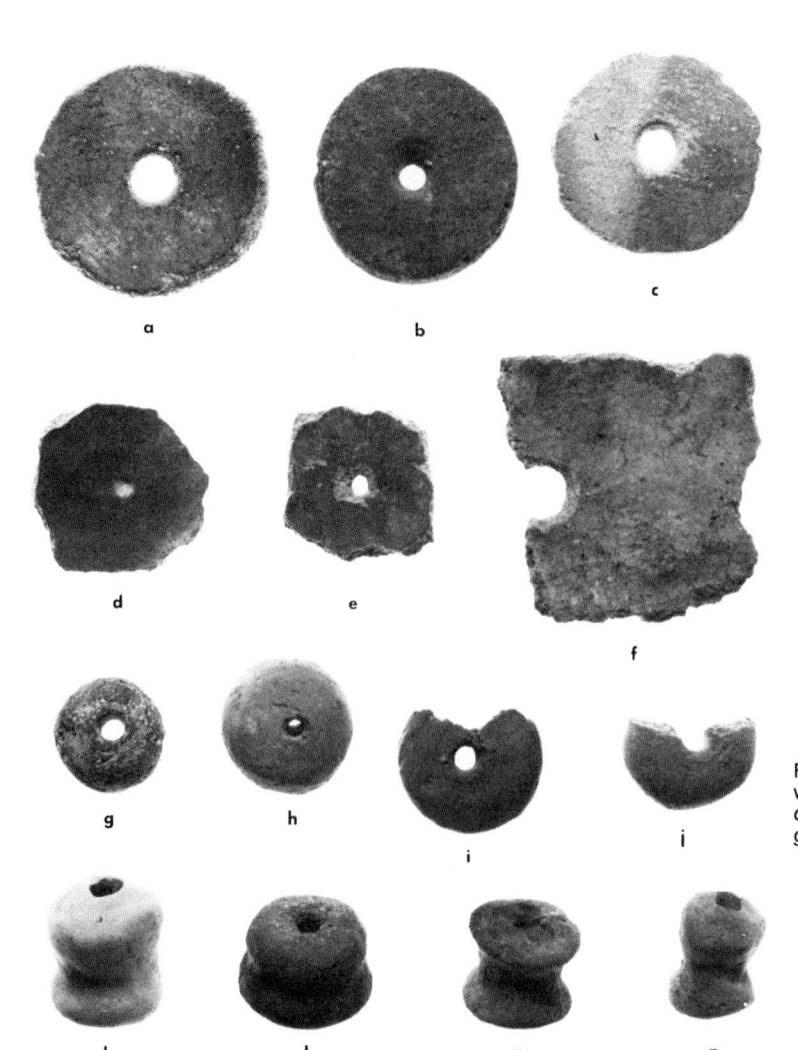

Fig. 4.1. Spindle whorls. *a-c*, Ceramic spindle whorls cut from plainware sherds; *d-f*, Technological stages of manufacture; *g-n*, Modeled spindle whorls.

All of the specimens were unpainted and they exhibited no incising or other decoration. The fragmentary discoidal whorl from Trench 10 (Arizona BB:13:41) was actually plano-convex in cross section. None of the whorls were symmetrical. Instead, rough surfaces and irregular shapes were the norm.

Generally, the introduction of modeled spindle whorls to southern Arizona possibly from the Guasave area of Sinaloa, has been ascribed to the late Sedentary period (Haury 1945:119). That they came into more prominence in the Classic period has been shown by DiPeso (1956:387-394) at Paloparado, by Scantling (1940:38) at the Jackrabbit Ruin, and by Greenleaf (in press) at the Fortified site (Arizona T:13:8) near Gila Bend. Kelly (n.d.:IV:169) reported six spindle whorls from the Hodges site, although only one was accurately dated. Withers (1941:54-55) assigned two modeled whorls to the Topawa phase, which is roughly contemporary with the Tanque Verde phase at Punta de Agua.

The provenience of all the modeled whorls at late Rincon phase houses confirms the hypothesis outlined above.

HUMAN FIGURINES AND EFFIGIES

From all the sites reported here, 24 fragmentary human figurines of fired clay were retrieved. In addition, one fragment of a human effigy jar and one whole miniature ladle with a modeled human head are included under this heading (Fig. 4.2).

Arizona BB:13:50

The fragmentary nature and small sample of the human figurines precludes a good discussion of the art and styles favored by the villagers in the Punta de Agua district. However, the range of types indicated by the diversity of the remains is impressive. Those figurines in association with the floors or the fill from houses at Arizona BB:13:50 appear to relate to the Rincon and Tanque Verde phases. None of the human figurines showed the remains of paint. With few exceptions, all were roughly finished.

As far as can be determined, the majority of figurines, including those illustrated, were modeled from a single lump of clay. Of course, a headdress or other ornamentation could be added. In the total collection of 24 ceramic figures, two fragmentary pieces were constructed by the method of joining two rods of clay. The bond was clearly visible along the spine of each.

The trunk and legs found on the floor of the transitional House 13 (Fig. 4.2h) is, perhaps, one of the latest models at Punta de Agua with good provenience. It was made with the legs foreshortened.

Fig. 4.2. Human figurines and effigies. *a,* Head and shoulders with headband, ear spool, and necklace; *b,* Head and shoulders of female figurine; *c,* Oval head; *d,* Miniature ladle; *e,* Long torso; *f, g,* Female torso; *h,* Trunk and legs; *i,* Small leg fragment; *j, k,* Large leg fragments.

The female figurine from House 18 (Fig. 4.2b) had lost most of the facial features and the left breast through erosion. The head was a flattened oval with a characteristic upraised chin. Only the nose, high and beaked, was modeled. The arms were indicated by two short stumps. The general features of this figurine seem to crosscut others found in phases contemporary with

80 CERAMIC ARTIFACTS

the Rincon phase in adjacent areas of southern Arizona (Kelly n.d.:II:19; Tuthill 1947:Plate 23; and Fulton and Tuthill 1940:Plate 16). These are all examples without applied "coffee bean" eyes and other elaborate details which were more common in preceding Rillito times.

From the fill of Trash Pit 2 and from House 22 fragments of larger figurines were recovered (Fig. 4.2j and k). Each of these was a fragment of a long leg with a crude approximation of a foot attached. In the first example the leg was slightly curved without an indication of a knee. The foot was flattened and flared with a rough attempt to represent toes. The second example was done in the same proportions. Both were parts of much larger figures. The best analogy would seem to be the elaborate figurines discovered in a cache on the Santa Cruz River north of the confluence with the Rillito. Photographs of this group, known as the Vaughn collection, are on file in the Arizona State Museum. The exact provenience of these figurines is unknown, but they best relate to the late Rincon phase.

From the entry of House 25 came a fine fragment of the head and shoulders of a figurine, showing a headband, ear spool, and necklace (Figs. 4.2a and 4.3a, b). It was the most elaborately modeled figure discovered at any of the Punta de Agua sites. The head was formed in a manner typical of the Sedentary period, with a beaked nose and protruding chin. In this case, however, a headband that consisted of an extra coil of clay had been applied over the forehead. A series of small incisions were impressed on the top of the band probably representing twisted and woven cloth. In this example, the eyes were fashioned by slightly downward sloping slots on each side of the broken, beaked nose.

A shaped ear spool was inserted in the right ear lobe. A necklace was indicated by a series of light incisions under the chin. Hanging from the necklace was a pendant modeled from a dab of applied clay. Three incisions were made on the pendant as if imitating an inlaid shell. Apparently no arms were on the original; only a stub was indicated on the unbroken right side.

This rare find has a parallel in a modeled figure from Tres Alamos on the San Pedro River (Tuthill 1947; Plate 23a). In the details of the adornments, this head repeats the refinements usually associated with the transitional Pre-Classic figurines in the Valley of Mexico (Vaillant 1966: Plates 15 and 17).

Two fragments of female figures were recovered in Trash Pit 1 (Fig. 4.2f and g). The larger torso was carefully and gracefully formed. As in other figurines, the arms were marked by pinched stumps of clay. The second torso was more crudely made and more generalized in anatomical details. Typologically, the large female torso recalls the form and attention to

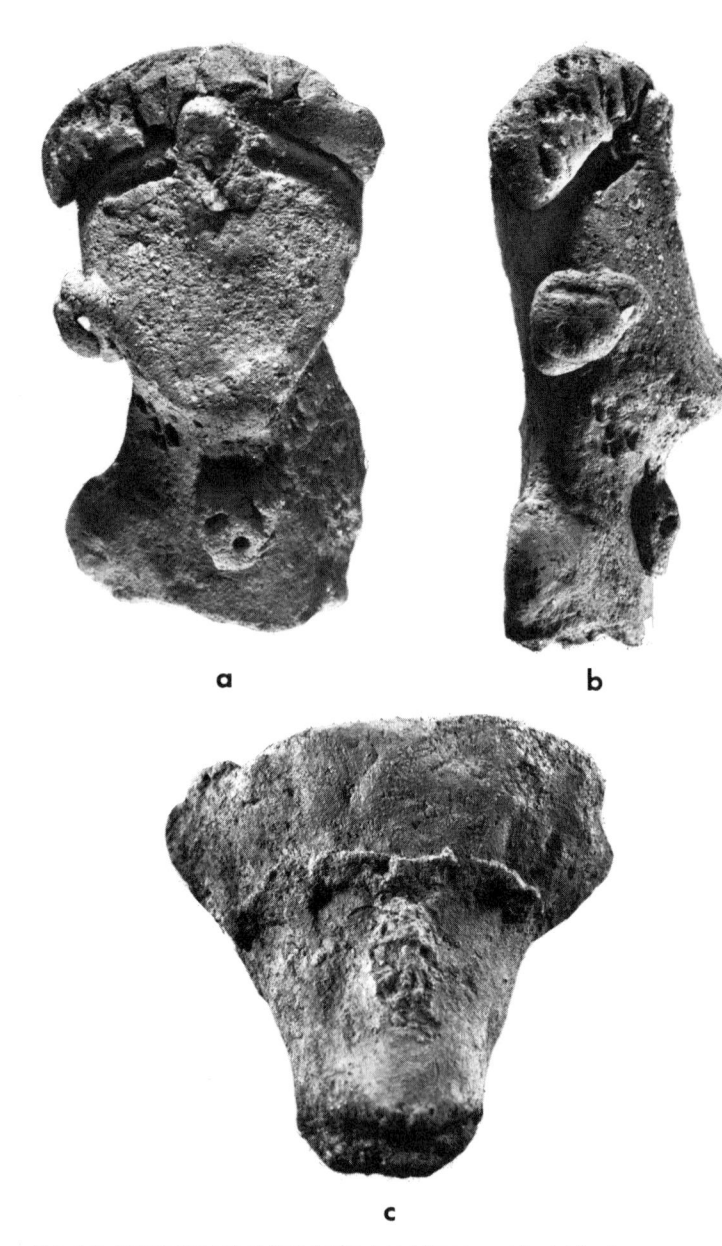

Fig. 4.3. Enlargement of head with headdress and facial features (front and side views), and fragmentary adorno. a, Front view; b, Right side; c, Fragmentary adorno.

detail found in Santa Cruz phase figurines at Snaketown (Gladwin and others 1937; Plate CXCVII). However, without the distinguishing characteristics of the head, the same body form is common to Colonial and Sedentary period figures.

Quite different from the figurines that were modeled in the round, was the head from Trash Pit 1 at BB:13:50 (Fig. 4.3c). The fragment, which has lost the beaked nose, carried a representation of a feathered headdress and decorated band over the forehead. Moreover, the reverse side shows that the head was applied separately

CERAMIC ARTIFACTS 81

as an *adorno* to a vessel. There was probably no body attached. Only the edges of the headdress touched the vessel, thus leaving a cup-like basin between it and the container.

Clay lobes that are barely distinguishable rise from the band. It is these that resemble the lower portions of feathers. The band itself is probably a representation of woven and twisted cloth. It bears a few irregular punctate depressions. The only facial contour, except for the broken nose, is the protruding chin. The face itself is of the same shape as those found on the normal figurines of the Sedentary period.

No exact analogue could be discovered in the literature. The closest resemblance seems to be to certain figurines with headdresses from Teotihuacan and to a type of Toltec mold-made figure (Vaillant 1966:78, 89).

The long torso (Fig. 4.2e) recovered from Trash Pit 4 was the lone example of its type. The fragment extends from the arm projections to the middle of the upper leg. The sex cannot be determined; the surface is rough. In form, this figure is analogous to some found at the Hodges site and at Tres Alamos, and best fits a Rincon phase date.

The last human representation at Arizona BB:13:50 was a fragment of a plain effigy jar from Trench 9. It consists of a rim sherd representing an ear with a pierced lobe.

Arizona BB:13:16

At the adjacent site, Arizona BB:13:16, a well-preserved oval head was found in House 5 (Fig. 4.2c). The high, beaked nose is the only modeled feature. Again, this type was identified at the Hodges site at Gleeson, and at Tres Alamos in Sedentary period contexts.

Arizona BB:13:41 and BB:13:43

Only one leg fragment from Arizona BB:13:43 is illustrated (Fig. 4.2i). Remarkably, it was shaped in a fashion recalling a female figurine illustrated by Vaillant (1966: Plate 14).

An interesting complete miniature ladle, with a crude head modeled on the handle, was the sole figure from Arizona BB:13:41 (Fig. 4.2d). The archaeological associations for these last three examples are all middle to late Rincon phase.

ANIMAL FIGURINES AND EFFIGIES

The large fragment (Fig. 4.4d) from Pit 3 at Arizona BB:13:50 is similar to the "guanacos," probably deer, found at Los Guanacos (Haury 1945:174-176, Plate

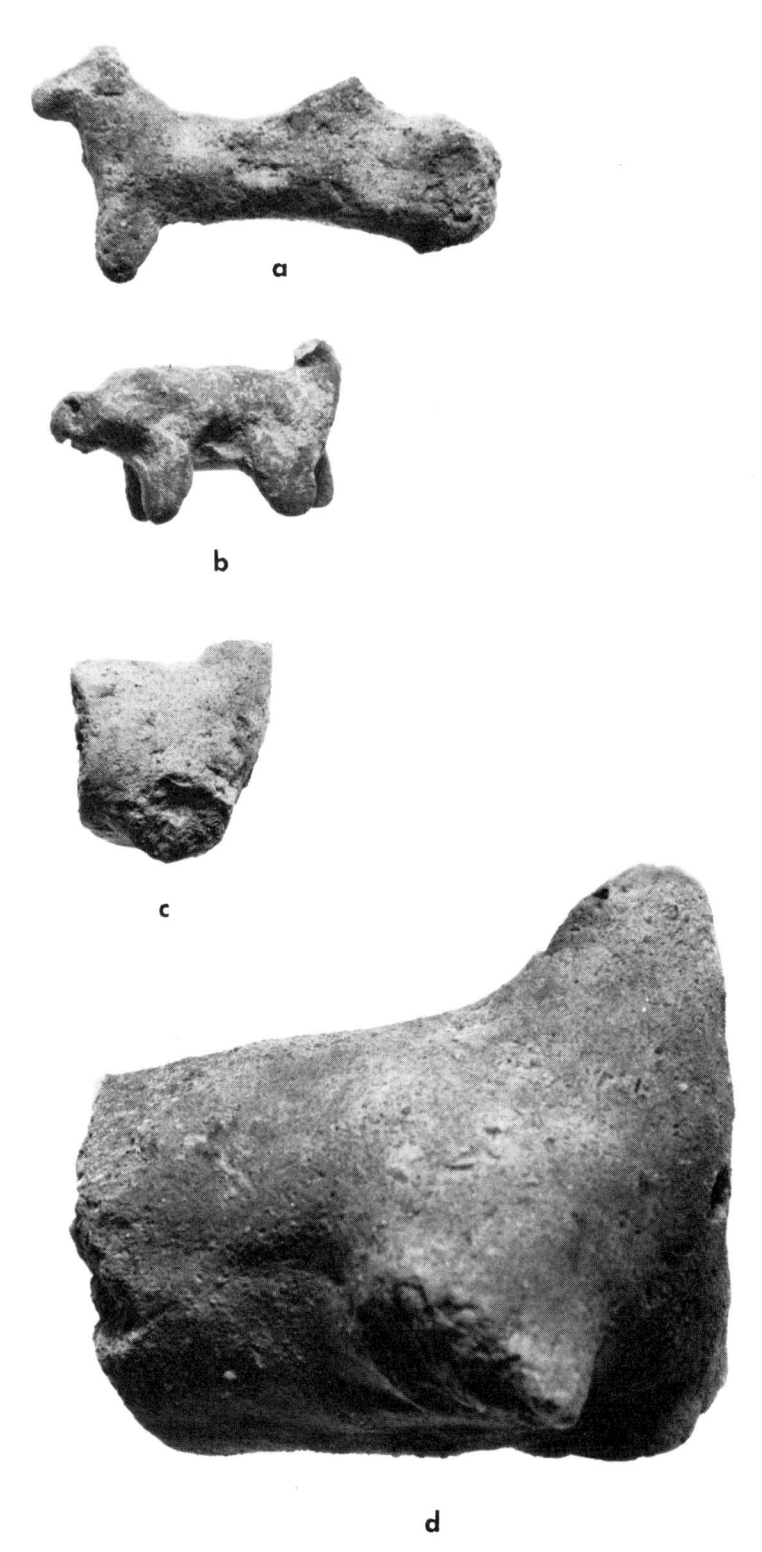

Fig. 4.4 Animal effigies. *a, b,* Crude, four-legged animals; *c,* Small fragment representing hindquarters of a four-legged animal; *d,* Larger version of "c."

82c), and at Snaketown (Gladwin and others 1937: Plate CCVIII). This fragment represents the hindquarters with raised tail. It is roughly finished and unslipped.

At Arizona BB:13:41, a smaller version of the same animal was recovered (Fig. 4.4c). It is a rear portion with an upraised tail. From Houses 2 and 11 at this site, two extremely crude four-legged animals were found (Fig. 4.4a, b). The former has a long humped body with three legs missing; the latter is complete except for the tip of its upraised tail.

Not many conclusions may be drawn from such a meager and varied assortment. As noted, most of this heterogeneous group are in association with Rincon phase houses and trash pits. Most figurines give the impression of having been formed from one piece of clay. A few exceptions, already noted, show two-rod construction.

An important fact is that the typical modeled head, peculiar to the Sacaton phase (Gladwin and others 1937:234, Plate CXCV) does not occur at Punta de Agua. Instead, a generalized oval head is dominant. This area divergence is in keeping with the material from the Hodges site, Tres Alamos, Gleeson, and Texas Canyon. In the case of the latter site, the lag in development has previously been called to our attention (Gladwin and others 1937:241).

PERFORATED DISCS

There is no question now that most of the circular discs with a ground and polished edge and with a biconical perforation at the center were used as spinning weights or spindle whorls. Thin pointed sticks were inserted through the center hole. That these flat or slightly concave discs were gradually replaced by the modeled spindle whorls in the Classic period has been confirmed at certain sites, such as Paloparado, Jackrabbit Ruin, and the Gila Bend Fortified site (Arizona T:13:8).

In the list and discussion following, there are certain discs which show spindle whorls in preliminary technical stages, and others which show more variation than would be expected and, therefore, are called problematical objects.

Of the two incipient whorls, one shows the start of a conical drill hole on the decorated side of a bowl sherd; the other has incomplete holes started on each side. There seems to be no significance in the choice of sherds for the spinning weight of a spindle whorl. Plain or decorated, thick or thin, smudged or unsmudged sherds were employed.

Quite large perforations (up to 1.0 cm) could be drilled. The approved method, where evidence remains, seems to be a biconical hole. There was a tendency for large diameter holes to be found in thick discs; in larger discs a more ragged circumference is often found. Apparently the desired centrifugal effect was not upset by crudely finished whorls.

Two large irregular plain sherds, each with a single biconical perforation (greater than 1.0 cm in diameter) were found in Houses 5 and 6 at Arizona BB:13:16. The fragment from House 5 had a rough circumference and was broken near the perforation. In concept, this piece recalls the sherd disc used as backing in the construction of a mosaic plaque (Gladwin and others 1937:243, Plate CCIX).

OTHER CLASSES OF WORKED SHERDS

A wide range of other types of worked sherds was evident at Punta de Agua. This category included rounded discs (unperforated), subrectangular forms, oval shapes, and odd geometrical sherds. The majority of all the shapes do not have smoothed or polished edges (Fig. 4.la-f). Not illustrated are a collection of large irregular concave sherds which served as obvious scraping tools as one or more facets were beveled through use.

From most of the large sites across the greater Southwest analogous worked sherds have been recovered. Three detailed reviews of these problematical artifacts have been published from the Swartz Ruin (Cosgrove and Cosgrove 1932:87-88), Pecos (Kidder 1932:154-155), and Snaketown (Gladwin and others 1937:242-243). Most authors refer to the familiar forms as gaming pieces if they lack beveled surfaces.

Even though so-called gaming markers have rarely been found in a properly identifiable context, the ascription remains. Another alternative is exemplified by the discovery, in a cave in the Winchester Mountains in southeastern Arizona, of plain and decorated discs, wrapped in pairs (Fulton 1941:24, Plate VII). These were in association with an assemblage of other ceremonial artifacts.

Smaller pieces that fit the hand well and exhibit beveled facets are often called pottery scraping tools.

Discs

From our sites a total of 74 whole and fragmentary plain discs and 29 decorated discs were collected. The range in size is reflected in Figure 4.5a-1. The smaller discs tend to have more carefully smoothed edges. Six of the discs were prepared from rim sherds from both bowls and jars. Each showed a more well shaped circumference and the form probably functioned as a scraper (Fig. 4.5a'-d'). We are left, therefore, with most of the illustrated discs still unexplained.

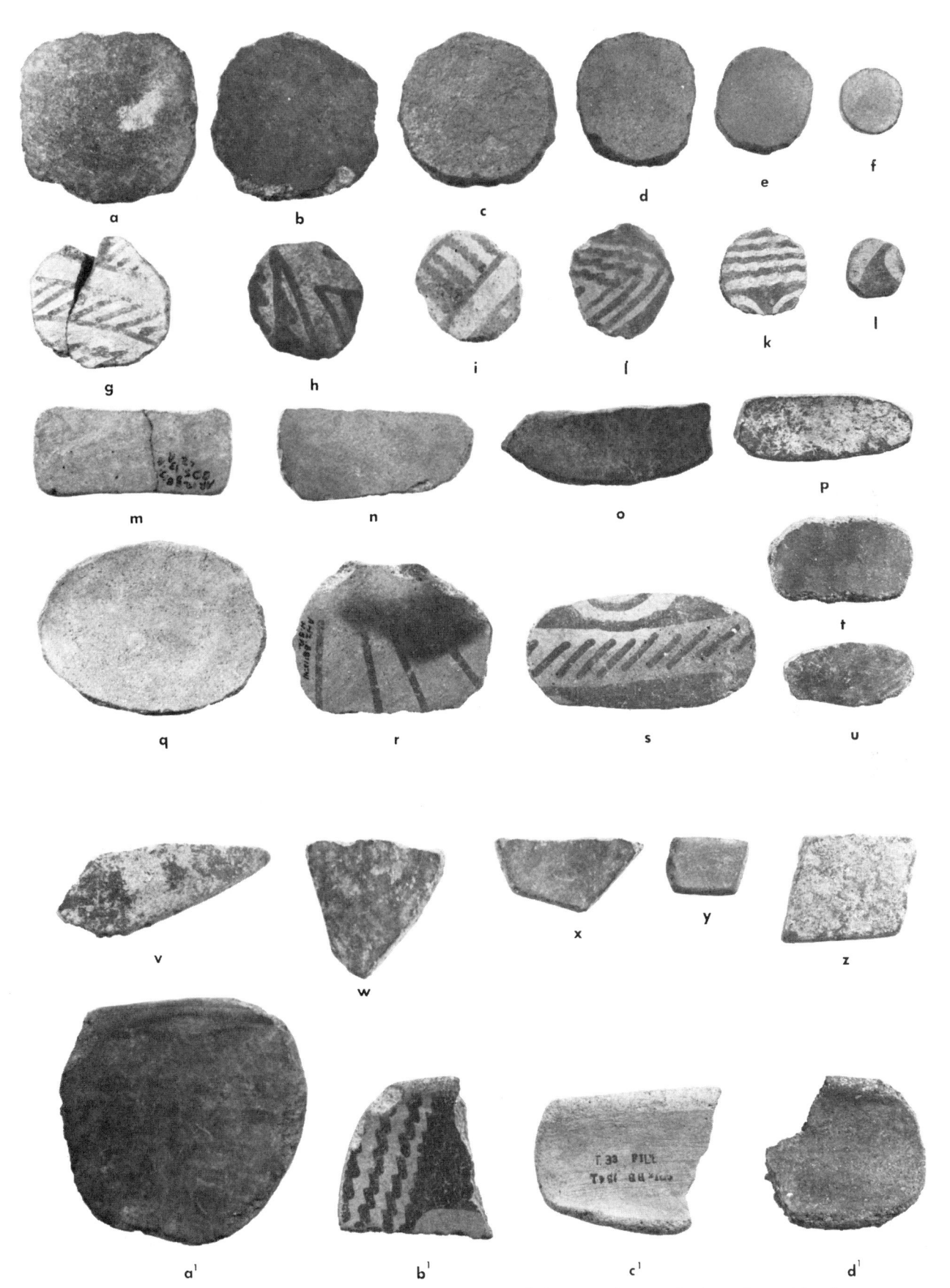

Fig. 4.5. Ceramic artifacts. *a-l*, Gaming discs; *m-p*, Subrectangular; *q-u*, Oval; *v-z*, Geometric; *a¹-d¹*, Scrapers.

84 CERAMIC ARTIFACTS

Oval. A series of 20 oval discs formed a subgroup. Some are found in Figure 4.5q-u. All except one had rough edges. No specific purpose has been proved for this form.

Subrectangular. Another variety of shaped sherds was isolated. These were elongated subrectangular sherds that included skewed forms. Only 4 of 28 from Punta de Agua are illustrated (Fig. 4.5m-p). Rillito Red-on-brown and Rincon Red-on-brown are represented but are not figured. An interesting characteristic, common to all except four, is that each was fashioned from a part of a smudged vessel. In the discussion to follow, the possible use of these specialized sherds as gaming devices will be considered.

Geometric. A few rare shapes of worked sherds are worthy of mention. Two small rhomboid sherds, one trapezoid form, and two triangular shapes stand out (Fig. 4.5v-z). Most of the edges were smoothed but no beveling from use as a pottery scraper, for instance, was evident.

Discussion. In most archaeological reports the odd-shaped worked sherds, except for discs, have been assigned to a class of pottery scraping tools in a perfunctory manner. Investigators were faced with a lack of good data in ethnographic descriptions of games throughout the Southwest showing the use of ceramic markers or dice. However, two reports of surviving games making use of ceramic discs provide interesting clues. Russell (1908:177-178) cites pottery discs being employed among the Pima, while Culin (1907:799-800) notes similar use at Zuni.

It is more difficult to account for the oval, rhomboid, or the ubiquitous rectangular variations as gaming pieces for one principal reason. The shapes were used ethnographically, but wood was the material, not ceramics. Nonetheless, the most widespread game was a derivative of patolli (Tylor 1878:116-131). Sets of painted wooden stick dice were catapulted into the air by a variety of means. Culin (1907:120, 216) reviewed this popular pastime. A preference for wood dice painted black on one side was the rule. Analogies were cited at Zuni and some Keresan pueblos as well as among the Mohave and Yuma (Culin 1907:205-209). It is significant that 20 of 28 rectangular ceramic pieces were fashioned from smudged sherds. A survival of the wood dice with one black side, used in patolli, might be suggested.

Jar Cover: Unfired

In a storage area outside House 21 (Arizona BB:13:50) an almost complete unfired adobe lid lay next to a group of smashed ollas. It was slightly convex in cross section, 2 cm in thickness and 30 cm in diameter. A small shoulder had been created on the underside when the damp clay cover was placed on a storage vessel. (Not illustrated.)

5. STONE ARTIFACTS

It is remarkable that from the Punta de Agua sites such a relatively small collection of stone tools was found. Projectile points and metates were especially notable for their scarcity. Only from two locations was anything found resembling a complete assemblage of normal household tools. For all intents and purposes, it seems the villagers always had time to remove valuable tools from an abandoned house.

Of more than passing interest were two slate palettes of Rillito phase cremations, a good range of stone bowls, an interesting mortar for red pigment, and a well-executed bird effigy.

PROJECTILE POINTS AND DRILLS

From the five larger sites only eight complete and three fragmentary points were collected. Four of these were gathered from the surface. There was a wide range of sizes and shapes involved (Fig. 5.1).

Arizona BB:13:50

The single point from this large site came from Test 3. It is leaf-shaped with a concave base, measures 4 by 2.2 cm, and is made from light brown chert (Fig. 5.lc).

Fig. 5.1. Projectile points. *a,* Thick, leaf-shaped with slight side notches; *b,* Triangular with side notches and concave base forming long basal spurs; *c,* Leaf-shaped with concave base; *d,* Drill; *e,* Small, triangular, serrated, fire-blackened; *f,* Small, triangular, serrated; *g,* Thin, triangular, serrated with concave base; *h,* Large, leaf-shaped.

86 STONE ARTIFACTS

Arizona BB:13:16

From House 6 came a small, triangular, serrated point of chert. It is fire-blackened (Fig. 5.1e).

Arizona BB:13:41

On the surface was an essentially triangular, siltstone point with wide side notches and concave base forming long basal spurs (Fig. 5.1b). On the floor of House 15 lay a thick leaf-shaped point with slight side notches (Fig. 5.1a). The last point came from House 11. It is a common, small, triangular type with serrations and a concave base (Fig. 5.1f).

Arizona BB:13:43

Two dissimilar points were recovered—one a thin, serrated, triangular chalcedony point with the tip missing and a concave base (Fig. 5.1g); the other, a large leaf-shaped blade, with secondary flake removal and retouched edges, was perhaps used as a knife or could have been hafted (Fig. 5.1h).

The only two surviving stone drills were both from Arizona BB:13:41. A complete specimen picked up on the surface was formed from a flake of fine-grained quartzite. The upper body is oval; the point was pressure flaked to form a four-sided tip (Fig. 5.1d).

TURQUOISE
Arizona BB:13:50

Turquoise Beads. Two perforated beads came from Test 41 and House 22 respectively. The former measures 4 mm and the latter 7 mm in diameter. (Not illustrated.)

Turquoise Disc. From House 2 a thick, polished, disc 8 mm in diameter was recovered. It is a finished piece, but one surface is rougher than the other. The disc might have been prepared for inlay. (Not illustrated.)

Arizona BB:13:16

Turquoise Beads. Two thin perforated beads, one 4 mm and the other 6 mm in diameter, were the only pieces at this site. The larger specimen is fragmentary. (Not illustrated.)

CARVED STONE ORNAMENTS
Arizona BB:13:50

Nose Plug. From House 2 a nearly complete, carved, red siltstone nose plug was found. Its dimensions are 1.8 cm in length and 8 mm in diameter. In the center portion, a deep low U-shaped cut, 6 mm long and 3 mm deep, had been removed. (Not illustrated.)

Bird Effigy Pendant. In Test 1, near House 2, a complete highly stylized, red siltstone bird pendant was found (Fig. 5.2). Through the body a biconical transverse hole had been drilled. The effigy is triangular in cross section. The head is set off by a deep incision around the circumference. On the back one vertical line with three and four diagonal flanking lines on the sides appear to be formal representations of folded wings. Below these a horizontal incision separates the tail from the back, both being in the same plane. The breast is keel-shaped and curves down under the tail. Cross dimensions are height, 3.1 cm; width, 1.7 cm; and thickness, 1.5 cm.

Although a search was made for similar stone effigies in archaeological contexts, nothing was found. However, descriptions of Zuni fetishes made by Cushing (1883:Plates I, II, III, and VII, 29-31) almost exactly fit the specimen from Arizona BB:13:50. It is, according to Cushing, a representation of the eagle, the Hunter God of the upper regions. The Zuni in historic times chose a similar red stone and made simple but effective stylized incisions for the wings and tail. The Zuni fetishes were also pierced through the breast for suspension from the roof of a house. The groove about the tail and the flat back facilitated the placement of a stone point and wrapping.

Fig. 5.2. Bird effigy pendant.

Arizona BB:13:16

Mica Disc. A large perforated mica disc about 4.5 cm in diameter was saved from House 6. (Not illustrated.)

PALETTES

The series of slate and schist palettes from the Punta de Agua sites parallels the sequence originally proposed so concisely by Haury (Gladwin and others 1937:121-126). Only the types belonging to the Rillito and Rincon phases are represented. These are strictly analogous to those found in the Santa Cruz and Sacaton phases in the Gila Basin. The palettes from the Hodges site stand in the same relationship (Officer 1961:I:50-53). The inven-

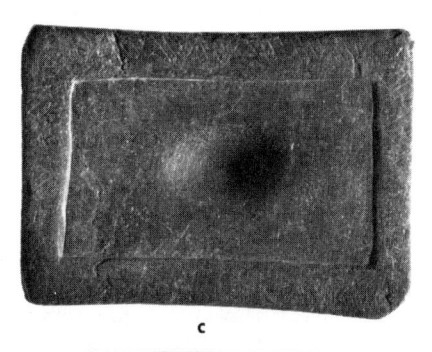

STONE ARTIFACTS

The one whole palette came from House 12, a storehouse that produced a large assortment of ollas, vegetal material, minerals, and carved stone bowls (Fig. 5.3c). The mixing surface is set off by a low sculptured border of hatched triangles. The sides are slightly concave and lack any notching or grooves on the edge. The interesting feature of this palette is an oval basin in the center of the grinding surface. The dimensions are 12 by 8.5 by 1.0 cm.

A corner fragment from House 10 is similar in concept to the complete specimen, but the border is higher. Poorly executed hatched triangles are analogous to the previous design. The sides are also concave.

The three remaining fragments are dissimilar and the only common trait is their crudeness. Test 50 produced a corner fragment of a thin 4 mm, flat, undecorated palette. It is a slab of schist with no improvement other than its smoothed edges.

The fragments from Houses 22 and 23 bear out the degeneration in palette style at the end of the Sedentary period. These two houses formed a cultural unit of the late Rincon phase. The palette from House 22 is composed of an irregular slab of slate 8 mm thick that bears no decorative elements. The edges have been roughly shaped. The specimen from House 23 is a corner piece of a sandstone slab 1.3 cm thick. The edges were trimmed by the removal of flakes.

Arizona BB:13:16
RILLITO PHASE

The two surviving complete (repaired) palettes of late Colonial period type (Gladwin and others 1937:Plate CL) were fine examples of the carefully carved variety with integral sculptured bird or snake forms at one or both ends (Fig. 5.3b, a). The first, from Broadside 11, has concave sides and a raised border with four longitudinal grooves, side notches, and a conventionalized bird carved at each end. An X-ray photograph indicated that an incrustation was probably a lead compound. Its dimensions are 14 by 8.5 by 1.0 cm. The second, from House 4, is longer and narrower and was apparently discarded after a hole had worn through the concave grinding surface. Its border is incised with hatched opposed triangles in a running pattern. Ends and sides are concave. At one end a pair of abstract snakes was sculptured. A biconical hole pierces each body. The head was carved as if one viewed the snake from above, both eyes being visible. The dimensions of the specimen are 15.3 by 7.5 by 1.0 cm. The lower part of the mixing surface is incrusted with lead as revealed by an X-ray photograph. Some of this lead compound had been transformed into a green glaze (a lead silicate). [The X-ray photographs cited above

Fig. 5.3 Palettes. *a, b,* Carved schist palettes with animal effigy handles (Rillito phase); *c,* Schist palette with shallow basin (Rincon phase); *d,* Flat slab without a raised border (Rincon phase).

tory comprises ten whole or fragmentary palettes, two of which are good examples of Rillito phase types; the remainder are all of Rincon provenience. The four best examples are shown in Figure 5.3.

Arizona BB:13:50
RINCON PHASE

One complete palette and four fragments from this large site reveal the typical Sedentary period characteristics.

were taken by Dr. Walter Birkby, Human Identification Laboratory, Department of Anthropology, University of Arizona, negative numbers 442 and 443.]

The use of lead carbonates on palettes led Haury (Gladwin and others 1937:163-167) to some interesting speculation on the character of the physical effects resulting from heating such a compound in a hot fire. It was suggested that, since most palettes bearing the incrustation were associated with cremations as offerings, the startling changes in color and the pyrotechnics accompanying the heating might have been part of a shaman's bag of tricks.

In any event, of the two incrusted palettes discussed above, only one, from Broadside 11, was found in the vicinity of a cremation offering. Just 50 cm away from Cremation 4 a small collection of stone (one handstone and one cylindrical bowl) had been assembled as a burial offering. The close proximity of the broken palette to this cremation might indicate it was originally a part of the cache. The second lead incrusted palette came from a mixed fill position near the late Rincon House 4, the construction of which could have been disturbed by an earlier burial just a few meters west of the main zone.

It should be noted that the fragment of a palette found in a cache with Cremation 7 could have been used in a similar burial rite. This cremation was dated to the first part of the Rincon phase and thus, by inference, indicated a persistence of two traditions—both the desire for magical effects and the placement of a stone offering cache near the deceased at the same time or after the burial.

RINCON PHASE

In the late proveniences at Arizona BB:13:16, one complete specimen and three fragments were identified typologically as belonging with the carelessly made palettes of the Sedentary period.

On the floor of House 4 was a rectangular, flat slab without a raised border (Fig. 5.3d). The grinding surface is, however, outlined by incised margins containing squared, interlocking scrolls.

A corner of a Rincon phase palette was part of a stone offering accompanying Cremation 7. This specimen is the only one fashioned from a fine-grained stone resembling quartzite. The border is on the same plane as the mixing surface with a running design of chevrons comprising the decoration. The palette is about 1.0 cm thick.

In the fill of House 6, part of an edge of a thin, schist palette shows a slightly raised border with hatched pendant triangles. It is 3 mm in thickness.

A corner fragment of a thin palette similar to the complete one above was also found in the fill of House 4. The border was, again, not raised. It is outlined by narrow incisions which owe their alignment to a chevron pattern originating at the corner. It is also 3 mm thick.

Arizona BB:13:41
RINCON PHASE

Half of a characteristic Sedentary period palette was recovered on the surface of this site. This slab also has a slightly raised border set off from the mixing surface by a deeper incision. The running design on the border consists of crudely etched pendant triangles filled with irregular hatching. The dimensions of the existing half are 6 by 6.8 by 0.5 cm.

STONE BOWLS
Arizona BB:13:50

Four complete carved stone bowls (Fig. 5.4a, b, and f) and one fragment survived. The ornamentation is all of simple geometric elements except for the crude bowl from House 25 (Fig. 5.4a) which bears discontinuous, incised lines about the circumference, giving an impression of a snake.

HOUSE 5: FILL

A small low bowl of sandstone had a deep incision about the circumference near the flat base (Fig. 5.4b). The upper portion of the exterior is decorated with a continual series of Xs. The rim is flat and smooth.

HOUSE 12: FLOOR

Two whole vessels were on the floor of this storeroom. The first is a heavy, bulbous bowl with incised triangles, each pendant from a horizontal line near the rim. The second bowl, flattened oval in shape, has a flat rim that originally was embellished by a running zigzag line which has been worn away except for one section comprising about 60 degrees of arc. The dimensions are 8.0 cm in greatest diameter, 2.5 cm in height, and 1.5 cm in depth.

A fragment, containing part of the exterior cross-hatched incisions on a high, slightly bulbous bowl, was found outside House 12.

HOUSE 25: FLOOR

A crude, asymmetrical bowl had withstood a fire which blackened one side and the base (Fig. 5.4a). One edge of the rim is about 1.0 cm higher than the opposite rim. Undulating, discontinuous, horizontal incisions might have been an attempt to represent the common snake symbol. A few groups of three or more vertical lines were cut near the base and up to the rim, where they created small notches.

STONE ARTIFACTS 89

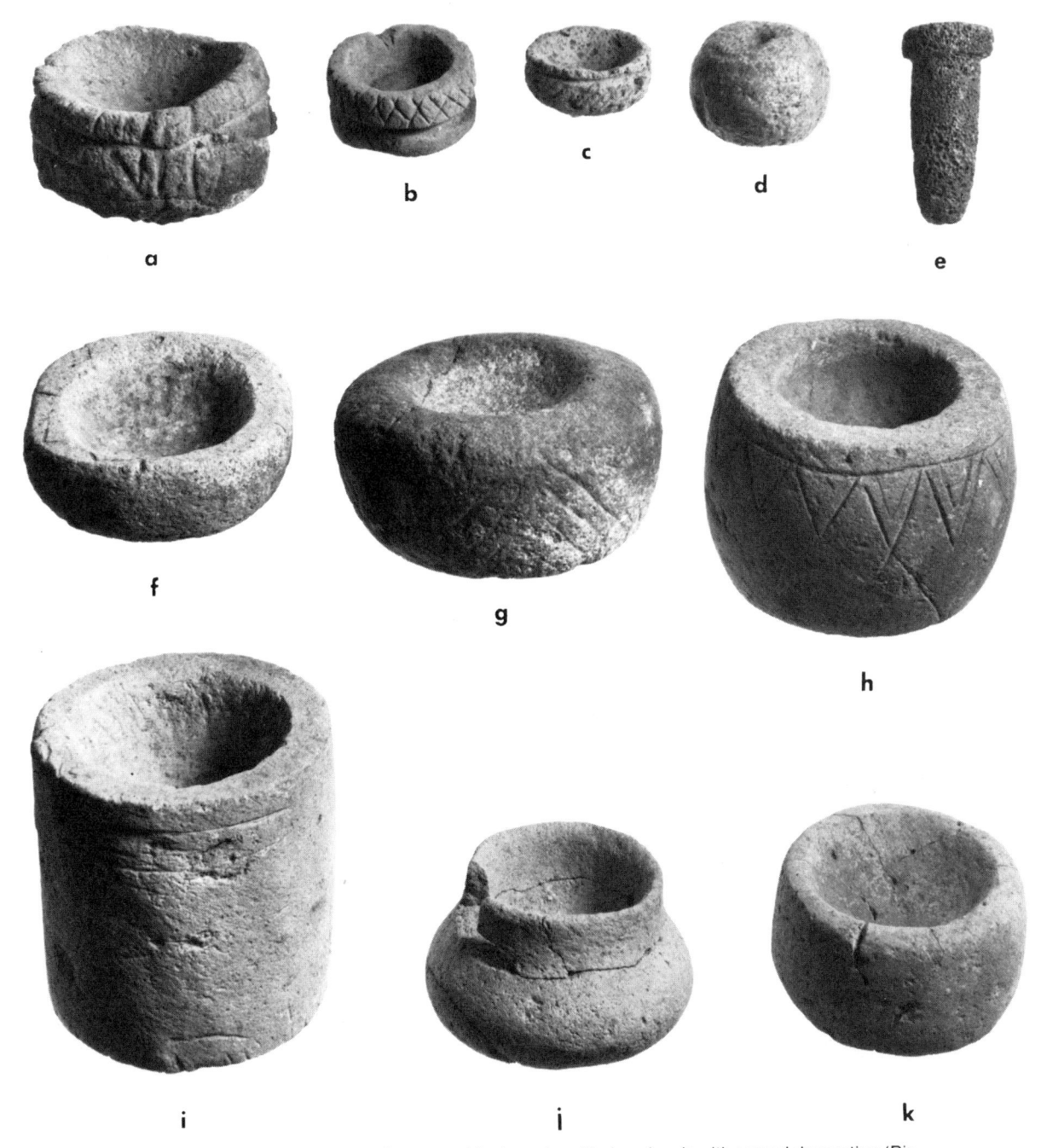

Fig. 5.4. Stone bowls and miscellaneous objects. *a, b, c,* Various bowls with carved decoration (Rincon phase); *d,* Rounded stone with small depression; *e,* "Medicine stone" of carved tuff; *g,* Shallow bowl or *incensario; f, h,* Bowls for paint preparation (House 12, Arizona BB:13:50); *i-k,* Plain stone bowls from cremation caches (Arizona BB:13:16).

Arizona BB:13:16
CREMATION 4: CACHE

One tall, cylindrical bowl, poorly finished, was in association with a small handstone and with a sculptured schist palette (Fig. 5.4i) as part of Cremation 4, an offering cache just 50 cm away from the urn. Of sandstone and easily carved, this bowl might have been specially prepared for the burial. The cremation belonged to the Rillito phase.

CREMATION 7: CACHE

Two small, plain, carved bowls were in a context similar to Cremation 4. The fragmentary quartzite palette (mentioned on page 88) was with the bowls. The first is low and cylindrical in shape, slightly convex, with a shallow basin (Fig. 5.4k). The second is shaped as a miniature globular jar (Fig. 5.4j). Perhaps these two bowls were also completed expressly for the burial. Both bowls were found in fractured condition and had perhaps passed through the crematory fire.

Arizona BB:13:41
HOUSE 13: FLOOR

A miniature bowl of tuff bears exterior incisions consisting of a horizontal line near the rim and a band of continuous chevron elements below (Fig. 5.4c).

Arizona BB:13:43
HOUSE 2: FLOOR

A rounded stone had been pecked to shape with a flat base (Fig. 5.4g). Further pecking made a shallow basin set within a wide rim. The type has often been labeled an *incensario*. Exterior incisions are a series of nested chevrons pendant from the rim.

AXES AND MAULS
Arizona BB:13:50
HOUSE 3: FILL

A complete three-quarter grooved axe was recovered here (Fig. 5.5b). It showed secondary use as a hammer on both ends. The original blade on the bit end had been modified by this use. Interestingly, the axe is not symmetrical at the head. The original piece of diorite carries flake scars from ancient fractures, which give the head a lopsided outline.

HOUSE 22

An excellent complete axe lay on the remains of a caliche mixing basin outside the entry of House 22 (Fig. 5.5a). Of green diorite, it is well polished with a three-quarter groove measuring 3.0 cm.

Arizona BB:13:16

Two small pieces of broken axes comprise the total from this site. One, bearing part of the three-quarter groove, was located in Trench 9 (Fig. 5.5d). The fragment from House 6 has a raised ridge on both sides of the groove.

TEST 89

A complete three-quarter grooved maul made from vesicular basalt came from this late Rincon provenience (Fig. 5.5c). The maul was hafted not in the center but near one end. It was pecked to shape, but the nature of the rough rock precludes a regular form.

ARROWSHAFT TOOLS
Arizona BB:13:16
TRENCH 9

A broken water-smoothed pebble with a transverse groove is the only tool of its kind found at Punta de Agua. It was made from granite with a groove 2.0 cm

Fig. 5.5 Axes and mauls. *a*, Three-quarter groove axe of green diorite; *b*, Three-quarter groove axe with battering on both ends; *c*, Three-quarter groove maul; *d*, Fragmentary three-quarter groove axe.

wide and about 3 mm deep. Its dimensions are 10 by 6 by 4.5 cm. (Not illustrated.)

HOUSE 6: FLOOR

From this unit came an oval sandstone pebble with a smoothed transverse groove. Erosion had obliterated part of the groove. The abrasive quality of the stone would place this tool in the category of a shaft smoother. Its dimensions are 10 by 7.5 by 2.5 cm with the groove being 6 mm deep. (Not illustrated.)

MISCELLANEOUS STONE ARTIFACTS
Arizona BB:13:16
TEST 10

From this site came the single example of a class of objects commonly designated "medicine stones" (Fig. 5.4e). Of dark porous lava, it features a flat round base and an undercut shoulder from which a long tapering body extends.

Arizona BB:13:49
MOUND I

A shaped, discoidal, polished stone with a conical drilled hole at the top and base cannot be properly classified (Fig. 5.4d).

METATES

Surprisingly, from all the habitation sites, just four of the 22 metate specimens are complete. For analysis in this section, three types of basic grinding implements are included in the metate category:

Types	Number Found
Trough Metates	
(a) fully shaped	15
(b) trough in boulder	1
Basin Metates	2
Slab Metates	
(a) thin slab with flat grinding surface	3
(b) slab on boulder	1

As the greatest number of houses belong to the Rincon phase, no clear changes in the use of the metates or in activities associated with their use are obvious. The scarcity of these tools was noted previously. After a death and before a house was burned, the important tools and vessels were removed to be used again.

Of the 16 examples of trough metates, 15 were pecked to shape, while the other one was set in a large unshaped boulder (Fig. 5.6b). The latter was found with the original mano (Fig. 5.6d) in association. The boulder slab metate (Fig. 5.6a) was also found in

Fig. 5.6. Metate-mano pairs. *a, c,* Found in association (House 9, Arizona BB:13:50); *b, d,* Found in association (House 9, Arizona BB:13:16).

92 STONE ARTIFACTS

association with a mano (Fig. 5.6c). Four of the trough metates should be classed as incipient types since wear had not produced a deep enough channel to leave vertical edges.

The well-worn trough metates tend to be wider and would require a two-hand mano. The surviving boulder metates and the fragments of incipient trough types are narrower and a smaller one-hand mano would be sufficient.

MANOS

All the manos from the sites near Punta de Agua will be grouped together for analysis. A selection showing the range of size and shape is illustrated in Figure 5.7. Of the 102 whole or fragmentary specimens, all had a single working face. The lengths range from about 10 cm to 23 cm. An arbitrary division was set up here to separate one-hand from two-hand manos. Those measuring about 20 cm or more (29 percent) are considered two hand manos. They fit the deeper trough metates which average about 20 cm in width.

Fig. 5.7. Manos. *a-h*, Unifacial manos; *i*, Natural triface mano; only one facet used.

A few manos have natural depressions along an edge which had been enlarged as finger holds. Some of the natural pebbles were selected for their triangular cross section which afforded better gripping quality. One in particular gives the impression of a triface mano, but only one of the faces was used for grinding (Fig. 5.7i).

Most manos are well-worn specimens of vesicular basalt (average dimensions 18 by 10 by 3 cm), quite flat transversely, and convex in longitudinal cross section with ends curved and smoothed from use in trough metates. This type had been originally pecked over the entire body to obtain the desire shape. A few mano blanks, showing the unused shape, confirm this technique. The balance of the manos are shaped from andesite, granite, quartzite, and sandstone.

Occasionally a water-smoothed stone of suitable shape was picked up and used without alteration. The mano found in a pit with the boulder metate in House 9 (Arizona BB:13:16) is a good example of such practice (Fig. 5.6d).

MORTARS

Four whole or fragmentary mortars were identified. Of these, the sole complete specimen is a specialized paint grinder which has two small grinding stones in association from House 19A at Arizona BB:13:50 (Fig. 5.8).

The scarcity of mortars probably reflects the same conditions noted in the metate discussion—they were valuable property and were portable. No bedrock mortars exist along this part of the Santa Cruz River. That a greater number of portable mortars existed may be inferred from the discovery of at least 17 large and small pestles in and around the Punta de Agua sites. That many species of beans and seeds, in addition to corn, were crushed to be utilized by the Indians is evident from the description of charred remains in Chapter 8.

Arizona BB:13:50
HOUSES 15 and 16

From each of these units a fragment of a deep vesicular basalt mortar was found; one was on the floor, the other in the fill. The portions fitted together. The houses were about 15 m apart, but the former was Rincon and the latter was Rillito in date.

HOUSE 19A

The small mortar found inverted on the floor of this Rillito phase unit is notable for the direct association of two well-shaped small pestles or hand-held grinders. The mortar and grinders are stained red from reduction of hematite for paint (Fig. 5.8).

STONE ARTIFACTS 93

Fig. 5.8. Mortar with two grinding stones.

Fig. 5.9. Large pestles.

Fig. 5.10. Small pestles. *a,* Small, irregular, fist-sized with convex grinding face; *b-e,* Shaped, tapering with working area on narrow end; *f,* Completely finished working tip.

The round hole is a relatively shallow, smooth depression with a smaller nipple-like concavity at the bottom. Evidently the larger pestle, which fits the larger diameter, was a primary grinder and the smaller became the secondary grinder for use in the lower concavity.

The mortar is shaped from an irregular slab of volcanic rock, 28 by 20 by 6 cm. Only the top of the slab has been pecked and smoothed to form a basin-like surface over most of the area.

PESTLES

The total of 18 pestles from all the sites may be grouped into three types. The first comprises long, crude basaltic stones which have been shaped by pecking. These show use as pounders on both ends. The lengths vary from about 26 to 40 cm. These heavy tools probably were not utilized with a mortar but served as a general crushing implement (Fig. 5.9).

The second most common type may be described as a shaped, tapering pestle with the principal working area on the narrow end. These were made from naturally tapering stones that required minimum effort to complete. A variety of this type shows a completely finished and rounded working tip (Fig. 5.10f).

A third type was a small, irregular, fist-sized stone with a well-smoothed convex grinding face (Fig. 5.10a). The illustrated example still bears the evidence of red paint and most likely was utilized in the same manner as the two paint grinders with the mortar at House 19A (Arizona BB:13:50).

ANVILS

In unrecorded numbers many large irregular stone blocks or water-worn cobbles were a common feature on floors of houses at each site. They were usually situated near the hearth and often surrounded by a variety of smaller stone tools. (Not illustrated.)

Their flat exposed surfaces appear to have served as an anvil (nether stone) upon which flaking or hammering took place. Only one specimen had been shaped to any degree. From House 2 (Arizona BB:13:41) a large (25 by 15 by 10 cm) loaf-shaped quartzite stone had been pecked about its circumference. The top surface carries the typical pitting from use as an anvil.

HANDSTONES

The handstones include a wide range of tools that have performed, in many cases, more than one function. The common denominator for all is that each could be held in one hand while completing a variety of tasks. The variety of types chosen from 94 examples is shown in Figure 5.11.

For identification, the main characteristic is a generally round-to-oval stone which has been shaped by pecking (Fig. 5.11g-i). Often, in the case of irregular shapes, it is impossible to tell whether or not the final shape was reached by purposeful shaping or through use.

Most seem to have been used as abraders or pecking stones and were worked around the whole circumference. In addition, some of the oval stones bear one or two polished surfaces that probably were the result of use on a slab metate.

There is a smaller group that resembles miniature manos. The common shape is subrectangular with one or two polished surfaces (Fig. 5.11a-f).

The range in diameter of the round or oval type extends from about 6 to 12 cm. A wide range of natural material was used, the most numerous being quartzite, granite, sandstone, and fine-grained basalt. Apparently stones were chosen for specific tasks that could be better accomplished by using either a fine-grained or coarse-grained tool.

Fig. 5.11. Handstones, hammerstones, chopper. *a-f,* Subrectangular handstones; *g-i,* Round-to-oval handstones; *j, k,* Hammerstones; *l,* Chopper.

CHOPPERS

The tools designated choppers are the conventional flaked pebbles, either uniface of biface in cross section. The flakes were removed in a manner which created sharp working edges on pebbles that originally had the same characteristics as those called hammerstones. Only 22 choppers were retrieved from all the sites. Of these, just four are of the bifacial variety. A typical unifacial chopper is illustrated in Figure 5.11 l.

HAMMERSTONES

This group is another general classification for 55 specimens used for hammering or abrading, but of irregular shapes.

The type is characterized by fist-sized, water-worn cobbles, of fine-grained volcanic materials, which have had flakes removed either during or before use; pounding surface may occur completely around the body. Less common were a wide selection of natural elongated stones often showing use at both ends (Fig. 5.11j and k).

POTTERY POLISHERS

This classification includes the series of natural water-worn pebbles that nearly fit the hand and bear one or more polished facets. By convention they are labeled pottery polishers and ethnographic analogies do exist for this use. Such interpretation does not rule out alternate functions for other jobs. Many of these pebbles originally had attractive shapes, probably causing them to be picked up, at first, as curiosities. Literally hundreds of similar stones were found at these sites which did not show indications of use.

A cache of these stones from House 6 (Arizona BB:13:43) revealed 6 polishers of varying shapes with some still carrying traces of red pigment. Five additional polishers were in the fill nearby. These are all illustrated in Figure 5.12. In spite of the great divergence of shapes, by inference these were all used at different stages of pottery fabricating. The majority of the polishers are generally categorized as elongated pebbles averaging about 8 cm in length.

KNIVES AND SAWS

In Figure 5.13 a selection of eight knives and saws are shown from a total of 35 implements or fragments. The larger type (Fig. 5.13d and f) is, by convention, designated a mescal knife. Throughout southern Arizona from the Gila Basin to Paloparado, these tools were made from tabular or schistose gray or reddish slabs. The thin cutting edge may be a natural fracture or may be retouched. A smaller variety, fitting the hand, often was made from siltstone (Fig. 5.13a).

Fig. 5.12. Polishing tools.

Fig. 5.13. Knives and saws. *a*, Small knife; *b, c, e*, Saws; *d, f*, Large knives; *g*, Specialized knife.

The saws were commonly made from the same material (Fig. 5.13b, c, and e). Common to all these cutting tools was a tapering cross section. The small variation of each type tended to be concave on the cutting edge. One combination tool from House 2 (Arizona BB:13:16) exhibited dual working edges—a saw on one side, a knife on the other. (Not illustrated.)

To make a saw, transverse incisions about 4 mm apart were cut on the thin edge. An interesting example (Fig. 5.13e) had incisions, as decoration, running up the short sides and across the top.

A specialized knife (incomplete: Fig. 5.13g) from House 5 (Arizona BB:13:16) could be a representation of a knife-scraper. Perhaps the wide protruding lugs at the top also supported a haft. This type has only been reported from the Papaguería. Specimens from Paloparado (DiPeso 1956:454) are direct analogies. Wear striations run perpendicular to the cutting edge.

A COMPLETE STONE TOOL "KIT"
Arizona BB:13:41
HOUSE 15

In Figure 5.14 a complete stone tool "kit" is portrayed. All the tools were on the floor of House 15. The structure had been consumed by a hot fire before the tools could be removed. This illustration shows, better than words, the range of stone to be expected in any family inventory. Flakes, gouges, knives, scrapers, choppers, handstones, hammerstones, manos, and pottery polishers are included.

It goes without saying that many items had no one specific function. Our impression is that there has been an excess of typology and taxonomy for generalized stone tools. We have, therefore, tried to keep the descriptions here to a minimum.

MINERALS

The recovery of minerals from each of the principal sites at Punta de Agua did not reveal any unusual ores or associated practices. The samples were, in descending frequency of their occurrence, red hematite, azurite, malachite, specular hematite, and limonite.

Arizona BB:13:50

House 12, an obvious storeroom, had a group of ollas which contained all of the minerals mentioned above. They were accompanied by an assortment of grinding bowls and palettes. Moreover, hematite occurred in Houses 5, 6, 7, 11, 16, and 20 as well as in

Fig. 5.14. Stone tool kit from Arizona BB:13:41, House 15.

Tests 27 and 63. Azurite was found in Houses 10 and 20; malachite was located in House 16 and 20.

Arizona BB:13:16

Hematite was used in House 4, Test 89 (a ramada work area), and was dumped in Trash Pit 2 near House 5. Azurite was found in Test 6, while a mixture of chrysocolla and malachite was located in Trench 17, Level 2.

Arizona BB:13:41

Hematite was found only in House 9 and in Trench 19.

Arizona BB:13:43

Cache 3 contained azurite and malachite. House 4 had malachite on the floor. Only in House 7 did hematite occur.

Comment

The sources of the hematites are unknown. These minerals were commonly distributed through the Southwest and enjoyed much trade popularity. As for the different copper ores, the indigenous people did not have to look far for outcrops. About one mile to the west lay the Twin Buttes mining district that gave rise to the open pits of today.

6. OTHER TECHNOLOGY

BONE ARTIFACTS

Just six cut bone artifacts were recovered from all the Punta de Agua sites. Each of these is a fragment of a bone awl. They all appear to have been manufactured from split metapodials of either deer or mountain sheep. Five of the specimens were charred by fire; the remaining one consists of only the tip.

SHELL ARTIFACTS

Considering the extent of testing at Punta de Agua, not many examples of complete shell items were found. There was, however, good evidence that shell working was practiced at the sites. Partly finished ornaments and discarded pieces testify to local enterprise. The following species were identified.

Marine	Freshwater	Terrestrial
Glycymeris gigantea	Anodonta sp.	Succinea sp.
Glycymeris maculatus		
Laevicardium		
Haliotis cracherodii		
Haliotis sp.		
Olivella gracilis		
Trigoniocardia biangulata		
Conus sp.		
Pyrene sp.		
Spondylus		

Of the marine species, all may be found in the Gulf of California with the exception of *Haliotis,* which is coastal Californian in habitat.

The well preserved *Succinea* shell was not in an archaeological context. It is a recent land snail.

In Figure 6.1 examples of the most popular ornaments, fashioned from *Glycymeris* shells, are depicted. By convention, the larger specimens are usually called bracelets (Fig. 6.1c, d, and e). These three were found in a cache at Arizona BB:13:16. Grinding has exposed a hole through each umbo; the holes were enlarged by a reaming operation. This fact has led some archaeologists to consider the ornaments as large pendants. One of the cut shells has four parallel incisions arranged in clusters of two on the lower edge.

A smaller *Glycymeris* bracelet (Fig. 6.1a) with a perforated umbo was found in House 22 (Arizona BB:13:50). The smallest shell (Fig. 6.1b) is the best example of nine fragments of immature *Glycymeris* shells cut for a ring.

A wide variety of carved shell ornaments are shown in Figure 6.2. The first is a polished *Glycymeris* pendant (Fig. 6.2a) from House 3 at Arizona BB:13:50. The next two (Fig. 6.2b and c) are *Laevicardium* pendants discovered near House 7 at Arizona BB:13:16. The purpose of the central hole in the larger is unknown. A typical *Conus* tinkler (Fig. 6.2d) had the spire ground off and a conical hole drilled at the tip.

An unusual *Trigoniocardia* pendant (Fig. 6.2e) from House 15 at Arizona BB:13:50 had the hinge removed before an irregular suspension hole was cut. The next specimen carved from a large *Glycymeris* valve (Fig. 6.2f) is well shaped and polished but its final use is problematical. A series of short, parallel incisions appear on the bottom edge. The *Laevicardium* (Fig. 6.2g) disc has well polished edges and is also difficult to classify. Perhaps these last two were potter's tools.

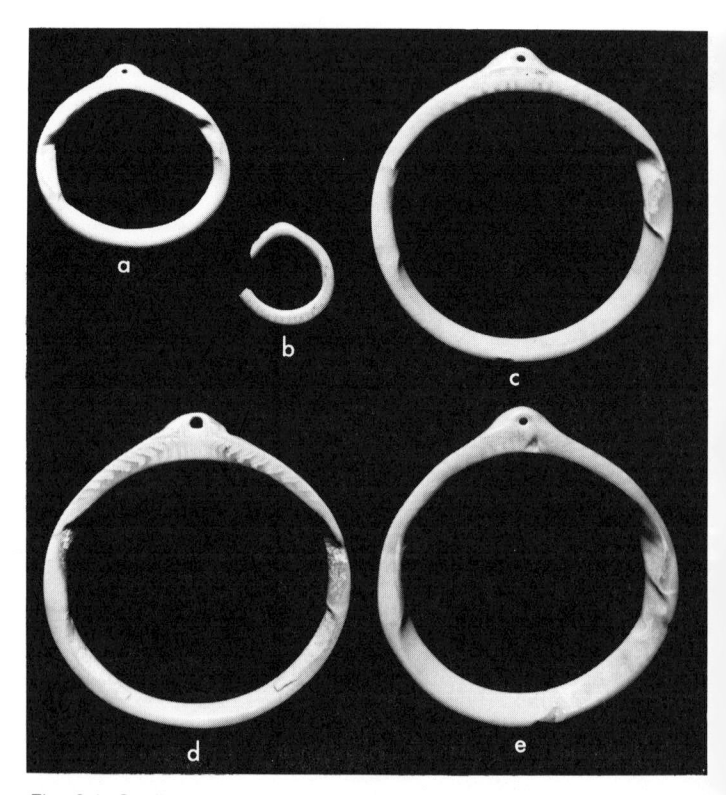

Fig. 6.1. Shell bracelets. *a,* Small *Glycymeris* bracelet; *b,* Fragmentary *Glycymeris* ring; *c, d, e,* Large *Glycymeris* bracelets.

Fig. 6.2. Various shell ornaments. *a, Glycymeris* pendant; *b, c, Laevicardium* pendants; *d, Conus* tinkler; *e, Trigoniocardia* pendant; *f,* Shaped and polished *Glycymeris* shell; *g, Laevicardium* disc; *h, Anodonta* pendant in the shape of a snake; *i, Anodonta* pendant; *j-m, Haliotis* pendants.

In the storeroom at Arizona BB:13:50 (House 12) a delicate pendant in the form of a coiled snake was made from a part of a nacreous *Anodonta* shell (Fig. 6.2h). From another piece of this fragile irridescent shell, a crude pendant was formed (Fig. 6.2i). The *Anodonta*, a fresh water clam, is an excellent supplementary food supply where found in abundance.

The last four illustrated shells are all examples of *Haliotis* pendants of varying sizes. Two shells (Fig. 6.2j and l), accompanied Cremation 1 in the fill of House 2 (Arizona BB:13:50). When the burial was exposed, parts of at least three broken pendants were leaning vertically against an inverted late Rincon cover bowl. Each pendant probably had a biconical hole drilled at the narrow end as seen in Figure 6.21. Another broken pendant (Fig. 6.2k) was discovered in House 3 at Arizona BB:13:50, presumably the dwelling in which the deceased person (Cremation 1) had lived.

The last *Haliotis* pendant (repaired) came from the late trash dumps at Arizona BB:13:49 (Fig. 6.2m).

The people at Punta de Agua did much of their own shell carving. Considerable residue from fabricating operations was strewn throughout the villages. The most interesting example of incomplete manufacture was a small *Glycymeris* valve that has the crown ground flat almost to the point of producing an opening in the center of the shell.

In the shell inventory, but not illustrated, were three *Olivella* beads that had the spires removed for stringing, two incomplete needles or awls made from *Glycymeris* shells or broken bracelets, and from House 13 (Arizona BB:13:41) 81 unidentified shell beads which might have been shaped from *Spondylus* shells. The beads, averaging 5 mm in diameter, had been exposed to fire but the dominance of pink, orange, and yellowish colors suggest this genus.

This modest collection shows only rudimentary carved decorations. Most common were short incised lines on the edges of discs and bracelets. The coiled snake pendant is the exception.

7. MORTUARY PRACTICES

CREMATIONS

Work at the four major sites at Punta de Agua revealed 18 cremations and two inhumations. The limits imposed by the highway right-of-way precluded the discovery of any burial zones at Arizona BB:13:41 and BB:13:43. At the latter site, in a large arroyo east of the village, one cremation exposed by erosion was salvaged. Three interesting Rillito Red-on-brown vessels were saved and are illustrated in Figure 3.2a, c, and d. This same area contained much evidence of Rillito and Tanque Verde phase occupation while the excavated portion was exclusively of the Rincon phase.

Most of the cremations were encountered at Arizona BB:13:16. Of the 15 burials, 14 were within a 22 by 16 m area suggesting a planned interment zone (Fig. 7.1). One cremation was isolated from this central burial ground. The zone was located ten meters east of the settlement on the slope leading to the upper terrace of the Santa Cruz River and represented two phases. The 7 Rillito phase burials were grouped together on higher ground, while the 7 Rincon cremations lay slightly downslope to the east. The separation of the burials into two different time periods might indicate either that perishable markers were employed or that an oral tradition persisted.

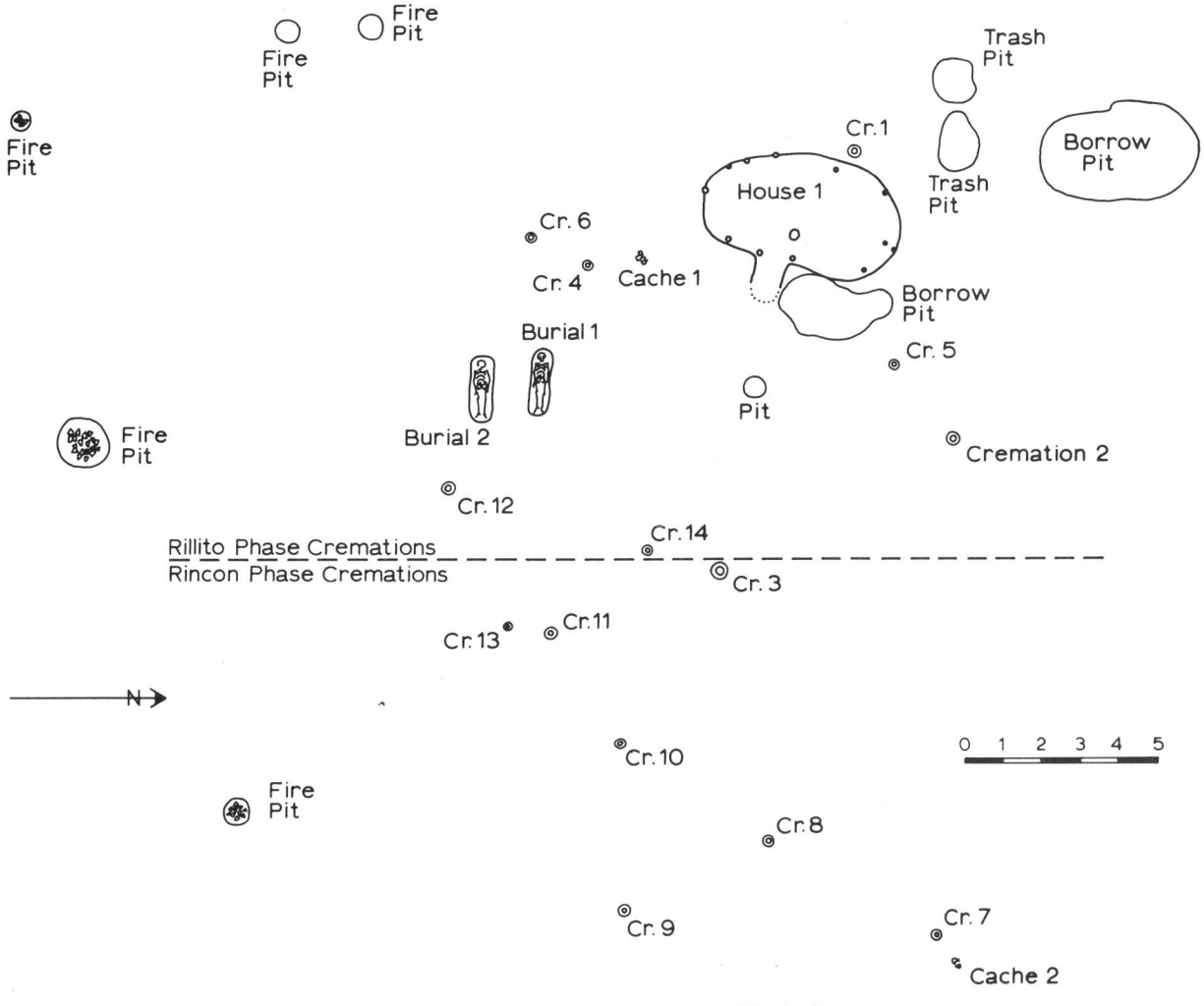

Fig. 7.1. Cremation area at Arizona BB:13:16.

The 3 remaining cremations were found at Arizona BB:13:50. The first, in the fill of House 2, was of late Rincon or perhaps early Tanque Verde date. The others, associated together on the floor of House 22, were Tanque Verde phase burials that probably represented the deceased occupants of House 18, the latest building encountered during these operations.

Even though Arizona BB:13:50 was extensively tested, the burial zones for the Rillito and the Rincon phase occupation were not revealed. As a result, we lack important data for the rapidly evolving Rincon phase occupation. Therefore, the information gathered for this phase at the Hodges site assumes greater significance in the discussion below.

Arizona BB:13:16

Each of the 14 cremations in the main zone was deposited in a small pit averaging about 50 cm deep and 30 cm wide at the bottom where the outline could be distinguished. Most pits were sunk into trash and loose fill on the edge of the ridge with only four pits reaching down to the sterile red native soil. There appeared to be no significant variations in pit shape or depth. The depth of trash and the degree of erosion of the slope determined the depth of each cremation.

All the cremations were secondary burials with two principal variations in the method of disposal. The calcined bone was gathered at the crematorium site or sites (which remain undiscovered), and then was deposited in a jar or bowl which, in turn, was set into the burial pit. When a jar was used, it was usually placed upright in the pit and it might or might not have a cover bowl (Type 1) (Fig. 7.2a). Alternatively, when the bone was set in a bowl, the bowl was inverted in the pit and often a second bowl was set in place over the first (Type 2) (Fig. 7.2b). Three of the seven Rillito phase cremations employed upright jars, while only one of the seven Rincon phase burials was placed in a jar.

The lack of personal ornaments and ceramic or stone offerings, except in two cases, is quite in contrast to burial practices in the Gila Basin and at the Hodges site. Basically, all the cremations at Punta de Agua consisted solely of the bone, a container, and usually, a cover bowl. A cache of carved stone offerings lay about 50 cm from and slightly above Cremation 4 (Rillito phase) (Fig. 7.2c) with a similar situation occurring near Cremation 7 (Rincon phase).

The isolated cremation at Arizona BB:13:16 was, technically, another variation. The bone at the bottom of the pit was covered by a variety of broken sherds. No whole or fragmentary vessel could be reconstructed.

Further details showed that four inverted bowl cremations had been "killed" by a sharp blow that pierced a hole in the base of each. These examples were equally divided between the Rillito and Rincon phases.

The containers and the cover bowls in no instance showed evidence of having passed through the orginal crematory fire.

Arizona BB:13:50

The three cremations from this site belonged to a later time period than those at Arizona BB:13:16. Cremation 1 (Type 1) consisted of an inverted early Tanque Verde phase Red-on-brown bowl over the bone. Leaning against the bowl, in a vertical position, were at least three fragments of *Haliotis* pendants. This burial was dug down into the fill of the late Rincon phase House 2. As the latest dwelling at Unit 1 was the neighboring House 3 where other *Haliotis* fragments were found, it is safe to assume House 3 to have been the house of the deceased.

Cremations 2 and 3, both Type 2, were situated opposite the entry to Tanque Verde phase House 18. They were aligned together, only 50 cm apart, resting directly on the floor of the late Rincon House 22 (Fig. 7.2d). Each of these burials was placed in an upright jar. Cremation 2 consisted of an upright large plain jar. Cremation 3 contained the remains of two or more individuals in a small plain jar with a Tanque Verde Red-on-brown cover bowl. No other offerings accompanied these late cremations. As in the first situation, we may identify House 18 as the dwelling of the deceased. Detailed provenience data on all cremations are presented in Appendix C.

Discussion

The evidence from this relatively small group of cremations covers parts of three phases, reaching from about A.D. 800 to 1200. During this stretch of time along the Santa Cruz River near historic Punta de Agua, the mode of interment showed great persistency. The same variations of urn burial were practiced, to different degrees, in each of the phases for which we have evidence.

If any selective features may be isolated from only 18 burials, the most obvious is the numerical superiority of upright jars in the Rillito phase, their eclipse during the Rincon phase, and their re-establishment as the preferred custom in the Tanque Verde phase. In order to determine the importance of this sequence, a review of the burials from the Hodges site is in order.

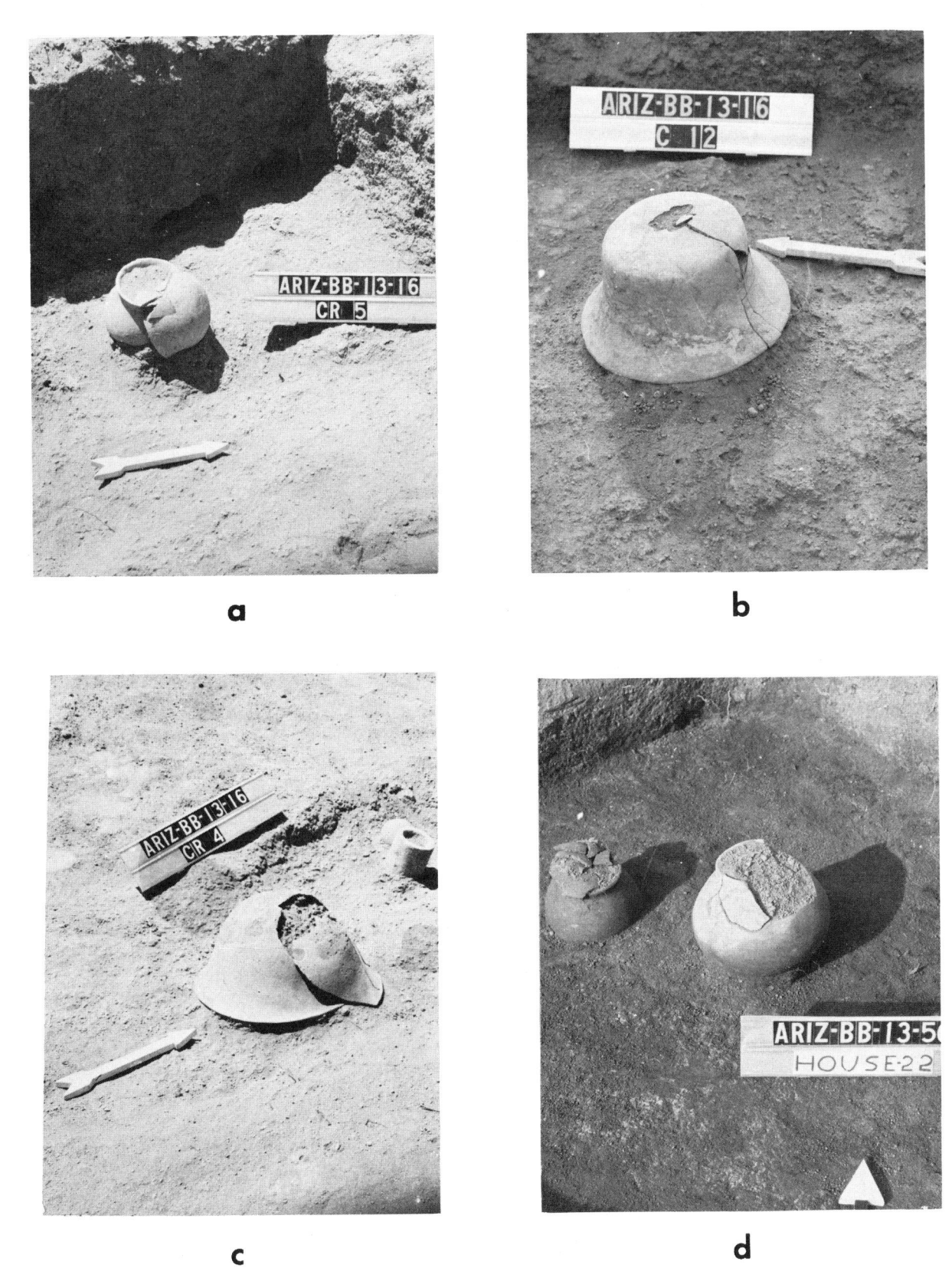

Fig. 7.2. Examples of cremations from the Rillito and Tanque Verde phases.

In general, the interments at Hodges were more varied and more elaborate. In these respects, they show more similarity to those of the Gila Basin. At Hodges, six cremations could be related to the end of the Pioneer period. The most popular were mixed burials with bone and sherds or crushed pots intermingled. One urn burial (bone in an upright jar with a cover bowl) and one primary cremation (Wasley and Johnson 1965:66-67) were found. The larger sample from the Colonial period revealed 14 mixed burials, 8 primary cremations, and 6 urn burials. The urn burials consisted of two variations similar to those at Punta de Agua. Two were in upright bowls (no jars were discovered) and 4 had inverted bowls or jar sherds over the residual bone.

During the Sedentary period the emphasis changed so that in addition to 4 primary cremations and 16 mixed burials, 21 urn burials were found. Of these, 6 were in upright jars and 15 were placed under inverted bowls or large sherds. The smaller early Classic period sample consisted of 8 urn-type and 5 mixed burials. Urn variations included 6 with upright jars and 2 with inverted bowls.

In summary, throughout the sequence at the Hodges site, the mixed burials, analogous to those in the Gila Basin, were more numerous up to the end of the Rincon phase. At that time and into the succeeding Classic period, the urn burials and their varieties replaced the other types in popularity.

Looking at the urn burials more closely, we find that the earliest were single examples of upright jar cremations occurring in the Snaketown and Cañada del Oro phases. In the Rillito phase, the innovation of inverted bowls over the bone was introduced. However, all types of urn burials still comprised a minority. Later, in the Rincon phase, all types of urn burials outnumbered all others combined. Fifteen of the 21 urn burials were of the inverted bowl type. The dominance of all kinds of urn burials continued in the early Tanque Verde phase.

The trend at Punta de Agua, therefore, generally follows the trend at Hodges. Most important is the emphasis at both sites, during the Rincon phase, of inverted bowl burials. In contrast, at Punta de Agua there was only one mixed burial encountered. The presence of mixed burials in large numbers at Hodges indicates closer ties with and influences from the Gila Basin.

Urn burials, along with inhumations, became the rule in all Hohokam early Classic period sites. In searching for the origin of urn burials, which (with one exception), are absent in the Gila district in the Sacaton phase (Johnson 1964:147-48) the data from Paloparado assume great significance. There, at a time corresponding to the Colonial and Sedentary periods, the urn burial was the dominant mode. Of 63 cremations, 44 were in upright jars and only 9 were associated with either upright or inverted bowls (DiPeso 1956:545-552). Perhaps a few of these could be of a time contemporary with the end of the Pioneer period. The indication, then, is that the area of concentration and earliest occurrence of urn burials are at Paloparado and at Hodges.

The data from the Punta de Agua district agree with the southern tradition and further concur by exhibiting the same scarcity of grave goods. The connection between the widespread use of urn cremations in the Classic period in the Hohokam homeland and its earlier acceptance across a long arc of southern Arizona was explored by DiPeso (1956:544-557).

More than ever, the settlement at Hodges, and the Tucson area in general, seem to bear material witness to the meeting of two cultural traditions, that of the Gila Basin and that of a southerly indigenous people. The evidence from Punta de Agua emphasizes the differences of burial practices in a great area which fell under Hohokam hegemony.

INHUMATIONS

Two inhumations were discovered in the cremation zone at Arizona BB:13:16. They were in parallel pits only 1 m apart near the southern edge of the burial ground (Fig. 7.1). Each was a fully extended supine burial. The skeletal material is discussed in more detail in Appendix D.

Both inhumations were lying with the head due west. This rather unusual situation plus the lack of any burial offerings or sherd material suggests that the interments may have been relatively recent. The historic Punta de Agua ranch house was just a few meters north of the site. House 2, the historic dwelling, was situated 28 m to the south.

In spite of the above observations, there is no proper reason for not considering that these two inhumations were placed in the known burial zone during the late Rincon or early Tanque Verde phase. For instance, during the 1940 season at the University Indian Ruin (Hayden 1957:97-98) one inhumation was disclosed in a similar condition with head due west. It was in an ill-defined pit with no grave furniture or associated material.

Burials 1 and 2 at Punta de Agua were, respectively, a young adult and a juvenile. The former was in a pit measuring 1.75 m in length and 25 cm in depth; the latter lay in a pit 1.60 m long and 35 cm deep with the head facing south. The pits had been cut into sterile soil from the old ground level which, in turn, was covered by about 50 cm of trashy fill.

Adding more circumstantial evidence for evaluating these inhumations as prehistoric is the recording from Snaketown of three supine burials, with the heads facing east (Gladwin and others 1937:93). One of these lacked any accompanying sherds or offerings. They were all estimated to belong to the Sacaton phase.

DEATH PRACTICES

As most of the 62 houses at Punta de Agua showed that burning completed their destruction, the question of how this occurred needs to be discussed. As only 3 houses possessed a full complement of tools and household material in place, the suggestion can be made that the houses were abandoned before burning.

In relation to this problem, the following quotation, from the journal of Father Joseph Och (1965:129) between 1755 and 1767 when he served among the Pima and Opata in Sonora, assumes more significance. The translation is by Treutlein.

They also burned a house whenever anyone died in it. At first I did not understand what caused so many fire-damaged villages. But I learned the cause, for they explained to me they no longer desired to live in a certain place because the dead one had returned to it. . . . This constant changing of huts irked me . . . . Since I forbade the burning of individual huts, and forced them to live in their old dwellings, they managed piece by piece to make over a house, even to the extent of digging out the floor deeply, to give it a different appearance and so to prevent the deceased from recognizing it.

8. FOOD RESOURCES

FAUNAL REMAINS

The meager collection of faunal bones from two seasons' work is presented in Table 8.1.

The Harris ground squirrel, cottontail, tortoise, and mule deer may still be found in the vicinity of Punta de Agua. However, it is not absolutely certain that the remains of the first three animals are prehistoric as each is a burrowing species.

The wolf-size bones are quite rare in an archaeological context. It was noted that they are larger than an average coyote.

The presence of cow bones must be connected with either the historic adobe house or the historic Punta de Agua Ranch (Arizona BB:13:18). There is no reason to suspect that they date to the Spanish frontier period.

Even though there is not much supporting evidence from the faunal remains, one would expect that the local villagers were successful hunters in their quest for rabbit, deer, and mountain sheep. It was pointed out earlier that all these species were common in the adjacent mesquite forest and in the surrounding mountains.

TABLE 8.1
Faunal Remains From Punta de Agua

Site	Provenience	Bone(s)	Common Name	Species
BB:13:16	Test 10	Skull	Harris ground squirrel	*Citellus harrisii*
	Test 8	Astragalus	Cow	*Bos*
	Trench 10	Cannon	Cow	*Bos*
	House 10	Left tibia, distal end	Desert cottontail	*Sylvilagus* sp.
	Test 7	Carrapace, plastron	Desert tortoise	*Gopherus* sp.
BB:13:41	House 14	Metapodials	Deer	*Odocoileus* sp.
BB:13:50	House 15	Scapula and fragments	Wolf	*Canis lupus* (?)

VEGETAL REMAINS

The fact that the Punta de Agua district offered a variety of opportunities for the success of cultivated plants has already been reviewed. Fortunately, from four locations, samples of carbonized plant remains were recovered. The presence of three cultigens and five wild plants has been published by Bohrer and others (1969: Table 3).

The storeroom (House 12 at Arizona BB:13:50) provided the greater part of the inventory (Table 8.2). Six of the seven identified species were found in separate storage jars. Remains of single species were found in Test 63 and House 11 at the same site. Two varieties of maize and tansy-mustard seed were stored in ollas at House 14 (Arizona BB:13:41).

There were two types of maize *(Zea mays)*. Samples of both Reventador, a popcorn, and of Onaveño, a flint corn, were distinguished. The investigators inferred that caches of Onaveño of uniform size probably were stored for planting; while Onaveño kernels showing a wide range in size most likely were stored for consumption (Bohrer and others 1969:3-4).

An important contribution to the prehistoric record for southern Arizona was the discovery of a concentration of stick-leaf *(Mentzelia* sp.*)* seeds in the large storeroom. This is the first documentation of its use in the Lower Sonoran life zone.

Jack beans *(Canavalia ensiformis)* were recovered from the same provenience. However, the researchers (Bohrer and others 1969) were cautious in their con-

TABLE 8.2
Vegetal Remains From Punta de Agua

Scientific Name	Common Name	Provenience
Descurainia sp.	Tansy-mustard	House 14 (Ariz. BB:13:41)
		Test 63 (Ariz. BB:13:50)
Zea mays 1. Reventador 2. Onaveño	Maize	House 14 (Ariz. BB:13:41) House 14 (Ariz. BB:13:41) House 11 (Ariz. BB:13:50) House 12 (Ariz. BB:13:50)
Phaseolus acutifolius var. *latifolius*	Tepary bean	House 12 (Ariz. BB:13:50)
Canavalia ensiformis	Jack bean	House 12 (Ariz. BB:13:50)
Amaranthus or *Chenopodium*	Amaranth or goosefoot	House 12 (Ariz. BB:13:50)
Prosopis	Mesquite	House 12 (Ariz. BB:13:50)
Mentzelia sp.	Stick-leaf	House 12 (Ariz. BB:13:50)
Cylindropuntia	Cholla	House 12 (Ariz. BB:13:50)

clusions. Because of a paucity of historic or prehistoric use of the species, especially in the Southwest, it was felt that the utilization of Jack beans for food was not proven.

Storage vessels filled with tansy-mustard *(Descurainia* sp.), tepary beans *(Phaseolus acutifolius* var. *latifolius),* and pigweed *(Amaranthus* or *Chenopodium)* reinforce the popularity of these staples in the drainages of the Gila and Santa Cruz rivers.

The reference to mesquite *(Prosopis juliflora)* is based on the recovery of a single pod. It is probable that the villagers depended much more on this food than the evidence shows. Of course, the most recent utilization of mesquite by the Papago depends on grinding up the pods, not the beans.

The charred cholla buds *(Cylindropuntia* sp.) are, in a fashion, another first for the record. Their use had been inferred before but this discovery provides more reliable evidence than pollen (Bohrer and others 1969:7). Of all these foods, only cholla buds are collected by the Papago today.

Notable for its absence at Punta de Agua was any residue of sahuaro seed *(Cereus giganteus).* This condition must be due to incomplete sampling of the villages. The plant was easily accessible on the slopes of nearby Black Mountain. It was a common staple at Snaketown in the Gila Basin (Bohrer and others 1969:8-9).

9. CONCLUSIONS

The nature of salvage archaeology is that it is often performed under difficult and rather restrictive conditions. Therefore, the data recovered do not always offer new insight or even permit speculations into the lifeways of past societies. An investigator is, in fact, lucky if he can expose and define new material traits. At Punta de Agua, tantalizing glimpses of new traits did present themselves. They cannot certainly be attributed to any single source, but probably are products of local innovation, of new population increments joining the existing community, or reflect indirect influence from adjacent cultural areas. In addition, a few bits of evidence hinted at the manner in which the communities at that time may have been organized.

It is clear that the excavated sites at Punta de Agua were first occupied in the Rillito phase. The architecture was conservative, preserving forms of the Pioneer period. As far as can be told, the sites reflect the growth of agricultural pursuits by indigenous people at a location with good water sources. The ceramic inventory had already diverged from that of the Hohokam proper in the Gila Basin by resuming the Red-on-brown tradition of the Mogollon or Sonoran Brownware school. The decorative elements, however, echoed the dominant traits of the Gila Basin homeland. The paucity of Pioneer settlements in southern Arizona has led most reporters to the conclusion that actual colonists from the Gila Basin acted as culture bringers, as it were, to the foragers of the southern river basins.

The most important details for understanding the culture-history at Punta de Agua were revealed by the long development during the Rincon phase. It should be noted that the estimated dates and duration of all phases, with the exception of the last part of the Rincon phase, are all extrapolations based on relative dating and comparisons of traits with the original Snaketown sequence. Pottery, cross-dated by other types secure in tree-ring placement, still is the point of departure for all correlations.

The internal changes in the Rincon phase were clearly marked by pottery seriation, architectural superposition, introduction of new architectural shapes and stylistic embellishments, change of construction methods and remodeling, and, finally, by some transitional architectural experiments. The late structures were effectively dated by archaeomagnetic dates which extended the end of the Rincon phase into the beginning of the thirteenth century.

The growing divergence of the Tucson area from the Gila Basin was emphasized by the persistence of urn burials. Invariably, cremated bone was gathered up and placed in a bowl or jar usually with another bowl as a cover. This was a favored method of disposal in prehistoric southern Arizona up to and into the Classic period. At that time, the Western Pueblo and Upper Piman practice of inhumation became widespread.

The transitional years between the late Rincon phase and the start of the Tanque Verde phase brought most of the unexpected traits including architectural innovation and ceramic experimentation.

The new architectural manifestations which were discovered consisted of raised adobe cones encasing the base of vertical roof supports. Sometimes the supports were an integral part of the structure, but this was not always the case. The interior surface of the adobe cones was impressed with reeds suggesting that the supports were either bundles of reeds or wooden poles enclosed by a reed casing. From the work at Punta de Agua no evidence of any intervillage ceremonial apparatus was forthcoming, but it is suggested here that the adobe cones are examples of the extra care one might expect to find in an intravillage structure intended for ceremonial purposes.

Ballcourts (or dance plazas) were absent. It was noted, notwithstanding, that near Martinez Hill, ballcourts have been identified. It is possible that during the Rillito and Rincon phases intervillage activities took place at such a central location. We do not know whether use of ballcourts continued into the early Classic period in the Tucson Basin. This point is stressed because so many of the transitional traits leading to the architectural and ceramic changes of the Tanque Verde phase were encountered at Punta de Agua.

The ceramic experimentation mentioned above was confined to a variety of post-reinforced, adobe-walled houses (two with a survival of the Hohokam bulbous entry). Strictly angular designs on jars and small bowls were noted together with boldly decorated outcurved bowls having designs on the interior only. No fully developed Tanque Verde Red-on-brown was associated with this late Rincon transitional variation. The exclusive geometric decoration appears to be a revival of the early Mogollon Red-on-brown tradition.

This late Rincon type was usually associated with a new polychrome composed of black and white decorations applied to Rincon red. The analysis of Rincon Polychrome, as this new type is called, showed that it reflected designs and elements found in widely disparate geographical zones. Most notable, when seeking antecedents, was the fact that two polychrome styles, Escondida Polychrome and St. Johns Polychrome, bore some of the same distinguishing characteristics.

The focal point of those sites bearing Rincon Polychrome lay along the Santa Cruz River near Tucson. In fact, the Santa Cruz River seemed to be the line of communication for the dissemination of the new pottery type. Vessels were found at the north and south extremities—one near Cashion where the Santa Cruz joins the Gila, and the other at Paloparado.

The type had a short life and narrow distribution. What motivation can be invoked for this unusual experimentation 50 to 75 years before the horizon of Gila Polychrome? If not experimentation, was it material evidence of an economic or religious elite making its presence felt and further identified by architectural innovation and concentrated settlements?

The question has been raised whether it would be better to define a new phase for this transition. Kelly (n.d.:III:71-72) tentatively proposed a Cortaro phase to balance the hypothetical Santan phase in the eastern part of the Gila Basin (Gladwin and others 1937:264). However, to base a new phase exclusively on a late type of Rincon Red-on-brown and on the elusive Rincon Polychrome seems to us to be a form of ceramic determinism.

The single piece of evidence from the Punta de Agua excavations reflecting social organization suggests that the accretion of population in the villages followed a set pattern throughout the Rincon phase. Clusters of two or more houses that seemed to be functionally and socially related were a recurring feature within the units of the individual sites. Perhaps these clusters had only an economic relationship that crosscut social ties. By now it is generally implicit in the literature that the prehistoric societies of this region were organized similarly to historic ones. Unfortunately only meager historical data are available, but patrilocality and the extended family are two basic aspects assumed to have been present. Therefore, a cluster could represent a patrilocal extended family. The basic unit, of course, was the nuclear family, the presence of which would be inferred by single or isolated houses. The suggestion is offered that the house clusters acted as an integrating factor within the villages. The length of time involved in the transformation of the Rincon ceramic, architectural, and settlement styles into those which heralded the Tanque Verde is uncertain. According to archaeomagnetic dates (Table 2.1) the typical bulbous entry, late Rincon phase home was in use up to A.D. 1215. Regrettably, no dates were obtained for the critical transition structures—Houses 3 and 13 at Arizona BB:13:50, and House 13 at Arizona BB:13:41. The culmination of the transitional period was marked by the solid-walled Tanque Verde structure—House 18 at Arizona BB:13:50—which is dated at A.D. 1240. Apparently, then, a 25 year span was required for the various changes to become formalized, standard features.

Until more Tucson Basin sites are exposed showing a similar development, the desirability of a new interim phase is questionable. It is more than likely, if events in the Tucson area provided the catalyst for the new features of the Tanque Verde phase, that the material evidence from areas outside the basin may be out of synchronization. Such lack of synchronization should hold true for analogous architectural changes in the early Soho phase of the Gila Basin.

The situation could, perhaps, be best explained by an illuminating concept proposed for rapid changes in the Tsegi phase in northeastern Arizona (Dean 1969:197-198). In that area it was demonstrated that sites with equivalent archaeological components were not necessarily contemporaneous. In that report, dendrochronology provided the determinant for absolute dating of sites. Until more precise dating methods can be used throughout the Hohokam district, we cannot safely propose that the sequence of events in the Tucson Basin was synchronous with changes in adjacent areas. It would also be too much to expect that all new archaeological material traits should be discovered at each developing site. Following this reasoning, the Rincon phase is extended to about A.D. 1215 at Punta de Agua. Other late transitional sites should probably show intraphase variability.

The concentration of true Tanque Verde phase settlements possibly shows a higher form of social integration than previously had existed in the scattered ranchería-type communities. There is no reason to believe the accessible and well-watered Punta de Agua suffered from arroyo cutting or a falling water table. Nor do we have data on possible adverse precipitation or temperature conditions. The latter effects often are invoked to account for the concentration of population in pueblos or contiguous compounds.

In review, the great technical effort behind the relocation of Tanque Verde phase villages and the attendant change to solid or post-reinforced wall architecture must have demanded much greater social coordination than was present in the villages of the Rincon phase. Furthermore, the extensive aesthetic development required for the emergence of Tanque Verde Red-on-brown required an area-wide cooperative endeavor. It was shown that elements of San Carlos Red-on-brown and Topawa Red-on-brown were synthesized into the final product.

Whereas in the Colonial period the establishment of villages of actual colonizers along the southern Arizona water courses has been accepted by convention, the data now emerging foretell the appearance of cultural forces from the middle Gila district—Bylas to Safford—as well as from the Upper Pima area and the Papaguería to the south.

When the rancherías were abandoned, the villagers concentrated at Martinez Hill, a site composed of several compounds. At this time, in addition to the emergence of a stronger political leadership, it is probable that a more formal hierarchical social structure, encompassing groups of extended families, was present in each compound. Thus, the base was formed for a relatively stable community for two hundred more years.

APPENDIX A
ARCHITECTURAL DATA
Series of House Superimposition

Site	House Number	Over Number	Over Number	Over Number
Ariz. BB:13:50	House 2	House 1		
	House 19B	House 19A		
	House 13	House 21		
	House 13	House 13A		
	House 18	House 15		
	House 18	House 22	House 20A	House 20B
Ariz. BB:13:16	House 6	House 7		

Phase Assignment and House Details at Ariz. BB:13:41

	Rillito	Early Rincon	Middle Rincon	Late Rincon	Tanque Verde	Comments
House 1			Sub-rectangular			Short entry
House 2				Sub-rectangular		Bulbous entry
House 3				Sub-rectangular		Long entry
House 4				Sub-rectangular		Bulbous entry
House 5			Sub-rectangular			Short entry
House 6				Sub-rectangular		Bulbous entry
House 7				Sub-rectangular		Bulbous entry
House 8			Sub-rectangular			Short entry
House 9			Oval ——————————→			Hearth superimposed
House 10 (Ramada)						
House 11				Sub-rectangular		Bulbous entry
House 12				Sub-rectangular		Bulbous entry
House 13				Sub-rectangular	House enlarged	Hearth relocated
House 14			Sub-rectangular			Entry eroded
House 15			Sub-rectangular ——→			Hearth superimposed, entry eroded

Phase Assignment and House Details at Ariz. BB:13:50

	Rillito	Early Rincon	Middle Rincon	Late Rincon	Tanque Verde	Comments
House 1			Sub-rectangular			Entry destroyed
House 2				Sub-rectangular		Over House 1, bulbous entry
House 3					Ovoid	Transitional
House 4	Squared					
House 5			Sub-rectangular	Sub-rectangular		Short entry
House 6				Sub-rectangular		Bulbous entry
House 7			Sub-rectangular			Bulbous entry
House 8		Oval				Hearth relocated
House 9		Sub-rectangular				Bulbous entry
House 10				Sub-rectangular		Entry obliterated
House 11	Sub-rectangular ——————————→					Short entry
House 12			Sub-rectangular ——————→			Storehouse, bulbous entry
House 13A					Rectangular	Transitional, over House 21, House 13A
House 13B				Sub-rectangular		Partly excavated

(continued)

Phase Assignment and House Details at Ariz. BB:13:50 (Continued)

	Rillito	Early Rincon	Middle Rincon	Late Rincon	Tanque Verde	Comments
House 14				Sub-rectangular		Long entry
House 15*			Sub-rectangular			
House 16	Squared					Long entry, 4 corner posts
House 17	(not excavated)					
House 18*					Rectangular	
House 19A	Squared					Short entry
House 19B		Oval				Over House 19A
House 20A*			Sub-rectangular			Short entry
House 20B*	Squared					
House 21			Sub-rectangular			Short entry
House 22*				Sub-rectangular		Bulbous entry
House 23				Sub-rectangular		Bulbous entry
House 24				Sub-rectangular		Long entry
House 25			Sub-rectangular ⟶			Short entry, irreg. post pattern

*Superimposed series.

Phase Assignment and House Details at Ariz. BB:13:16

	Rillito	Early Rincon	Middle Rincon	Late Rincon	Tanque Verde	Comments
House 1	Oval					Eroded
House 2						Historic
House 3		Sub-rectangular				Short entry
House 4				Rectangular ⟶		Long entry
House 5			Squared ⟶			Curb rim
House 6				Rectangular		Long entry
House 7	Oval ⟶					Hearth remodeled
House 8	Sub-rectangular					Entry at end
House 9			Oval			Eroded
House 10	Squared					Long entry with adobe sill; bell-shaped pit

Phase Assignment and House Details at Ariz. BB:13:43

	Rillito	Early Rincon	Middle Rincon	Late Rincon	Tanque Verde	Comments
House 1			Sub-rectangular ⟶			Entry eroded; hearth relocated
House 2				Sub-rectangular		Bulbous entry
House 3		Oval				Pit
House 4		Oval				Pit
House 5			Sub-rectangular			Bulbous entry; plug set in old hearth
House 6			Rectangular			Entry eroded
House 7		Oval				Bell-shaped pit
House 8		Oval				
House 9			Oval			
House 10		Oval				Bell-shaped pit

APPENDIX B
RINCON POLYCHROME SUMMARY
Provenience of All Known Specimens

Site	Phase	Description	Comments
GILA DRAINAGE:			
Snaketown 1934-5	Sacaton	1 jar sherd	Shouldered, interior slipped (ASM 27206).
Snaketown 1964-5	Sacaton	1 jar sherd	Shouldered, int. unslipped.
1964-5	Sacaton	1 bowl sherd	Hemispherical (ASM 26982).
Cashion-Gila Pueblo	Sacaton-Soho	Bowl-restored	Hemispherical (Amerind 3892).
SANTA CRUZ DRAINAGE:			
Ariz. AA:12:57 Survey 1969	Rincon	1 jar sherd	Shouldered, int. slipped.
Ariz. AA:12:36 Survey 1934	Rincon (?)	30 bowl sherds	All from same vessel. Hemispherical; direct rim; int. decoration only. Rim thickened. Designs: (1) diagonal panels & strips filled w/angular elements, & (2) remains of broad curvilinear strips w/hatching. Rim painted black.
St. Mary's Ruin	Rincon (?)	Jar	Shouldered, interior unslipped (ASM 20144).
		1 bowl sherd	Hemispherical, rim.
Paloparado Cremation Area 1		Bowl-restored	Low shoulder; slightly flared rim; interior B/W band (ASM P/7).
Ariz. BB:14:24 trash	Rincon	2 bowl sherds	
trash	Rincon	1 jar sherd	Shouldered, interior unslipped (ASM 47400).
Ariz. DD:4:5	Rincon (?)	1 jar sherd	Shouldered, interior unslipped.
Ariz. DD:8:60	Rincon (?)	7 bowl sherds	Two direct rim; one flared rim w/interior B/W band.
Hodges-Cremation 182	Rincon	2 bowl sherds	One slight flare rim; interior band of pendent triangles (ASM 22685 x-2, x-33).
Burial 1	Rincon	2 bowl sherds	Rim w/interior band pendent triangles; white paint used in primary design as arm of interlocked scroll (ASM 22685, x-16, x-20).
House 59 Floor	Rincon	1 bowl sherd	Direct rim; interior & exterior decoration (ASM 22685 x-23).
(?)	Rincon	1 bowl sherd	(ASM 22687 x-2).
PUNTA DE AGUA:			
BB:13:50 House 3 Fill	Late Rincon	3 bowl sherds	Low shoulder, flared rim; red slip oxidized; vertical panels; exterior decoration.
		1 bowl sherd	Hemispherical

(continued)

Provenience of All Known Specimens (Continued)

	Site	Phase	Description	Comments
	House 25 Fill	Rincon	1 bowl sherd	Hemispherical; appears to be part of same vessel as in House 3.
	House 18 Floor	Tanque Verde	1 bowl sherd	Hemispherical (?)
	House 18 Fill	Tanque Verde	1 bowl sherd	This & above appear to be from same vessel.
	House 20 Fill	Rincon	1 bowl sherd	Interior B/W band; exterior unslipped; low outcurved bowl.
	House 23 Fill	Late Rincon	1 bowl sherd	Rim everted; body hemispherical.
	Trash Pit #4	Rincon	1 bowl sherd	Relatively straight-sided.
BB:13:49	Mound II	Late Rincon	1 jar sherd	
BB:13:45	Surface	Rincon	2 jar sherds	Large fragments from same shouldered, incurved jar.
BB:13:43	House 9 Floor	Rincon	1 bowl sherd	Rim slightly everted; hemispherical.
BB:13:16	House 4 Fill	Late Rincon	1 jar sherd	

Shapes of Specimens from Punta de Agua

JARS (EXTERIOR DECORATION)

Shouldered, incurved	Jar shape indeterminate
1 complete 6 sherds	3 sherds

BOWLS

Principal decoration: Exterior		Principal decoration: Interior	
Hemispherical		Shouldered	Hemispherical	Outcurved
Direct rim	Everted rim	Flared rim	Direct rim	Direct rim
1 complete	4 sherds	1 complete	30 sherds (same vessel)	1 sherd
3 sherds		4 sherds		

INDETERMINATE SHAPE

15 sherds

APPENDIX C
CREMATION AND INHUMATION DATA

ARIZ. BB:13:16
(See Figure 7.1)

Cremation	Phase	Urn in Pit Type 1 — Bone in Upright jar	Urn in Pit Type 2 — Bowl (or jar) inverted over Bone	Variation — Bone mixed with sherds	Remarks
1	Rillito	Jar ASM 30718			No cover bowl
2	Rillito	Jar ASM 30728			Cover bowl (ASM 30728). Crude stone bowl was assoc. (ASM 30828).
3	Early Rincon		Bowl ASM 30703		Shouldered jar (ASM 30706) assoc.
4	Rillito		Bowl ASM 30702		Cache #1, 50 cm North: stone bowl (ASM 30801), hand stone palette (ASM 30737).
5	Rillito	Jar ASM 30707			Cover bowl (ASM 30711).
6	Rillito		Bowl ASM 30725		Cover bowl "killed"
7	Early Rincon		2 Nested Bowls ASM 30705, above ASM 30701		Cache #2, 60 cm NE. Stone incensario (ASM 30802,X-2), stone bowl (ASM 30802,X-1), palette frag. (ASM 30802, X-3).
8	Early Rincon		ASM 30709		Cover bowl "killed"
9	Early Rincon	Seed Jar ASM 30700			Cover bowl (ASM 30726); bowl (ASM 30724) assoc.; plus frag. split bone awl.

(continued)

[115]

ARIZ. BB:13:16 *(Continued)*

Cremation	Phase	Urn in Pit — Type 1: Bone in Upright jar	Urn in Pit — Type 2: Bowl (or jar) inverted over Bone	Variation: Bone mixed with sherds	Remarks
10	Rincon		Bowl ASM 30710		Plainware, crude
11	Rincon		Jar ASM 30712		Wide-mouthed jar, inverted.
12	Rillito		Bowl ASM 30709		Cover bowl "killed"
13	Rincon		Bowl ASM 30727		Cover bowl in Dragoon red-on-brown style.
14	Rillito		Bowl ASM 30708		
15	Rincon			Sherds under & over bone	Isolated from main zone.
TOTALS		4	10	1	

ARIZ. BB:13:50

Cremation	Phase	Urn in Pit — Type 1	Urn in Pit — Type 2	Variation	Remarks
1	Late Rincon		Bowl ASM 30899		Cover bowl in Rincon-Tanque Verde transitional style. *Haliotis* shell ornaments propped against bowl.
2	Tanque Verde	Large jar ASM 30894			No cover bowl
3	Tanque Verde	Small jar ASM 30903 Cover Bowl ASM 30901			Cover bowl decorated Cr. 3 placed next to Cr. 2 (above) on floor of House 22.
TOTALS		2	1	--	

ARIZ. BB:13:43

Cremation	Phase	Urn in Pit — Type 1	Urn in Pit — Type 2	Variation	Remarks
1	Rillito		Bowl ASM 30715		2 plates assoc.; standing vertically next to bowl (ASM 30716-30729).
TOTAL			1		

REFERENCES

Ambler, Richard
1961   Archaeological Survey and Excavations at Casa Grande National Monument, Arizona. MS, Master's thesis, Department of Anthropology, University of Arizona, Tucson.

Arnold, Lee W.
1940   An Ecological Study of the Vertebrate Animals of the Mesquite Forest. MS, Master's thesis, Department of Entomology and Economic Zoology, University of Arizona, Tucson.

Bohrer, Vorsila L., Hugh C. Cutler, and Jonathan D. Sauer
1969   Carbonized Plant Remains from Two Hohokam Sites, Arizona BB:13:41 and Arizona BB:13:50. *The Kiva* Vol. 35, No. 1:1-10.

Bolton, Hubert E.
1936   *Rim of Christendom*. The MacMillan Company, New York.

Breternitz, David
1966   An Appraisal of Tree-Ring Dated Pottery in the Southwest. *Anthropological Papers of the University of Arizona* No. 10, University of Arizona Press, Tucson.

Carlson, Roy L.
1970   White Mountain Redware: A Pottery Tradition of East-Central Arizona and Western New Mexico. *Anthropological Papers of the University of Arizona* No. 19, University of Arizona Press, Tucson.

Cosgrove, H.S. and C.B. Cosgrove
1932   The Swarts Ruin: A Typical Mimbres Site in Southwestern New Mexico. *Papers of the Peabody Museum of American Archaeology and Ethnology* Vol. 15, No. 1, Harvard University, Cambridge.

Culin, Stewart
1907   Games of the North American Indians. *Twenty-fourth Annual Report of the Bureau of American Ethnology*. Government Printing Office, Washington.

Cushing, Frank
1883   Zuni Fetiches. *Second Annual Report of the Bureau of American Ethnology*, pp. 3-50. Government Printing Office, Washington.

Danson, Edward B.
1940   An Archaeological Survey of the Santa Cruz River Valley from the Headwaters to the Town of Tubac in Arizona. MS, Department of Anthropology, University of Arizona, Tucson.

1957   Pottery Type Descriptions. In "Excavations, 1940, at University Indian Ruin, Tucson, Arizona" by Julian D. Hayden, pp. 219-231. *Southwestern Monuments Association, Technical Series* Vol. 5, Gila Pueblo, Globe.

Danson, Edward B. and Roberts M. Wallace
1956   A Petrographic Study of Gila Polychrome. *American Antiquity* Vol. 22, No. 2:180-83.

Dean, Jeffrey S.
1969   Chronological Analysis of Tsegi Phase Sites in Northeastern Arizona. *Papers of the Laboratory of Tree-Ring Research* No. 3, University of Arizona Press, Tucson.

Dice, L.R.
1943   *The Biotic Provinces of North America*. University of Michigan Press, Ann Arbor.

DiPeso, Charles C.
1953   The Sobaipuri Indians of the Upper San Pedro River Valley, Southeastern Arizona. *The Amerind Foundation, Inc.* No. 6, Dragoon.

1956   The Upper Pima of San Cayetano del Tumacacori: An Archaeological Reconstruction of the Ootam of Pimería Alta. *The Amerind Foundation, Inc.* No. 7, Dragoon.

1958   The Reeve Ruin of Southeastern Arizona: A Study of a Prehistoric Western Pueblo Migration into the Middle San Pedro Valley. *The Amerind Foundation, Inc.* No. 8, Dragoon.

DuBois, Robert L.
1968   Letter to Greenleaf written August 5, 1968.

Eddy, Frank
1958   A Sequence of Cultural and Alluvial Deposits in the Cienega Creek Basin, Southeastern Arizona. MS, Master's thesis, Department of Anthropology, University of Arizona, Tucson.

Ekholm, George F.
1942   Excavations at Guasave, Sinaloa, Mexico. *Anthropological Papers of the American Museum of Natural History* Vol. 38, Part 2:23-140.

Ezell, Paul
1955   The Archaeological Delineation of a Cultural Boundary in Papaguería, *American Antiquity* Vol. 20, No. 4:367-74.

Ferdon, Edwin N., Jr.
1967   The Hohokam "Ball Court": An Alternative View of its Function. *The Kiva* Vol. 33, No. 1:1-14.

Ferguson, Charles W.
1950   An Ecological Analysis of Lower Sonoran Zone Relic Vegetation In South-Central Arizona. MS, Master's thesis, Department of Botany and Range Ecology, University of Arizona, Tucson.

Fontana, Bernard L., J. Cameron Greenleaf, and Donnelly D. Cassidy
1959   A Fortified Arizona Mountain. *The Kiva* Vol. 25, No. 2:41-52.

Fontana, Bernard L., William J. Robinson, Charles W. Cormack, and Ernest E. Leavitt, Jr.
1962   *Papago Indian Pottery*. University of Washington Press, Seattle.

Fraps, Clara Lee (see Tanner, Clara Lee)

REFERENCES

Frick, Paul S.
1954 An Archaeological Survey of the Central Santa Cruz Valley, Southern Arizona. MS, Master's thesis, Department of Anthropology, University of Arizona, Tucson.

Fulton, William S. and Carr Tuthill
1940 An Archaeological Site near Gleeson, Arizona. *The Amerind Foundation, Inc.* No. 1, Dragoon.

Gabel, Norman E.
1931 Martinez Hill Ruins. MS, Master's thesis, Department of Anthropology, University of Arizona, Tucson.

Getty, Harry T.
1934 Arizona State Museum Site Card No. AA:12:36.

Gladwin, Harold S., Emil Haury, E.B. Sayles, and Nora Gladwin
1937 Excavations at Snaketown, I: Material Culture. *Medallion Papers* No. 25, Gila Pueblo, Globe.

Gladwin, Winifred and Harold S. Gladwin
1929 The Red-on-Buff Culture of the Papaguería. *Medallion Papers* No. 4, Gila Pueblo, Globe.

Grebinger, Paul F.
1971 *Hohokam Cultural Development in the Middle Santa Cruz Valley, Arizona.* Doctoral dissertation, Department of Anthropology, University of Arizona, Tucson, and University Microfilms, Ann Arbor.

Greenleaf, J. Cameron
1975 Excavation of the Gila Bend Fortified Hill Site, Western Arizona. *The Kiva* Vol. 40, No. 4: 213–282.

Hammack, Laurens C.
n.d. AA:12:46 (Rabid Ruin). Excavated January-March 1969. Field notes on file, Arizona State Museum, University of Arizona, Tucson.

1971 *The Peppersauce Wash Project. A Preliminary Report on the Salvage Excavation of Four Archaeological Sites in the San Pedro Valley, Southeastern Arizona.* Arizona State Museum, University of Arizona, Tucson.

Hastings, James R. and Raymond M. Turner
1965 *The Changing Mile: An Ecological Study of Vegetation Change with Time in the Lower Mile of an Arid and Semiarid Region.* University of Arizona Press, Tucson.

Haury, Emil W.
1928 The Succession of House Types in the Pueblo Area. MS, Master's thesis, Department of Anthropology, University of Arizona, Tucson.

1932 Roosevelt 9:6. A Hohokam Site of the Colonial Period. *Medallion Papers* No. 11, Gila Pueblo Globe.

1936 Some Southwestern Pottery Types. *Medallion Papers* No. 19, Gila Pueblo, Globe.

1945 The Excavation of Los Muertos and Neighboring Ruins in the Salt River Valley, Southern Arizona. *Papers of the Peabody Museum of Archaeology and Ethnology* Vol. 24, No. 1, Harvard University, Cambridge.

1950 *The Stratigraphy and Archaeology of Ventana Cave, Arizona.* University of Arizona Press, Tucson, and University of New Mexico Press, Albuquerque.

Hayden, Julian D.
1957 Excavations, 1940, at University Indian Ruin, Tucson, Arizona. *Southwestern Monuments Association, Technical Series* Vol. 5, Gila Pueblo, Globe.

1970 Of Hohokam Origins and Other Matters. *American Antiquity* Vol. 35, No. 1:87-93.

Heindl, L.A.
1959 Geology of the San Xavier Indian Reservation. In *Southern Arizona Guidebook II* edited by L.A. Heindl, pp. 153-159. Arizona Geological Society.

Johnson, Alfred E.
1964 Archaeological Excavations in Hohokam Sites of Southern Arizona. *American Antiquity* Vol. 30. No. 2, Part 1:145-161.

1965 *The Development of Western Pueblo Culture.* Doctoral dissertation, Department of Anthropology, University of Arizona, Tucson, and University Microfilms, Ann Arbor.

Johnson, Alfred E. and William W. Wasley
1966 Archaeological Excavations near Bylas, Arizona. *The Kiva* Vol. 31, No. 4:205-253.

Kelly, Isabel
n.d. Hodges Site Materials. MS, Arizona State Museum, University of Arizona, Tucson.

Kelly, Roger E.
1963 The Socio-Religious Roles of Ballcourts and Great Kivas in the Prehistoric Southwest. MS, Master's thesis, Department of Anthropology, University of Arizona, Tucson.

Kelly, William S.
1936 University Ruin. *The Kiva* Vol. 1, No. 8:1-4.

Kidder, Alfred V.
1932 *The Artifacts of Pecos.* Published for the Phillips Academy by Yale University Press, New Haven.

Lindsay, Alexander, J., Jr., and Calvin H. Jennings (eds.)
1968 Ninth Southwestern Ceramic Seminar: Salado Redware Conference, Oct. 13-14, 1967. *Museum of Northern Arizona Ceramic Series* No. 4, Northern Arizona Society of Science and Art, Inc., Flagstaff.

Lowe, Charles H.
1964 *Arizona's Natural Environment.* University of Arizona Press, Tucson.

Och, Joseph
1965 *Missionary in Sonora; the travel reports of Joseph Och, S.J., 1755-1767.* Translated and annotated by Theodore E. Treutlein, California Historical Society, San Francisco.

Officer, James E.
1961 Hodges Site Materials. MS, revision of manuscript by Isabel Kelly, Arizona State Museum, University of Arizona, Tucson.

Olberg, C.R. and F.R. Schanck
1913 *Special Report on Irrigation and Flood Protection, Papago Indian Reservation.* 62nd Congress, 3rd Session, Senate Ex. Doc. Vol. 24. Government Printing Office, Washington.

Pomeroy, J.A.
1962 A Study of Black-on-White Painted Pottery in the Tonto Basin, Arizona. MS, Master's thesis, Department of Anthropology, University of Arizona, Tucson.

Robinson, William J.
1963 Excavations at San Xavier del Bac, 1958. *The Kiva* Vol. 29, No. 2:35-57.
1969 Letter to Greenleaf written December 9, 1969.

Rogers, Malcolm J.
1958 San Dieguito Implements from the Terraces of the Rincon-Pantano and Rillito Drainage Systems. *The Kiva* Vol. 24, No. 1:1-23.
1966 *Ancient Hunters of the Far West.* Union-Tribune Publishing Co., San Diego.

Russell, Frank
1908 The Pima Indians. *Twenty-Sixth Annual Report of the Bureau of American Ethnology.* Government Printing Office, Washington.

Sayles E.B.
1945 The San Simon Branch, Excavations at Cave Creek and in the San Simon Valley: Part I, Material Culture. *Medallion Papers* No. 34, Gila Pueblo, Globe.

Sayles, E.B. and Ernst Antevs
1944 The Cochise Culture. *Medallion Papers* No. 29, Gila Pueblo, Globe.

Scantling, Frederick H.
1939 Jackrabbit Ruin. *The Kiva* Vol. 5, No. 3:9-12.
1940 Excavations at the Jackrabbit Ruin, Papago Indian Reservation, Arizona. MS, Master's thesis, Department of Anthropology, University of Arizona, Tucson.

Sellers, William D. (ed.)
1960 *Arizona Climate.* University of Arizona Press, Tucson.

Shreve, Margaret B.
1943 Modern Papago Basketry. MS, Master's thesis, Department of Anthropology, University of Arizona, Tucson.

Smith, H.V.
1956 The Climate of Arizona. *Arizona Experiment Station Bulletin* No. 279, University of Arizona, Tucson.

Spicer, Edward H.
1941 The Papago Indians. *The Kiva* Vol. 6, No. 6:21-24.

Swanson, Earl H., Jr.
1951 An Archaeological Survey of the Empire Valley, Arizona. MS, Master's thesis, Department of Anthropology, University of Arizona, Tucson.

Tanner, Clara Lee (Fraps)
1935 Tanque Verde Ruins. *The Kiva* Vol. 1, No. 4.
1936 Blackstone Ruin. *The Kiva* Vol. 2, No. 3:9-12.

Tuthill, Carr
1947 The Tres Alamos Site on the San Pedro River, Southeastern Arizona. *The Amerind Foundation, Inc.* No. 4, Dragoon.

Tylor, Edward B.
1878 *Researches into the Early History of Mankind and the Development of Civilization.* John Murray, London.

Vaillant, George C.
1966 *Aztecs of Mexico.* Doubleday and Company, Inc., Pelican Books, New York.

Wallace, Roberts M.
1957 Petrographic Analysis of Pottery from University Indian Ruins. In "Excavations, 1940, at University Indian Ruin, Tucson, Arizona" by Julian D. Hayden, pp. 209-219. *Southwestern Monuments Association, Technical Series* Vol. 5, Gila Pueblo, Globe.

Wasley, William W. and Alfred E. Johnson
1965 Salvage Archaeology in Painted Rocks Reservoir, Western Arizona. *Anthropological Papers of the University of Arizona* No. 9, University of Arizona Press, Tucson.

Wheat, Joe Ben
1955 Mogollon Culture Prior to A.D. 1000. *American Anthropological Association Memoir* No. 82.

Withers, Arnold M.
1941 Excavations at the Valshni Village, Papago Indian Reservation, Arizona. MS, Master's thesis, Department of Anthropology, University of Arizona, Tucson.
1944 Excavations at Valshni Village, a Site on the Papago Indian Reservation. *American Antiquity* Vol. 10, No. 1:33-47.

Wright, Barton A. and Rex E. Gerald
1950 The Zanardelli Site. *The Kiva* Vol. 16, No. 3:8-15.

Zahniser, Jack L.
1966 Late Prehistoric Villages Southeast of Tucson, Arizona and the Archaeology of the Tanque Verde Phase. *The Kiva* Vol. 31, No. 3:103-204.

INDEX

Adobe cones, 20, 23, 29, 30, 31, 35, 41-43; with fluting, 23, 29, 35, 41
Amargosa I-II stage, 18
Amole Polychrome, stepped *Grecque* element, 72
Archaeomagnetic dates, Arizona BB:13:50, 21
Architectural wood, identification of, 43-44
Architecture: curb-rim plan, 35, 40, 41; summary, 35-40; transitional (Rincon-Tanque Verde phases), 23, 25, 31

Ballcourts, 19
Bidegain site, 37
Bird effigy pendant, stone, Zuni type, 86
Birkby, Walter, 88
Black Mountain, 11, 15, 16; relic vegetation, 16
Blackstone site, 37
Bulbous entry, earliest, 25
Burials, area comparisons, 104
Burial zones (cremations): Rillito phase, 47; Rincon phase, 49; Tanque Verde phase, 21, 22, 52-54
Bylas phase, 16, 17

Cache, accompanying cremations at Arizona BB:13:16, 89
Caliche mixing basins, 25, 31
Cañada del Oro phase, 11
Casa Grande National Monument, 37
Casa Grande Red-on-buff, 66; intrusive, 75
Cashion site (Gila River), 67
Ceramic types: comparison of taxonomy between Gila Basin and Tucson Basin, 45; red-on-brown continuity to Tanque Verde phase, 60
Ceramic types, abstracts from Hodges site report: Cañada del Oro phase, 45; plainware, 55-57; redware, 58-59; Rillito phase, 45, 47; Rincon phase, 48-49
Ceremonial houses, discussion, 43
Ceremonial structures, 19
Classic period, 16; at Arizona BB:13:50, 25
Cochise culture, 18
Colonial period, 18
Cortaro phase, proposed, 44, 60
Cortaro Red-on-brown, hypothetical type (synonym: Late Rincon Red-on-brown), 49, 60
Cremations: evidence of planned interment area (Arizona BB:13:16), 101; variations in disposal of calcined bone, 102, 104, Appendix C

Discs, ceramic, as gaming pieces, 82-84
Dos Cabezas phase, 18
Dragoon Red-on-brown, 77

Empire Valley sites, 18
Escondida Polychrome (synonym: Animas Polychrome), 72
Estrella phase, 18

Figurines, ceramic, affinity to Mexican Pre-classic, 80

Gila Plain (Tucson variety), 56
Gila Polychrome, local varieties, 73-75
Guasave Red (Huatabampo district), 59
Guasave Redware (Huatabampo complex), as prototype for Rincon Redware, 72

Hodges site, 11, 16, 17
Hohokam: Gila River, 11, 18; colonists, 18
House cluster, 20
House, Papago, 35
Houses, post-reinforced (Rincon-Tanque Verde transition), 40
House superimposition, Rincon phase, 20, 22, 23, 24, Appendix A

Irrigation: historic, 19; Hohokam, 18; potential at Arizona BB:13:16, 19

Jackrabbit Ruin, 16

Kelly, Isabel, abstracts of ceramics from Hodges site. *See* Ceramic types

Lower Sonoran Life Zone, 15

Maize, varieties stored for seed corn or consumption, 106
Martinez Hill Ruin, 16; Classic period compounds, 26
Mimbres Black-on-white, 76-77
Mimbres cultural dispersal, 77
Modeled spindle whorls, as Classic period horizon marker, 79
Mogollon red-on-brown, 18
McGee, W.J., expedition (1894-1895), 35

Oval houses: Peñasco and Dos Cabezas phases, 37; Rillito phase, 32; with storage cists, 28

Palettes, carved slate, with lead (Pb) carbonates, 87-88
Paloparado site, 16, 18, 67
Peñasco phase, 18
Papago ethnography, myths, 19
Papago Indians, 16, 18, 19
Papaguería, archaeology, 16
Phase synchronization between Gila Basin and Tucson Basin, 44
Picacho Red-on-brown (hypothetical type), 48
Pima ethnography, myths, 19
Pima Indians, 18, 19
Pioneer period, 17, 18
Plainware, micaceous variety (Rincon and Tanque Verde phases), 57, 58
Plant remains, carbonized, 25
Potrero Creek site, 18
Punta de Agua: acequia, 19; place name, 19; ranch, 19

Rabid Ruin, 17
Rainfall (bi-seasonal), 15
Rillito phase houses, at Arizona BB:13:50, 22-25, Appendix A
Rincon phase, 18; earliest settlement (Arizona BB:13:43), 27; extension to about A.D. 1215 in Tucson area, 109; internal changes, 108
Rincon phase houses, chronological placement, 20, 21, Appendix A
Rincon Polychrome: combination of diverse elements, 73; development from Rincon Red shapes, 67, 68, 72; first description as unidentified polychrome, 67; variations due to oxidation and slip application, 67
Rincon Red, varieties (Rincon and Tanque Verde phases), 59, 60
Rincon Red-on-brown, varieties, 50
Rincon Red-on-brown (Late), characteristics, 60-66
Robinson, William J., 43-44
Roosevelt Black-on-white, 77
Roosevelt 9:6, 16, 43

Sacaton Red, 58
Sacaton Red-on-buff, 60, 66; late variety, 72
Sahuarita Butte (Martinez Hill), 11, 15, 16
St. Johns Polychrome, 73
San Carlos Red-on-brown, 51, 52, 54, 66
San Dieguito stage, 18
San Pedro River, 16-18
San Pedro stage, 18
San Simon phase, 18

Santa Cruz phase, 18
Santa Cruz River, 11, 15; east channel, 15; fauna, 16; west channel, 15
Santan phase, proposed, 44, 60
San Xavier Indian Reservation, 11, 15; geology, 15
San Xavier Mission, 11, 16
Sells Red, 57, 59
Shell, evidence for local carving, 99, 100
Site unit, 20
Snaketown phase, 18
Snaketown Red-on-brown (Tucson Basin), 45
Snaketown Red-on-buff (Gila Basin), 45
Snaketown site, 11, 16, 17
Sobaipuri Indians, 16, 18, 19
Stick-leaf (*Mentzelia* sp.) seeds, first record of use, 106
Stone tool "kit" (floor House 15, Arizona BB:13:41), 96, 97
Stratigraphic tests in borrow pits, 25, 26
Sweetwater phase, 18

Tanque Verde phase, 11, 16, 17; presence of new aesthetic traits, 108-109; type site, 16
Tanque Verde Red-on-brown, 16; inclusive dates and progenitors, 51-54; origin of exterior decoration, 66

Tonto Polychrome, 72
Topawa phase, 54, 76
Topawa Red-on-brown (Tucson variety), 54
Trash mounds, tests at Arizona BB:13:49, 26
Tres Alamos site, 16
Tucson Basin archaeology, 16, 17

University Indian Ruin, 16, 17

Valshni Red, 59
Valshni Village, 16
Ventana Cave, 16, 18
Vikita ceremony, 19

Western Pueblo intrusion, 37; during Bylas phase (A.D. 1100-1200), 51
Western Pueblo traits, 16, 18
Whiptail site (Arizona BB:10:3), 16, 17, 66
White Mountain Redware, 18